A PASSION FOR TRUTH

OTHER BOOKS BY ERIC BREINDEL

*The Venona Secrets: The Soviet Union's World War II Espionage
Campaign against the United States—and How America Fought
Back: A Story of Espionage, Counterespionage, and Betrayal*
(with Herbert Romerstein)

A PASSION FOR
TRUTH

THE SELECTED WRITINGS OF
ERIC BREINDEL

EDITED BY JOHN PODHORETZ

HarperCollins*Publishers*

HarperCollins books may be purchased for educational, business, or sales promotional use. For information please write: Special Markets Department, HarperCollins Publishers, Inc., 10 East 53rd Street, New York, NY 10022.

FIRST EDITION

Designed by Nancy B. Field

Library of Congress Cataloging-in-Publication Data

Breindel, Eric, 1955–1998.
    A passion for truth : the selected writings of Eric Breindel
[edited by] John Podhoretz.—1st ed.
        p.   cm.
    ISBN 0-06-019327-1
    1. Anti-communist movements—United States—History—20th century.
2. Communism—United States—History—20th Century. 3. New York (N.Y.)—
Social conditions. 4. New York (N.Y.)—Race relations. 5. Antisemitism—
History—20th century. 6. Israel—Politics and government. 7. Holocaust, Jewish
(1939-1945). 8. Breindel, Eric, 1955–1998. I. Podhoretz, John. II. Title.
E743.5.B72   1999
973.92—dc21

98-51059

99 00 01 02 03 ❖/RRD 10 9 8 7 6 5 4 3 2 1

CONTENTS

FOREWORD

Daniel Patrick Moynihan

Eric Breindel died March 7, 1998, at the age of forty-two. His was a short life, but in ways a singularly fulfilled one. He had spent a decade as editor of the Editorial Page of the *New York Post*. Its obituary noted that he had once said that life granted few gifts greater than the ability to influence the political debate in the greatest city in the world. He had surely done that, as evidenced by the great company of New Yorkers who came to his funeral service at the Park Avenue Synagogue. In placing this and other obituaries in the *Congressional Record*, I commented: "The Talmud teaches that fools measure their lives in years, while wise people measure them in days. Eric was wise in this respect as he was in so many others."

He had been a student of mine at Harvard, and at the funeral I stated in my remarks: "I taught him for two years . . . and learned from him for the next twenty." Dr. Johnson commented that "in lapidary inscriptions a man is not upon oath," but this was literally true with Eric. We met in the waning days of campus unrest, if that term will serve, when something subtler and far more consequential was taking place. The creeds and screeds of the 1950s were slowly being absorbed by the institutions against which they had originally been directed. In those years I recall scribbling a doggerel:

> *The SDS will soon desist*
> *Being so obstructionist.*
> *Made the City Fathers nervous;*
> *Ended up in the Civil Service.*

Well, yes. Indeed, there were those at the time who pro-pounded in Mao-speak the need to gird for "the long march through the institutions." Eric sensed this. He didn't say much about it, but he felt the tremors. In particular—I think I have this right—he sensed the degree to which a certain kind of political extremism passed from generation to generation, sometimes liter-ally in a family sense, at times mutating, but persisting. It was, after all, what the twentieth century had been all about up to that point.

And this he would not have. For the simplest reason. One I don't ever recall him mentioning and didn't fully appreciate until I read a column of May 18, 1995, entitled "François Mitterrand's Curious Paean":

> Nazi abominations in Germany. "Ethnic cleansing" in Bosnia. A pogrom in 1991 New York. It isn't necessary to reach into the distant past to find illustrations of violence animated by racial and ethnic hatred.
>
> But it remains important to stand fast against those who would rewrite history.
>
> Last month, on Armistice Day, French President François Mitterrand saw fit to lay a wreath at the grave of Marshal Philippe Pétain. Mitterrand's ostensible purpose was to honor Pétain as a World War I hero.
>
> But the notion of separating Pétain's illustrious military record from the horrors perpetrated in his name during the Vichy years is manifestly absurd. . . . France's need to bury its true past—and to invent the Gaullist myth of massive national resistance—is the primary legacy of Philippe Pétain.

Then this:

> Vichy's crimes were directly linked to Hitler's. Pétain's men rounded up the Jews and the gypsies. The French delivered them to the Germans: Adolf Eichmann, Klaus Barbie, Alois Brunner, and others. And the latter shipped their victims to Auschwitz.
>
> In the interest of full disclosure, I should acknowledge here that a grandfather I never met was one such victim. I also confess that my mother and grandmother would likewise have been vic-tims were it not for their own courage and ingenuity. I make no

pretense of neutrality or objectivity in treating the subject of wartime France and the crimes of Vichy.

But I'd like to think I would be writing this column anyway, even if I didn't feel personally offended by François Mitterrand's shamelessness and arrogance.

It was in the context of heritage that Eric was one of the rare persons of his generation who grasped the implication of the United Nations General Assembly Resolution of November 10, 1975—the anniversary of *Kristallnacht* in Hitler's Germany—claiming that "Zionism is a form of racism." I was then our UN ambassador—permanent representative, as the oxymoron goes. Chaim Herzog represented Israel. It took the utmost effort to arouse opposition among our contemporaries, not the least among Jewish organizations. But among students? Scarcely a word. Worse.

I was a graduate student in England in the late 1970s. And I watched in amazement as Left-dominated student unions, in university after university throughout the country, barred Israeli representatives from speaking on campuses.

The method used was always the same. Resolutions would be passed denying campus podiums to "racists." It would then be asserted—on the basis of the UN's Zionism resolution—that the ban applied automatically to Zionists, that is, Israelis.

The point here is that ideas have consequences. Eric understood this in the most profound and pervasive manner. The rest of the world, the United States included, pretty much decided to forget the whole thing. At a dinner party in New York a short while after the vote, my wife found herself seated next to the permanent representative of France, indeed an *ambassadeur de France*, of whom there are five at any given time. Liz remarked how hideous the vote had been. Alas, Madame, said the ambassadeur, we would never had lost had your husband not given such a provocative and undiplomatic speech. In point of fact, with just this in mind, I had spoken after the tally "In Explanation of Vote," as UN usage has it.

But Europeans, and for that matter Americans, were prepared to let it be over with. Herzog, however, would not give up. By then we knew the Soviet origins of the theme of Zionism-as-racism, a form also of capitalist imperialism. The UN resolution gave legitimacy to what soon became an international movement to delegitimate, and indeed exterminate, the Jewish state. And so Herzog got himself elected president of Israel and began a countercampaign. In time he was able to get the Australian Parliament to call for the repeal of the resolution. I was by then in the Senate and was able to get Congress to adopt the Australian resolution word for word. Our thought was to pass it on to other democratic polities. Nothing much happened. But in time the Soviet Union imploded, and in 1991 President George Bush went before the General Assembly and called for repeal, which occurred on December 16. Eric Breindel had helped. MAKE U.N. RESCIND ITS ZIONISM SLUR he thundered all that fall (see "The Shame of the United Nations," page 167). And it did. But it had taken the collapse of world communism to bring it about. Ideas can have awful consequences.

At home no less than abroad, Eric's encounter with "Left-dominated student unions" and his earlier brush with their counterparts in the United States imparted a lively sense of the continuity—again, often as not mutated, but continuous withal—of Communist influences, especially in New York City, which had been the epicenter of American communism in the early decades of the Soviet Union. Trade unions found themselves infiltrated—this was a political movement much given to conspiracy and dissimulation—by assorted political associations, even a considerable political force, the American Labor Party, founded in New York in 1936. First, there was the Communist Party itself, with its various youth groups and such and its publications, such as the *Daily Worker* and assorted journals.

From the 1930s forward, Communists infiltrated various activities of the national government, most notoriously atomic weapons development, but also various departments in Washington. The attack, if you like, was not large, but neither was it inconsequential, particularly in espionage. These activities emerged, notably with the charges made by Whittaker Chambers against Alger Hiss. A great uproar occurred in Congress, mostly associated with Senator Joseph R. McCarthy. McCarthy was a disaster, both personally and politically. Reckless, for the most part uninformed, and generally obnoxious. In the end, he was censured by the Senate, and the Red Scare (our second, if you go back to the years following World War I) subsided. But not without a sinister aftermath, as the cold war commenced.

Eric captured this situation perfectly in a column written for the *Post* in 1987, "Joe McCarthy's Don't-Say-It Legacy" (reprinted here under the title "Calling a Communist a Communist"). Seldom noted, however, is the Wisconsin senator's most insidious political legacy: As a consequence of the recklessness and seeming cruelty of his efforts to expose Communist infiltration in government, it became virtually impossible, in polite company, to call a Communist a Communist.

The prohibition on identifying Communists as such is a fact of American life—it obtains in journalism, in politics, in the academy, indeed in virtually all mainstream public discourse. It's a rule widely acknowledged and obeyed, rather like a taboo.

Almost a decade later, we would come upon how devastating that legacy was. In 1994 I was able to pass legislation creating the Commission on Protecting and Reducing Government Secrecy. My thought was that secrecy is a form of governmental regulation. Most such rules tell the citizen what may or may not be known. Secrecy determined what the citizen may know, a subtle, insidious threat to democratic processes when overdone, as surely we had overdone it during the cold war and continue to do. My report, *Secrecy*, was published in 1997 to ample notices, as you could say. But the run-up was far more exhilarating. In brief, the National Security Agency decided, a half century after the event, to release the Venona decryptions. "Venona" is a made-up word for the Soviet KGB code used to transmit radio messages from New York (mostly) and Washington during and just after World War II. Beginning in 1943, the Army Signals Intelligence Service began transcribing these messages, and in 1946 the first was decoded. There were the names of the principal scientists at Los Alamos. Of one hundred thousand or so cables, some two thousand were "broken"—an incredible feat. The secrecy problem was complex. The first cable was decoded by brilliant cryptanalyst Gardner Meredith in a girls' school, Arlington Hall, in Virginia, which had been taken over for the project. As Meredith toiled away, looking over his shoulder, providing sharpened pencils and fresh coffee, was an army cipher clerk, a corporal, a KGB agent who passed on the information. Also, some of the cable material was shared with the British Embassy, where word of the breakthrough reached Kim Philby. So fairly early, the United States knew that the Soviets knew, and that they knew we knew. Still the material remained classified.

Now, a half century later, it all came out. The army had been able to identify more than one hundred Soviet intelligence agents. With the exception of the Rosenbergs, none was prosecuted. Early on, the decryptions had to be kept secret (and probably would not have held up in court anyway). But they were kept secret within our government as well. People who needed to know about, say, Alger Hiss, did not. We have since learned that President Truman was not told—on orders from the Pentagon. Truman left the presidency thinking that Chambers and Elizabeth Bentley were crackpots or worse.

In October 1996 a conference on the Venona decryptions was held at the National War College in Washington. Eric was there and got it right away. The damage done to American liberalism by the withholding of this information was incalculable. By now he was an avowed conservative, but that made him no less sensitive to the damage. Too many good men and women had spent much of their political lives denying something their own government knew to be true. He said as much at the conference; it gave him no pleasure.

There were still resisters, and Eric wrote a column called "The Sad Delusions of Aging Stalinists" (here titled "Venona and the Stalinist Remnant"). For them, no great mercy; but the nation got a palpable sense of what was lost. Only a great spirit could have managed that. Eric's was one.

Harvard should be proud that it nurtured that spirit. After all, the university recognized it: He graduated magna cum laude in 1977, was editorial chairman of the *Harvard Crimson,* and from there went to the Law School. So ought we. The world will miss his influence. At the time of his death, Charlie Rose grieved, "His capacity to influence world affairs was growing." Let us then treasure what he did leave us. Not the least his capacity to seek truth wherever it led him and, in the end, to forgive so much that he found.

Washington, September 1998

PREFACE:
A MAN OF PASSION

Eric Breindel was only forty-two when he died on a sad Saturday morning at New York Hospital in March 1997, but he had already led the kind of full and dramatic life that would have made him a suitable protagonist for a panoramic novel about America at the close of the millennium.

Breindel was a child of privilege, became intimate with the powerful and the glamorous in his teenage years, and was laid to rest at a funeral attended by every major politician in his state—yet he had once been laid low and in full public view. Breindel traveled in rarefied social circles where politically conservative opinion is tantamount to heresy, and, what is more, he cared deeply about those connections, yet he was a full-throated and fearless advocate for pointedly unfashionable ideas. Breindel took great joy in getting his hands dirty in practical politics and made his living working for a daily newspaper— yet much of his intellectual life was spent mastering controversies and catastrophes that took place before his birth.

He was born in Manhattan in 1955 to Jewish parents who had survived the Holocaust. In that one sentence can be found the origin of the uncommon triad of intellectual obsessions that defined "Agendas," the weekly column he wrote for eleven years in the *New York Post*. The word *obsessions* is carefully chosen here. Most newspaper columnists are generalists who comment on events in the news in the widest possible sense. But in the five hundred-plus "Agenda" columns he wrote for the *Post*, Breindel kept coming back relentlessly and passionately to three and only three themes. That was much in keeping with his character—Breindel was the kind of person who would happily have eaten nothing but hamburgers or baked ziti every day of his life, and at every meal.

Sixty-nine of those columns appear in this book, and they are divided into three categories reflecting these themes.

As Breindel was the Editorial Page editor of a New York City newspaper from 1986 to 1997, it makes sense that he would have devoted much of his time to the issues facing the city of his birth—a city he loved dearly and (as New York City mayor Rudolph Giuliani made clear in his eulogy at Breindel's funeral, which appears in this volume's Epilogue) about which he was, perforce, a lay expert. Those columns are gathered in the section called "New York."

The other two themes that obsessed Breindel were highly unusual subject matter for someone of his age and station—and for any contemporary newspaper columnist of any age.

He was consumed with the Holocaust and its aftermath. Those columns appear in the section entitled "The Fate of the Jews." And he was consumed as well with setting the record straight on the nature of communism and the role of Communists in the United States during this century ("The Anti-Communist Crusade").

These two seemingly disparate themes—the legacy of the Holocaust and the legacy of communism—are, in fact, intrinsically linked. As Norman Podhoretz explained in his eulogy, Breindel took the post-Holocaust admonition "Never again!" with deadly seriousness. He believed it was the totalitarian system constructed by Hitler that made the Holocaust possible, and in the wake of World War II, the totalitarian force that posed the greatest danger to mankind was the Soviet Union.

Breindel also believed that those in the West who aligned themselves with the Soviet Union were not only throwing their support to an enemy of the United States, but had surrendered to an ideological impulse that, in its Nazi guise, had been directed toward the destruction of the Jewish people. In its Soviet guise, totalitarianism was a profound threat to the future of the Jews as well. In its policies toward Soviet Jews, its use of classic anti-Semitic rhetoric and scapegoating, and its hostility toward the state of Israel, the Soviet Union showed itself Hitler's successor.

Breindel became fascinated with the history of the American Communist movement during his high-school years at Philips Exeter Academy and continued to study the subject during his undergraduate studies at Harvard. It was at Harvard that Breindel made the acquaintance of his friend and mentor, Martin Peretz. Peretz shared Breindel's passionate commitment to Israel and to the Jewish people (as his posthumous tribute, first published in the *New Republic* and included in the Epilogue, makes clear) and encouraged him to write, study, and think deeply about these questions.

During his years in Cambridge, Breindel became editorial chairman of the *Harvard Crimson*—a tribute not only to the journalistic talents that led to his successful career at the *New York Post*, but to his remarkable social gifts. Breindel's capacity for friendship was legendary. Once you were his friend, you were his friend forever, and there was little he wouldn't do for you. He did not allow political or ideological differences to sour his relationships, as Robert F. Kennedy, Jr., made clear in his eulogy.

Breindel graduated from Harvard College in 1977 and studied at the London School of Economics before getting a Harvard law degree in 1982. His energies and ambitions pointed him to Washington, and he faced an interesting dilemma. His political views were clearly tending toward the neoconservative camp—he had begun writing regularly for Norman Podhoretz's magazine, *Commentary*, a few years before. The neoconservatives in Washington had all gone to work for the Reagan administration. But Breindel had formed a close association with New York senator Daniel Patrick Moynihan while at Harvard (Moynihan had been the employer of most of those Washington neoconservatives on their way from liberalism to Reaganism). Breindel did not join the Reagan administration; instead, he went to work for Moynihan on the Senate Intelligence Committee.

In Washington in the early 1980s, there was no more promising young Democrat than Breindel. But he was harboring a secret that would have an initially catastrophic and finally triumphant effect on his life.

From his high-school days onward, Breindel had been coping with a series of health problems—troubles with his kidney and, especially, a ruinous injury to his wrist—that kept him mired in a state of almost constant pain. Operations on the wrist failed to alleviate the suffering. In some ways, he lived a life more understandable in the nineteenth century than in the present day—physical pain was a constant companion.

He was introduced to powerful painkillers to help him cope, but they did not give him all that much relief. It may well have been the quest for more effective pain relief that led him to experiment with heroin, the ultimate opiate. And in 1983, while working for the Senate Intelligence Committee, Breindel was arrested while attempting to buy heroin from an undercover FBI agent.

It was a horrific blow for someone whose life had been, until that point, nothing but an upward climb. Yet the arrest may have been the best thing that ever happened to him. Breindel kicked his habit, and the only addictions he indulged in afterward were cigarettes—he chain-smoked with unholy glee—and the aforementioned hamburgers and baked ziti. He never took a sip of a drink.

More important, in the aftermath of the arrest, a career as a foreign policy maker was no longer a tenable option. This led Breindel away from government and into the world of journalism. After a brief stint as a television producer, he began writing editorials for the New York *Daily News.* In 1986, Rupert Murdoch chose him to be Editorial Page editor of the *New York Post,* and with Murdoch, as with Moynihan and Peretz and Norman Podhoretz before him, Breindel forged yet another of his extraordinary friendships.

The former Democratic staffer had become responsible for devising and structuring the editorial opinions in the city's conservative newspaper. He no longer stood on the dividing line between Left and Right, trying to determine which side to stand on. He was firmly in the conservative camp. And by moving decisively and unmistakably rightward, Breindel found his voice as a writer.

He remained as the *Post's* Editorial Page editor until early 1997, when he became a senior vice president of Murdoch's NewsCorp. Those eleven years were tempestuous ones for the newspaper he worked for—it had three owners and almost closed down twice before Murdoch purchased it again in 1993—and for the city he lived in. New York became the image of a civil society under siege. At the same time, Soviet communism was rapidly disintegrating, black anti-Semitism was on the rise, and Israel's future remained front-page news.

Breindel continued to cope with health problems. He was diagnosed with Hodgkin's disease in 1991 and suffered through chemotherapy before being pronounced in remission two years later. In the fall of 1997, he began to suffer spasms of pain and naturally feared a return of his cancer. But a battery of tests showed none; indeed, the tests could not determine the source of the pain.

In the last week of February 1998, Breindel collapsed from internal bleeding and was taken to the hospital, after months of pain his doctors could not diagnose. He remained in a coma for almost a week, then briefly recovered consciousness the morning he died.

His funeral was an extraordinary event. Twelve hundred people crowded Park Avenue Synagogue on a rainy Monday to pay their respects to a man who had touched them—either through his generous friendship, his sage and practical advice, or the uncompromising honesty of his writing.

John Podhoretz

A PASSION FOR TRUTH

PART 1

THE ANTI-COMMUNIST STRUGGLE

PARTY MEMBERS AND FELLOW TRAVELERS

What was it that the American Communist Party did that so aroused the ire of Breindel? In this series of columns, Breindel explains the intellectual corruption at the heart of the Party and the Party's uncanny ability to inspire deathless loyalty among not only those who signed up (its members) but those who did not and yet still shared its ideals and goals (fellow travelers).

Nazis of the Left

March 2, 1988

The Republican Party's condemnation of Ku Klux Klansman David Duke, who managed last month—running as a Republican—to snare a seat in the Louisiana state legislature, deserves more attention than it has received.

It would have been easy for the GOP simply to dismiss the Duke episode as a fluke and to try to ignore it. The Republicans did just the opposite, launching a major effort to defeat the former KKK Grand Dragon running on their line.

The GOP, at the direction of its new national chairman, Lee Atwater, even succeeded in drawing Presidents Bush and Reagan into the fray—both men issued statements condemning Duke and the KKK and urging voters to cast their ballots for Duke's opponent.

That it's altogether extraordinary for the White House to involve itself in a state legislative contest seems self-evident.

It's possible, of course, to explain the urgent Republican response to Duke's candidacy as a manifestation of Lee Atwater's plan to bring blacks and other minorities into GOP ranks. And that's what many pundits have done.

Certainly, there is such a plan. And the Republicans have no reason to be ashamed of the fact that they—at the instigation of Atwater, HUD Secretary Jack Kemp, and President Bush himself—mean to reach out to blacks in a serious way.

But there was also a political downside to the GOP's posture vis-à-vis Duke. The Republicans risked alienating those Southern whites to whom Duke obviously appeals—some of them actual racists, others bitter ex-Democrats who are convinced that they've been abandoned by the party into which they were born.

Thus, speaking out against Duke cannot be represented as a cold political calculation on the part of the GOP leadership. Bush, Reagan, et al., clearly saw a moral issue at stake.

David Duke—an overt racist, a recent KKK official, and ex-(American) Nazi—was seeking public office under the Republican banner. This placed on Republicans a moral obligation to speak out in defense of their party's good name—by separating themselves from Duke and by disavowing his ugly message.

How have the Democrats responded in parallel circumstances? How has the Democratic Party leadership behaved when faced with similar moral questions?

Not well, sad to say.

True, in Illinois, when followers of Lyndon LaRouche managed to win statewide Democratic primary races, the national party, at the behest of Democratic gubernatorial candidate Adlai Stevenson III— who wound up with LaRoucheites as his statewide running mates— distanced itself from the LaRouche candidates.

But New York Democrats evidenced no like concern when members of the recently dissolved Communist Workers Party (CWP), a violence-oriented Maoist sect, took over an important Democratic political club and even elected a CWP leader to the state Democratic Committee.

In failing to act, New York Democrats willfully ignored warnings issued by Stevenson himself. Indeed, for his effort to make clear that the Illinois-LaRouche episode and the New York–CWP controversy involved the same issues, Stevenson was censured as a "Red-baiter" by the New York County Democratic Committee.

Moreover, supporters of radical-Left totalitarianism have sought and won election—as Democrats—to local offices all across the country and to the U.S. Congress without a murmur of protest from the national party leadership.

In this category, of course, are men and women with close links to the Title Principle U.S.A. and its many fronts: Representative George Crockett of Michigan, a former attorney for the Title Principle, is an obvious example. Representative Charles Hayes of Illinois is another.

Ex-Massachusetts state representative Mel King is one of many Democratic politicians active in the Communist Party-controlled U.S. Peace Council. New York City Councilwoman Miriam Friedlander, elected and reelected as a Democrat, is a former member of the Communist Party national committee.

There is no record of Friedlander's ever breaking with or disavowing the Communist Party, yet neither Robert Strauss nor Paul Kirk ever spoke out against her on behalf of the national Democratic Party. And it doesn't seem likely that Ronald Brown, the new Democratic national chairman, will break the silence.

Is this a result of the taboo that makes it impossible, in polite company, to call a Communist a Communist (without being labeled a McCarthyite Red-baiter)? Only in part. The bottom line is that most Democratic leaders recognize no parallel between a Klansman riding to victory on the Republican ticket and a Communist winning public office as a Democrat.

This failure to see the Communist Party and the KKK as similarly pernicious political phenomena bespeaks a critical weakness in the worldview of mainstream Democratic Party leaders. It explains the party's sharp shift to the left and the rise within the national party of the Jesse Jackson forces.

Until Ron Brown is willing to deal with Crockett and Friedlander the way Lee Atwater approached David Duke, extremist elements in the Democratic Party will continue to gain strength. And the likelihood of the Democrats' capturing the White House any time soon will continue to diminish.

A Traitor's Secret Regrets

May 19, 1988

There is a good deal we don't know—and probably never will know—about H. A. R. (Kim) Philby, the legendary Soviet mole in British intelligence who died last week in Moscow at the age of seventy-six.

But not long before his death, an ill as well as aging Philby granted British journalist Phillip Knightley a series of extensive interviews. The talks with Knightley took place this past January. They were the first lengthy interviews granted to a recognized Western journalist since Philby fled to Moscow in 1963.

The final installment appeared in the *Sunday Times* (London) just last month. It seems plain that Philby knew he didn't have much time left—he discusses his illness in that last installment—and wanted to send out a final message.

Although attended by a fair bit of bluster and a fair bit of intelligence-related disinformation, Philby's intended message is plain: "No regrets" burden him, he tells Knightley, "no regrets."

No regrets about the deaths he caused—the deaths, for example, of the Albanian and other East European refugees who were shot on sight, thanks to Philby, after parachuting into their native lands in order to foment popular risings against newly installed Communist regimes.

As a senior British intelligence officer, Philby had helped plan these operations, even as he betrayed every detail to Moscow. But in his view, he merely helped "frustrate a Western-inspired plan for a bloodbath in the Balkans."

Nor does Philby regret having caused the murder of Konstantin Volkov, a Soviet intelligence officer who sought to defect in 1945. Volkov had appeared at the British consulate in Istanbul, begging for asylum and offering valuable information.

He asked that news of his offer not be telegraphed to London—Moscow, Volkov explained, had broken the British code. The Soviets, moreover—according to Volkov—had agents at the highest level of British intelligence.

London heeded Volkov's counsel and turned the case over to

Philby for expert handling. The British, needless to say, never saw or heard from Volkov again.

But "Volkov was a nasty piece of work," Philby tells Knightley. "No regrets there," either.

What Philby most wants us to know is that he doesn't regret having betrayed his country, that he has retained his faith in the Communist ideal. This is his principal intended message.

"In Gorbachev . . . I have a leader who has justified my years of faith," Philby explains at one point.

And at the close of the last interview, when Knightley asks if there's anything they haven't touched on, Philby tells the interviewer there is "one bone I want to pick with you."

He refers to Knightley's previously published assertion that Philby, living in Moscow, has "no home, no woman, no faith." After pointing out his flat and his Russian wife, Philby exclaims: "No faith? Come, come, only a fool would deny me my faith."

The KGB—in which Philby held the rank of general—probably authorized the Knightley interviews with some enthusiasm, pleased by the message Philby wanted to send. It's not often these days that Moscow can produce a cultivated Westerner who, after half a century of service to the Communist cause, remains a true believer.

But in the end, Philby's protestations with regard to guilt ("no regrets") and treason and faith have a decidedly hollow ring.

When Knightley asks him if he feels guilty about his "lack of patriotism," Philby's answer is rambling and tortured: "Patriotism is a very complex emotion," he contends. "The Russians have a great love for their country, but over the years many of them have emigrated. . . . Millions of people fight and die for their country, yet millions emigrate to found new nations. I'm from such ancestry myself. Our family was originally Filby and came from Denmark."

Philby goes on to explain that his "interest in patriotism" makes him "intrigued by Mrs. Thatcher when she says, 'I love my country passionately.'" He professes to wonder "which country she's talking about? Finchley and Dulwich? Or Liverpool and Glasgow?"

This verges on the pathetic—pointing to the fact that the UK is a big place in order to question the validity of a British patriotic sensibility. From a man like Philby, this is strikingly unconvincing stuff.

On reading these interviews, it's hard not to conclude that Philby never actually came to terms with what he had done. His disloyalty is often explained by reference to his father: St. John Philby was a minor Lawrence of Arabia, an angry misfit who lived in the Middle East, converted to Islam, and went about London, when he was there, cloaked in Arab garb.

But Kim Philby's unorthodox family background seems *not* to have insulated him fully from patriotic sentiment—he was evidently burdened by doubt right to the end.

He even reminds Knightley that "Trevor-Roper [the British historian] wrote that he thought I had never done England any harm." This apparently comforts Philby, who adds: "In my terms that is certainly true, but I was surprised and touched that he [Trevor-Roper] thought it was so in his terms."

In fact, of course, Philby and his cohorts did Britain and the West enormous harm, particularly by facilitating Soviet domination of Eastern Europe and by sowing mistrust between Britain and America.

What's interesting is the discovery that betraying his country continued to weigh upon Philby. Try as he might to rationalize it away, he knew he was a traitor, and that knowledge pained him. For all his claims to "no regrets," that's the essence of his final message, intended or not.

The Popular Front Raves On

November 24, 1989

"Anti-Communism is an exploitation of the deep structures of racism for the exploitation of the workers." So pronounced Joel Kovel, Alger Hiss Professor of Sociology at Bard College, at a conference on "Anti-Communism and the U.S.: History and Consequences," held at Harvard University earlier this month.

No, this is not a joke. That really is Professor Kovel's title—he really holds the "Alger Hiss Professorship." And Kovel really did utter the sentence quoted above—whatever it may mean.

There really was such a conference, moreover.

The "Anti-Communism" conference was sponsored by the Institute for Media Analysis, a left-wing press-monitoring group. Many of those who came, not surprisingly, are actual, self-professed Communists—including, for example, Gus Hall, general secretary of the Communist Party USA, whose speech was reported on the front page of the *People's Daily World*, the Party newspaper.

But most of the conferees—some of them well-known figures in political and intellectual life: John Kenneth Galbraith, William Styron, and Julian Bond, to name just a few—are not.

Their presence at the gathering, which was attended by twelve hundred people and was dedicated to the memory of Lenin Peace Prize winner and IRA staff chief Sean MacBride—marked it as an important Popular Front event.

The concept of the Popular Front dates back to 1935, at which time the international Communist movement decided to abandon the claim that social democrats were merely "social fascists" and to adopt a call for a united (or "popular") front against real fascism.

The Comintern had come to the conclusion that—contrary to its previous stance—Hitler was not a passing phase. The Communists determined that fascism was a decidedly more pernicious force even than liberal democracy and that it was worthwhile making alliances with non-Communist political elements wherever and whenever possible.

The strategic purpose of Popular Front activities has always been to use these non-Communist elements as beards—to see that the Party line is advanced by individuals and groups that enjoy independent reputations and can't, therefore, be written off as mere puppets of Moscow.

The message to participants at the Harvard conference from the organizers held that anticommunism is "a pathology . . . the civic religion of the U.S. . . . a justification for the scapegoating of radicals, progressives, leftists and, now, liberals."

Also at the conference, apart from those already mentioned, were CIA defector Phillip Agee; Old Left attorney Leonard Boudin; former Communist Party USA vice-presidential candidate Angela

Davis; Rainbow Coalition official Jack O'Dell; and Dr. Bernard Lown, founder of International Physicians for the Prevention of Nuclear War.

The panels addressed such themes as "Godlessness: Religion and Anti-Communism" (Joel Kovel, moderator); "The Role of the CIA" (William Schaap, Phillip Agee); and "What's Black and White and Red All Over? Anti-Communism and American Literature" (Howard Fast). Also treated were "The Rise of the American Empire," "The Culture of Anti-Communism," and "Anti-Sovietism in America."

While not surprising, given the nature of Popular Front activities, it is nonetheless worth noting that criticism of the Soviet Union, no matter how mild, was utterly taboo at this event.

Jack O'Dell argued that the USSR is constantly slandered in America—anticommunism, said O'Dell, "is the ideology of hatred that has been the spinoff of the big lie about the Soviet Union."

Kovel maintained that the entire concept of totalitarianism is "a fictional construct to promote anti-Communism."

And when journalist Carl Bernstein, of Watergate fame, suggested that the American press is free and independent—and isn't a participant in the ongoing anti-Soviet conspiracy—he was roundly booed.

Another theme made its way to the fore in the course of the conference. In a symposium on anticommunism and the media, Jane Hunter, the editor of *Israeli Foreign Affairs,* an anti-Israel periodical, allowed that "the greatest lie . . . around the coverage of Israel . . . is the notion of the uniqueness of the Holocaust."

Just why it is necessary to argue against the uniqueness of the Holocaust at a conference on the subject of anticommunism in American life would seem to be something of a mystery.

But later on in the discussions, another panelist took things even further along this path, delivering a disquisition on the theme that Jews are not genuine Semites; disliking Jews, therefore, can't properly be termed "anti-Semitism," this participant maintained.

This is ugly stuff—it sounds like it comes right out of the Soviet media. True, that's not surprising; indeed, it's an illustration of precisely what is meant to happen at events of this kind.

For outsiders, then, a conference of this kind represents a useful opportunity to get a glimpse at the Party line and at Communist priorities in America.

As for the non-Communists who lent their names and talent to this event, thereby giving it credibility—the various John Kenneth Galbraiths—they should be ashamed of themselves.

Why Moscow Funded Gus Hall & Co.

March 5, 1992

The discovery, in Mikhail Gorbachev's personal Politburo file, of a series of letters from Gus Hall—general secretary of the Communist Party USA—begging Moscow to rush delivery of the American Party's $2 million annual stipend, has created a story with an inherently comic aspect.

According to Michael Dobbs of the *Washington Post*, Hall—though only one of many recipients of secret Soviet funding—apparently issued his unending pleas in a particularly plaintive and abject fashion: He would claim, on the one hand, that the American Communist Party was on the verge of leading "a mass upsurge" against U.S. imperialism; he'd then shift gears and complain that Party leaders might have to resort to remortgaging their homes if cash from Moscow weren't forthcoming.

Less sophisticated even than Hall's agitprop-ridden letters was his tendency to provide the KGB couriers who gave him the money with handwritten, signed receipts acknowledging the sum that had been (illegally) transferred.

As the *Washington Post* notes, Western European Communists tended to be far more discreet. For example, a receipt discovered by Soviet prosecutors that had been signed by a French Communist leader reads simply "RECEIVED: two packets of paper." The signature itself is illegible.

Obviously, Hall's use of primitive Marxist jargon and his effort to pretend to Yuri Andropov and Mikhail Gorbachev that the Communist Party USA itself was a vital force in American political life—the "objective situation" was always about to turn in "our" favor—make for an easy laugh. Hall's insistence on the strategic significance of the Party's location—"in the decaying heart of imperialism"—must have given even the men in the Kremlin a chuckle.

But it remains that until 1990, the subsidy *was* provided—even if the Soviet ambassador to Washington, Anatoly Dobrynin, found it necessary to scotch Hall's 1988 effort to secure a 100 percent increase.

It also remains that the American Party was but one beneficiary of Soviet largess: Moscow supported client parties from India to El Salvador, demonstrating—as Dobbs puts it in the *Washington Post*—that an "'an international communist conspiracy' really did exist for much of the past seven decades."

Some things, it would seem, are true, even though J. Edgar Hoover said them.

But before we laugh too hard at Gus Hall's pronouncements about the impending triumph of the "working-class movement," it seems well to consider the implications of these archival discoveries. The extent of the funding and the political level in Moscow at which the decisions to continue it were taken are worth pondering.

For starters, it can be viewed as yet another comment on Mikhail Gorbachev's firm credentials as a Communist that he kept the subsidy program going all through the 1980s.

But there remains a larger question: What was Moscow's purpose? Leonid Brezhnev, Yuri Andropov, and Mikhail Gorbachev—along with their colleagues and predecessors—were serious men. It's unlikely that they took Hall's grandiose claims at face value. It's unlikely that they were inclined to waste valuable hard currency.

Indeed, it's unlikely that they were well disposed toward wasting their own time—and these issues, after all, required Politburo discussion. Did they provide the money out of a sense of moral obligation? Also not likely.

My guess? The Soviet leaders understood that the success of the Communist Party could not be measured in traditional terms: number of members, electoral victories, and so forth. The American Communist Party did play a dynamic role, far out of proportion to its numerical strength, in national political life; in fact, it helped set the American political agenda—mostly by creating and controlling front organizations.

Examples aren't hard to come by, although this is a subject that is often shouted down by cries of "Red-baiting."

The Communist Party USA—through the party-controlled U.S. Peace Council—played a major part in the 1982 nuclear-freeze campaign, even determining the nature of the rhetoric (condemnations of the USSR were virtually verboten) at the huge Nuclear Freeze Rally in Central Park that year.

The importance of tiny El Salvador in the U.S. political debate has had a great deal to do with a still-extant protest group called CISPES (Committee in Solidarity with the People of El Salvador), an outfit with close links to the U.S. and Salvadoran Communist parties.

And, of course, the role of the Communist Party USA in the 1984 creation of Jesse Jackson's Rainbow Coalition has been discussed in detail both in Party journals and in the non-Party left-wing literature.

More information on these themes may well emerge as documents are unsealed in Moscow.

But it's safe to assume that Gorbachev & Co. didn't allow Soviet money to be wasted on the tired, endless Gus Hall-for-president campaigns. The cash almost certainly went where cool heads believed it might do the cause some good.

And, notwithstanding communism's eventual demise—a historical development that even the U.S. Peace Council couldn't prevent—who's to say this particular assessment was incorrect?

The National Lawyers Guild

June 30, 1995

It seemed at least reasonable to hope that, after the demise of the Soviet Union, it would be possible to call a Communist a Communist—or to label a Communist-front group as such—without inviting charges of Red-baiting.

Not so, sad to say.

A recent *New York Post* editorial noting that Judge Kristin Booth Glen, the newly appointed dean at the City University Law School, is a member in good standing of the National Lawyers Guild proves the point. The *Post,* in the course of wondering whether or not left-of-center credentials were a prerequisite for the CUNY law deanship, pointed out that Glen has "long been active in the [National Lawyers] Guild," as well as in other political organizations with a left-wing bias.

The editorial described the guild as having been, for many years, the "legal arm of the American Communist Party"; it went on to suggest that the guild was now a "collective of ultra-Left lawyers."

The rush to deny was surprising, if not stunning. Martin A. Sanchez Rojas, the guild's executive director, wrote a letter to the editor asserting that "we would not describe the National Lawyers Guild as a collective of ultra-Left lawyers any more than we would assume every member of a right-of-center organization is planning on bombing a federal building." Thus, Rojas—not the *Post*—posits a moral equivalency between membership in an "ultra-Left collective" and a disposition to blow up buildings.

The bizarre illogic on exhibit here may not indicate anything more than an overwrought sensibility. But there's something decidedly strange about endeavoring simply to deny the guild's left-of-center orientation. And crying "McCarthyism," as does Rojas, to deflect discussion of the guild's historical ties to the Communist Party seems flatly dishonest.

Citing prior efforts to discredit the guild by depicting it as an "adjunct" of the Communist Party, Rojas reports that throughout its history the guild has had but one client: "the Bill of Rights." This empty platitude is no substitute for an effort to deal with the complicated story of the guild's relationship to the Communist Party. Yet it's unlikely that Rojas is ignorant as to the issue's significance in the history of the guild. Far more plausible is the notion that he finds the subject too embarrassing or too painful to explore.

In a letter attacking the same *Post* editorial, Professor Peter Erlinder of the William Mitchell College of Law in St. Paul, Minnesota, calls the suggestion that the guild is an ultra-Left collective "absurd"; Erlinder "proves" his point by noting that many guild members have served in political and judicial posts.

The professor seems to believe that the willingness of guild lawyers to represent witnesses called before the House Un-American Activities Committee—"when few [others] had the courage to do so"—led to the attorney general's decision to label it the "legal bulwark" of the Party.

He also asserts that "after years of intensive surveillance, FBI infiltration and disruption," the Justice Department had to admit that "the Lawyers Guild was not the legal arm of the Communist Party." This, of course, would be interesting—if it were true. Actually, it's utter nonsense: The Justice Department never issued any such finding.

The guild, as it happens, was formed in 1937 by pro-New Deal, pro-FDR attorneys—some of them Communists, others not. But a controversy about the Communist Party's role in the organization utterly fractured it a mere two years later. Early in 1939— and especially after the August Hitler-Stalin Pact—many of the leading non-Communists in the guild concluded that they'd been naive in believing they could work with Party members in a national political organization. The most noted of the New Dealers—Judge Jerome Frank, Abe Fortas, Morris Ernst, and Adolf A. Berle, Jr.—dropped out of the guild. At the leadership level, the guild came to be dominated by lawyers who were strictly devoted to the Party line.

True, the guild took pains to put non-Communists in some of its most public posts—usually, fellow travelers like Thomas Emerson of Yale Law School and Clifford Durr, a Roosevelt appointee to the Federal Communications Commission. And guild rank-and-filers always included non-Party "progressives."

But on key issues, the National Lawyers Guild stood shoulder to shoulder with the Party. In 1939, it refused to adopt a resolution condemning the Hitler-Stalin pact. It joined the Moscow-controlled International Association of Democratic Lawyers in 1946, just when the IADL was created. A year later, the guild condemned the Marshall Plan. Subsequently, at the IADL, it voted—in the aftermath of the Stalin-Tito split—to expel the Yugoslav (pro-Tito) delegation. And at the onset of the Korean War, the guild declared it couldn't "approve the military action of the United States" in Korea.

Communist front? You decide.

In the late 1950s, after the Communist Party transformed itself from a political movement into a pro-Moscow sect, the National Lawyers Guild gradually weakened its ties to the Party and sought to define a role for itself in the context of the civil rights movement, the New Left, and the campaign against the war in Vietnam. The influence of Stalinism remained strong. But new issues—and new allegiances—came to the fore.

One thing seems certain: At this stage, it should be possible to discuss these subjects with a measure of candor. Starting the discussion by denying that the National Lawyers Guild has a left-wing bias—even Judge Glen has called it the "leftist bar association"—is an early sign of bad faith. And denying the guild's historic ties to the Communist Party indicates that honest discussion is still a ways off.

THE LEGACY OF
McCARTHYISM

Nowhere can Breindel's nuanced but fierce anticommunism be seen better than in this series of columns, which explores the ways in which Joseph McCarthy's demagoguery ended up aiding the cause of the Communists he supposedly reviled—by making it hard to have an honest public conversation about who was and was not a American Communist and why being an American Communist was not a good thing.

Calling a Communist a Communist

May 9, 1987

This week saw the thirtieth anniversary of the death of Senator Joseph R. McCarthy, an anniversary scarcely acknowledged save for a small memorial mass at St. Patrick's Cathedral. McCarthy, censured by the Senate in 1954, was already dead as a political force by the time of his actual passing at the age of forty-seven.

He entered history, from the standpoint of the liberal establishment, as a symbol of evil incarnate—and as something of an embarrassment for most of the Republican Right.

In precious few circles has it been possible to hear a good word about Joe McCarthy in the three decades since his death. The term *McCarthyism* has entered the American language. It's used freely—as a synonym for character assassination, guilt by association, and innuendo—all across the political spectrum.

Seldom noted, however, is the Wisconsin senator's most insidious political legacy: As a consequence of the recklessness and seeming cruelty of his efforts to expose Communist infiltration in government, it became virtually impossible, in polite company, to call a Communist a Communist.

The prohibition on identifying Communists as such is a fact of American life—it obtains in journalism, in politics, in the academy, indeed in virtually all mainstream public discourse. It's a rule widely acknowledged and obeyed, rather like a taboo.

Ethics is a key factor here—perceived ethical issues, actually. In the wake of what are widely regarded as the excesses of the McCarthy era, many people tend to feel that by identifying someone as a Communist, they are doing something wrong—even when that identification is altogether accurate and even when making it in public is altogether relevant.

The second reason for the general reluctance to identify public figures as Communists—or organizations as Communist fronts—is that doing so is bad PR. It invites immediate accusations of Redbaiting and—even when the identification is accurate beyond doubt—tends to discredit not the Communists themselves, but those who identify them.

It isn't necessary to look very far to find an example of this inhibition at work. Consider the case, just this past week, of Benjamin Linder—the twenty-seven-year-old American engineer who was killed in a Contra grenade attack in northern Nicaragua.

For Linder's death to be used effectively in the effort to undermine U.S. support for the Contras, it was advantageous for family, friends, and the Sandinista propaganda apparatus to downplay his political ties—and to depict him as an innocent, well-intentioned young professional who simply wanted to donate his skills to making life better in a poor and war-ravaged country.

Although various press accounts did note Linder's ties, in college and in Nicaragua, to groups protesting U.S. policy in Latin America, the emphasis was always elsewhere—on his ability to entertain children by riding a unicycle and performing as a clown and on his desire to bring the benefits of electricity to the peasants of Nicaragua.

In this innocent and wholesome context, his brother's charge that

"Ben was murdered" by the U.S. government had considerably more force to it, as did his father's assertion that, ultimately, Ronald Reagan was to blame. A number of legislators on Capitol Hill took up this cry, as did editorial pages around the country.

It seems safe to say that the Linder case would have aroused far less public and congressional sympathy if it had been clear from the outset that this was a young man of decidedly pro-Marxist and anti-American views, that Linder had headed the University of Washington chapter of an organization—the Committee in Solidarity with the People of El Salvador (CISPES)—with close links to the American Communist Party, that he was in Nicaragua to help consolidate Sandinista rule, and that he came by his politics honestly: Benjamin Linder's parents are both activists devoted to far-Left causes.

His mother, in fact, is a leader of the Women's International League for Peace and Freedom, one of the oldest and most established international Soviet fronts.

Is all this relevant to who this young man was, how he came to be in Nicaragua, and what he stood for in life? You bet.

Was this readily available information put forward in a concerted fashion—even by Reagan administration officials—during the last week? No way.

That would have been Red-baiting.

It isn't fair to blame Joe McCarthy alone for the taboo on identifying Communists as Communists. He is merely the symbol of an entire era. But it seems safe to say that if it weren't for the fact that some people suffered unfairly during the McCarthy era, the contemporary political debate in America would be a whole lot more honest.

Memories of Metzenbaum

August 1, 1987

The latest "McCarthyism" furor—the Howard Metzenbaum affair—raises a number of questions that have been ignored by most of those commenting on the case.

First the facts: the National Republican Senatorial Committee prepared a seventy-two-page research report on Senator Howard Metzenbaum, a two-term Ohio Democrat who faces reelection next year. Such reports, which tend to focus on areas in which the targeted incumbent may be vulnerable, are standard practice for both parties.

This one was a bit rough. In a section headed "Early Political Affiliation: Communist Sympathizer," the report—which was given to Metzenbaum's two most likely Republican opponents—details the senator's past ties to what the study calls "Communist causes."

While urging that "caution be observed in order to avoid . . . looking 'McCarthyistic' [sic]," the report goes on to note that many of Metzenbaum's legislative initiatives can be represented as consistent with his early Communist leanings. The Ohio Democrat's call for a government-run national oil corporation is cited as an example.

Now this, in a sense, is dumb stuff. The political initiatives noted in the report are standard left-liberal fare. And Metzenbaum's overall Senate record is that of a Ted Kennedy liberal Democrat—not a Marxist.

The reaction to the report—a copy of which found its way to the *Cleveland Plain Dealer*—was entirely predictable. Rudy Boschwitz (R-Minnesota), the chairman of the National Republican Senatorial Committee, took to the Senate floor to apologize to Metzenbaum. Boschwitz called the study "insulting and outrageous."

Bob Dole (R-Kansas), the Senate Republican leader, echoed Boschwitz's sentiments, declaring, "I apologize to all my colleagues." Dole then strode across the Senate floor to shake Metzenbaum's hand.

Metzenbaum, for his part, accepted the apologies, but emphasized that he had "never seen a document that went to the depths this went to—to smear, to lie, to misrepresent."

And this points up the key undiscussed question: Where are the lies?

None of the Republican senators who apologized for the report, none of the Democrats who denounced it—and none of the news stories about the episode—challenged the document's factual accuracy.

Did Metzenbaum, as a young Ohio politician in the 1940s, have ties to the organizations cited in the report—the National Lawyers Guild, the Ohio School of Social Science, and the

Progressive Citizens Committee of Cleveland? The answer is yes. (None of the allegations are new; they are all amply documented, and Metzenbaum has never denied them.)

What about these groups—were they actually Communist fronts, controlled by the U.S. Communist Party? Again, the answer is yes—beyond the shadow of a doubt.

Yet, somehow, these matters continue to sow confusion. A *New York Times* editorial entitled "Campaign Sleaze and Mr. Metzenbaum" exclaims with sarcasm: "Imagine the mentality of the authors [of the report] who zeroed in on some of the peace and progressive 'Communist causes' that Mr. Metzenbaum joined in the 1940s. Perhaps they worry, too, about President Reagan's affiliation with the Screen Actors Guild in those years."

A strange analogy—the Screen Actors Guild was not a Communist front. Its minority Communist faction was routed in union election after union election. The pro-Communist character of the groups to which Metzenbaum had ties, on the other hand, has never seriously been disputed.

Even stranger, however, is the appearance in the *Times* editorial column of misleading terminology from the Old Left lexicon. For Communist fronts to be described in a *Times* editorial as "progressive" organizations or as "peace causes" represents a bizarre instance of semantic infiltration.

The point of this whole affair is unclear. Perhaps it was unseemly to link Metzenbaum's current political posture to his past Communist-front ties, but that's obviously not the only message those who have attacked the report are trying to send.

The manifest implication is that raising this history is automatically illegitimate. This seems especially odd at a time when those who aspire to public office are subjected to every conceivable intrusion—into their personal lives and into their private financial circumstances.

But beyond the ethos of the moment, why should a politician's political history ever be deemed taboo terrain? Is it wrong to raise these matters because Metzenbaum was affiliated with the groups in question a long time ago? That might be a reasonable position if the senator had subsequently repudiated these ties.

But he's never even explained them—not how he came to serve as secretary of the Ohio National Lawyers Guild, the legal arm of the Communist Party, and not how he and Hyman Lumer, later the Communist Party's national education director, came to found the Ohio School of Social Science.

These were organizations that devoted themselves to justifying the crimes of Stalin. Why shouldn't a U.S. senator be called upon to explain his involvement with them?

Roy Cohn and His Enemies

March 24, 1988

The appearance of two new books on the late Roy Cohn promises to make the ex-chief counsel to Senator Joseph McCarthy a subject of considerable attention in the months ahead.

Attention, of course, wouldn't have been anything new for Cohn, who died nearly two years ago. He went from early headlines as a boy prosecutor—at the age of twenty-two, he helped send Julius and Ethel Rosenberg to the electric chair—to national celebrity, while still in his twenties, as McCarthy's top aide.

But the obloquy that descended upon Roy Cohn as a result of his activities during that period made it seem unlikely he'd ever again attain a place of prominence in mainstream society.

Yet despite an unorthodox lifestyle, several brushes with the law—he was indicted three times on multivaried financial charges, but was never convicted on a single count—and the constant presence of personal enemies in high places, Cohn became a preeminent power broker, a man of rare political influence.

Much of the discussion about Cohn will center on his seemingly paradoxical journey to power and influence, his controversial career in law and finance, and his life as a first-echelon jet-setter.

Sidney Zion's *Autobiography of Roy Cohn* consists largely of Cohn speaking in his own, albeit edited, voice—in response to questions put to him by Zion. The project took this form after it became clear that Cohn's battle with AIDS would prevent him from completing the autobiography he'd begun.

The book also includes background biographical passages written by Zion to add context to Cohn's reminiscences.

Citizen Cohn, by Nicholas von Hoffman, is a more traditional biography, based largely on interviews conducted by the author. But many of the interviewees—friends of Cohn, as well as foes—apparently requested anonymity, a circumstance that makes the book somewhat difficult to evaluate.

Citizen Cohn seeks to reconcile Cohn's ultrapatriotic, staunchly anti-Communist political sensibility with his unconventional personal and sexual mores—this, in fact, is the book's overriding concern.

Von Hoffman also grapples with the question of how Cohn achieved the influence he came to wield, an issue the Zion book treats in its own way—by means of anecdote.

Both books examine, in some detail, Cohn's role as a prosecutor and his work with McCarthy. But this material is unlikely to draw the same kind of popular interest as Cohn's life in the fast lane.

Yet that was the period in which Cohn purportedly engaged in the reckless "witch-hunting" that earned him the undying enmity of liberal society.

Those were the years in which he is said to have gone about leveling false charges against innocent people—destroying careers with carefree abandon by calling innocent people Communists.

That's the conventional wisdom, anyway.

But in neither of these books is there a single example of a case in which Cohn inaccurately labeled someone a Communist.

Of all the prosecutions Roy Cohn worked on—Hiss, the Rosenbergs, Remington, and more—and of all the cases Cohn pursued on Capitol Hill, from the army dentist Irving Peress to the teletype clerk Annie Lee Moss, there isn't one instance of someone Cohn labeled a Communist who turned out not to be a Communist.

In the Zion book, to be sure, Cohn acknowledges for the first time that he did, indeed—as critics have charged—hold *ex parte* communications with Judge Irving Kaufman during the Rosenberg trial. Cohn says he even counseled the judge that the magnitude of the crime made the death penalty appropriate.

Such communications between judges and prosecutors—though technically improper, then as now—were not uncommon at the time. And while Rosenberg-case activists will seize this tidbit as further evidence that the trial was a judicial miscarriage, it has no bearing whatever on the couple's guilt.

Why is this failure to identify innocent victims of Cohn's anti-Communist zealotry significant?

Cohn himself points to the answer in a discussion about McCarthy with Zion:

"I don't buy the liberals' line that they only opposed McCarthy's methods. I believe most of them opposed his ends—which was to expose and bring to justice Communist subversives.

"If it were the methods they didn't like, why didn't we hear from them when Kefauver investigated the mob? Well, we did hear from them. We heard cheers. And later, when McClellan went after the Teamsters, the liberals ran to orgasm."

During his years in public life, Roy Cohn stood for something—waging war against domestic communism. Cohn's chief enemies, apart from the Communists themselves, were people who didn't believe that war needed to be fought. Thus their enmity toward him—not his youth, not his arrogance, not his "methods."

Smearing Clarence Thomas

October 17, 1991

If ever a semantic term experienced a rebirth, *McCarthyism* enjoyed a new lease on life during the Clarence Thomas inquisition. And while pro- and anti-Thomas forces used the term with equal abandon, it's hard not to feel that contemporary American McCarthyism is practiced most enthusiastically, and most efficiently, by those who dwell in the precincts of the Left.

True, McCarthyism has come to mean different things to different people, so much so that it's been necessary to wonder whether the term actually denotes anything specific at all any-more—other than ugly political tactics with which the hurler of the epithet takes issue.

That this should be true forty-one years after Senator Joseph R. McCarthy (R-Wisconsin) entered the national political arena—by delivering a speech in Wheeling, West Virginia, in which he claimed he knew the names of Communists in the State Department—probably shouldn't be surprising.

Even during the McCarthy Era, McCarthyism had come to mean lots of different things: guilt by association, scurrilous charges, unscrupulous investigatory methods, inquisitorial congressional hearings in which the rules of evidence don't apply, sensationalism in an effort to play to the news media.

In fact, the late Richard Rovere, in his decidedly hostile biography of Joe McCarthy, made a strong case for the view that playing to the media by learning its news cycles and serving the deadline needs of working journalists was the Wisconsin senator's chief asset as he mounted his anti-Communist crusade.

McCarthy was among the first to recognize that mere allegations, if leveled by a public figure, represented a "legitimate" news story—from the standpoint of nearly all journalists.

The story would consist entirely in the allegation. The absence of documentation was a matter for another day (if that day ever came).

That Joseph R. McCarthy degraded the cause of anticommunism in America—eventually making it taboo even to identify real Communists as such—has been apparent for a long time.

But only in the last week did it become clear to what extent his tactics have been adopted by the political Left.

Judge Clarence Thomas, a public figure confirmed for high office four times by the United States Senate, was hauled before the Senate Judiciary Committee and asked, for starters, to do the impossible—by proving a negative.

Thomas, according to his accusers, needed to demonstrate that a series of unwitnessed and undated events, alleged to have occurred nine and ten years ago, did not take place. Try it in your head; it can't be done.

Senator Howell Heflin of Alabama implied repeatedly that

Thomas had been accused of "date rape"—a charge never leveled even by Anita Hill. Talk about ugly innuendo.

Thomas found strangers (perhaps reporters, perhaps not) rifling through the garbage pails outside his house, looking for God only knows what (pornographic magazines?). He chased them away. Talk about unscrupulous investigatory methods.

The liberal-Left lobbies that publicly professed a determination to defeat the Thomas nomination by exposing his views as extreme—one such lobbyist said her group would "Bork" that "Uncle Thomas"—scoured the country, telephoning former Thomas aides and even journalists who'd covered him, pleading for "dirt."

Juan Williams of the *Washington Post* received calls from Senate staffers who wanted to know if Thomas was a wife-beater, if he'd submitted phony expense-account claims, if he'd taken money from the government of South Africa. Finally, in exasperation, a caller asked if Williams had "anything we can use to stop Thomas."

Some, to be sure, profess to have seen McCarthyism within the pro-Thomas camp. Indeed, NBC correspondent Andrea Mitchell accused Wyoming Senator Alan Simpson of "McCarthyism of the worst order" during a television interview. Mitchell was referring to Simpson's declaration that he was "getting stuff over the transom about Professor Hill," including a good deal of "derogatory" information.

But it wasn't clear whether Mitchell deemed the mere fact that Simpson had referred to the material an illustration of McCarthyism or whether she objected chiefly to his indulgence in innuendo—to his failure, in other words, actually to produce the "stuff" he said was coming in "over the transom." (It's hard to believe Simpson wouldn't have been subjected to the very same charge—McCarthyism—if the senator had, in fact, chosen, perhaps on an interview program rather than during the hearings, to publicize the material in question.)

Speaking of introducing derogatory material during the hearings, for an example of McCarthyism in its purest form it was instructive to watch Senator Howard M. Metzenbaum slander a pro-Thomas witness, John Doggett, late Sunday night. Metzenbaum, rather than question Doggett about his testimony, asked the witness about an unsworn and utterly uncorroborated personal allegation concerning Doggett.

The question had nothing to do with anything (it didn't involve Thomas or Hill). The "charge" against Doggett had been made in a telephone interview with Senate staffers. Doggett had already denied it categorically. And merely by referring to it, Metzenbaum was violating the Judiciary Committee's agreed-upon evidentiary ground rules. The Ohio senator eventually "withdrew" the question—after a vigorous protest from Doggett in which even Judiciary Committee chairman Senator Joseph Biden concurred.

But the damage (despite Metzenbaum's subsequent public apology) had already been done. Metzenbaum—who has probably leveled the charge of McCarthyism more frequently than any other sitting member of the U.S. Senate—had slandered a young businessman from Austin, Texas, on national television for no reason beyond the fact that Doggett had come to Washington in support of Clarence Thomas (a fellow black alumnus of Yale Law School with whose political philosophy Doggett happens *not* to agree).

If McCarthyism—as a contemporary American political phenomenon—has, of late, been difficult to define, the foes of Clarence Thomas gave it all the meaning it needs by their conduct in recent weeks.

THE BLACKLIST REVISITED

The Hollywood blacklist, which effectively made unemployable anyone who had been an active Communist in the motion picture or television business, was a singular moment of injustice in American history— and therefore posed a difficult challenge for an anti-Communist like Breindel, who believed that investigations of American Communist Party members had been of vital importance in exposing Stalin's penetration of the U.S. government. In these columns, Breindel takes on the blacklist—and its utility in the 1980s and 1990s as a leftist martyrology for an increasingly anticonservative Hollywood.

Defaming Brent Bozell

October 12, 1989

L. Brent Bozell III is a young conservative publisher now under fire in Hollywood for an alleged effort to revive—in the words of the Screen Actors Guild (SAG)—"the dark blacklist days of the 1940s and 1950s."

What is it that Bozell's doing?

His new newsletter, *TV, etc.,* intends—according to Bozell himself—to "examine the political biases in the entertainment world, including prime-time network and cable television programming, recent movies and record releases and the activities of the stars themselves."

Bozell, in fact, has been even more specific about his purposes. Responding to the news that—in addition to the SAG's general opposition to "any form of blacklisting"—*TV, etc.,* was explicitly condemned in a recent AFTRA (American Federation of Television and Radio Artists) resolution, Bozell discussed his plans with the conservative weekly *Human Events.*

He said he opposed blacklisting and all efforts at state or federal censorship. And he made available to *Human Events* a letter he'd sent to AFTRA's new president after the resolution condemning his work was adopted this past summer.

In the letter, Bozell wrote: "Are we practicing censorship? If you mean censorship through legislation the answer is an emphatic: No. I will uphold anyone's right to free speech.

"But if that means Jackson Browne has a right to sell records with a vicious pro-Marxist message, I have the right to urge conservatives not buy his music.

"If HBO has the right to air anti-Contra movies on television, I have the right to urge pro-Contra supporters to change channels.

"If the cast and producers of 'Head of the Class' have the right to blast conservatives at every opportunity, I have the right to call [actor] Howard Hesseman & Co. liberals."

Is this nothing more than the revival of 1950s-style blacklisting, albeit with a new gloss? Are the ostensible distinctions mere semantics?

For someone with a right-of-center political perspective who's, nonetheless, decidedly uncomfortable with the blacklisting that took place during the 1950s—someone like myself—this is a question that can't be ignored.

Yes, the McCarthy-era blacklist was also boycott oriented. The organizers of the blacklists threatened the networks and the motion picture studios with public boycotts of productions featuring Communists.

But these people—private citizens, generally speaking, though they sometimes acted in collusion with governmental agencies—went a good deal further.

They threatened sponsors of TV programs with secondary boycotts: Unless the sponsor—whether a cereal company, an insurance agency, whatever—demanded that certain specified alleged Communists be removed from the program, a boycott of the sponsor's product would be organized.

The blacklisters often operated in secrecy, so that their role in enforcing the blacklists would not become known.

And they maintained specific, unchanging lists—once your name appeared on the list, that was that. Unless you complied with *their* "self-purification" procedure—a two-step process—you could not secure the removal of your name from the list.

As for the two steps: First it was necessary to acknowledge past or current membership in the Communist Party or its fronts and to renounce such ties.

Then it was necessary to "name names"—to provide, as a demonstration of seriousness of purpose, the names of others known to the "confessee" as Party members or sympathizers.

As for compliance, in some industries, these private citizens acted as judge and jury—in other circumstances, it was possible to make confession and "name names" before representatives of the FBI or congressional investigating committees. But the mandated procedure was roughly the same.

And all this took place in a climate in which refusal to comply could render an actor or a director permanently unemployed.

Bozell, of course, is operating in an entirely different political climate. There is, moreover, nothing secret about his work. And he isn't interested in secondary boycotts.

In fact, he's concerned primarily with productions that carry within them a political message—and far less with whether actor "X" has signed this or that petition.

It's also fair to ask whether Bozell's foes genuinely oppose black-listing per se or are actually opposed to the political disposition he represents.

After all, one of Bozell's leading critics—the man who introduced the AFTRA resolution, actor John Randolph—is a member of Athletes and Artists Against Apartheid and of TransAfrica. Both groups play key roles in enforcing the blacklisting of some two hundred athletes and entertainers who've appeared in South Africa.

This is a highly specific list—and to get off it, it's necessary to follow a prescribed ritual that involves promising never to perform in South Africa again.

It doesn't matter whether the artist has insisted on appearing before racially mixed audiences in South Africa, thereby, perhaps, contributing to the end of apartheid.

These groups believe in an absolute boycott. And if you've violated the boycott, you're on the list.

Now that's blacklisting, 1950s style. Bozell's efforts pale by comparison.

But AFTRA and the SAG don't seem to have much to say about the South Africa blacklist, perhaps because the leaders of the two unions share the political orientation of the men and women who organized it.

All of which leads to the conclusion that the uproar over *TV, etc.*, isn't about principle at all; it's about politics—Left-Right politics—plain and simple.

Brent Bozell, in other words, has gotten a raw deal—from biased folks invoking pious platitudes.

Dishonoring Robert Taylor

January 11, 1990

An extraordinary episode took place in Hollywood recently. Indeed, in light of the earthquake that shook the world in 1989—the popular revolt against communism in Eastern Europe—it's not unreasonable to term this Tinseltown tale downright bizarre.

Lorimar Studios, a major television and film production company (*Dallas, Falcon Crest,* and so forth), removed the name of the late screen actor Robert Taylor from its Hollywood office building.

Taylor has been dishonored posthumously, Lorimar explains, because he appeared as a cooperative witness before the House Committee on Un-American Activities (HUAC) in 1947.

It seems Lorimar recently purchased the building in question and the lot on which it is located from Metro-Goldwyn-Mayer—Taylor's home studio. But a group of Lorimar employees were displeased to find themselves working in a building bearing the name of a fervent anti-Communist who'd cooperated with HUAC.

Taylor—at the time (1947) an official of the Screen Actors Guild—had testified about the political struggle between Communists and anti-Communists in his union.

In the course of lengthy and general testimony, he named three Hollywood political activists—a screenwriter, an actor, and an actress—as people who seemed to him to be devotees of the Communist Party line.

Taylor made it plain he had no idea whether any of the three were Party members.

Still, in the eyes of the Left, he'd committed the unpardonable sin—Taylor was guilty of "naming names."

Lorimar employees in the Robert Taylor Building collected signatures and presented studio executives with a petition—signed by some fifty producers and screenwriters—demanding that the building's name be changed. Copies of Taylor's HUAC testimony were attached to the petition.

The company—which professes, in any event, to have been searching for a way to honor the late MGM director George Cukor—was apparently persuaded, and the Robert Taylor Building is now the George Cukor Building.

The ironies here are many and varied. In the first place, removing Taylor's name from the building—rendering him, in effect, a nonperson—is an emblematic Stalinist practice.

This mode of totalitarianism is just now being rejected by the very peoples long condemned to live under it—in Eastern Europe and in the Soviet Union itself.

Indeed, in the USSR, Mikhail Gorbachev's government is confronting the reality of Stalinist thought control by struggling to extract a genuine history of the past seventy years from the constantly rewritten versions prompted by changes in the Party line.

The USSR, in short, is endeavoring to determine whose names were erased from buildings, who was whited out of which photographs, and what the names of various cities were before they were renamed and renamed again.

But in Hollywood, they are erasing names from buildings.

And (to double the irony) they are removing the name of a

respected actor precisely because he was an active foe of Stalinism at the very moment (1947) when its pernicious nature had become blatantly clear to all but the willfully blind.

Yes, the constitutional legitimacy of the inquiry with which Robert Taylor cooperated can be questioned.

A persuasive case can be made for the view that while Congress had a right to investigate domestic communism—just as it investigated domestic fascism before World War II—summoning particular individuals and demanding, on pain of contempt citations, that they disclose their (altogether legal) political affiliations represented a violation of these people's constitutional rights.

Thus it's possible to defend the stance taken by subpoenaed witnesses who refused to cooperate with HUAC on First Amendment grounds, even though nearly all who followed this strategy actually *were* Party members, adhering to a line set (it was later changed) by Communist Party lawyers.

But it is quite another thing to brand as immoral someone who took a different view, let alone to subject that individual to posthumous ignominy.

After all, in the view of Robert Taylor and many other Americans (then and since), American Communists were the domestic advocates for a system that had already carried out mass murder on a scale rivaled only by Hitler, that had already turned half of Europe into a bloc of police states, and had already built a concentration-camp universe of a scope unprecedented in the history of man.

To have seen these concerns as paramount at the onset of the cold war seems—to say the least—entirely understandable.

And it's fair to ask the following question: Would there be a parallel controversy today if Taylor—or someone like him in a different industry—had cooperated with the prewar congressional inquiry into the activities of the (then altogether legal) German-American Bund, even to the point of identifying particular individuals as probable Bund sympathizers? Highly unlikely.

This suggests that the real issue here, for the Left, isn't civil liberties at all—it's that HUAC and folks like Robert Taylor opposed domestic communism, a movement those who gathered the signatures at Lorimar *don't* view in a profoundly negative light.

Their claim that Taylor's testimony contributed to the eventual Hollywood blacklist is refuted by a mere glance at what he actually said to HUAC.

In any case, it seems odd for people who are engaged in removing names from buildings for political reasons to represent themselves as animated by an opposition to blacklisting. Very odd.

Why Did They Hide?

November 6, 1997

"Hollywood," the writer James Lardner noted earlier this week, "knows how to make a fuss." He was referring to movieland's "fuss" over the fiftieth anniversary of the House Committee on Un-American Activities (HUAC) probe into communism in Hollywood. The first HUAC hearings turned the "Hollywood 10"—Jim's father, Ring Lardner Jr., now eighty-two, and nine industry colleagues—into liberal-left martyrs.

True, Hollywood has been apologizing to the "10"—and to other "blacklistees"—for more than two decades. The effort to celebrate them has included *Scoundrel Time* (Lillian Hellman's manifestly dishonest 1976 memoir), error-ridden pseudo-histories (like Victor Navasky's *Naming Names*), and full-length feature films (starting with Woody Allen's *The Front*). By now, therefore, it is received wisdom that the film-world Communists who refused to respond to HUAC's questions were genuine defenders of the Bill of Rights (an especially delicious bit of irony, in view of their fealty to Soviet totalitarianism).

Still, James Lardner is correct in pointing out that the fiftieth anniversary extravaganza has dimensions larger than anything heretofore undertaken. One of the galas—a multimedia event grounded in film clips, live commentary, and dramatic re-creations—included many of Tinseltown's brightest young stars: Billy Crystal, Kevin Spacey, John Lithgow, Kathy Baker, James Cromwell, and others.

Last week, these artists performed before a packed house at the

Samuel Goldwyn Theater. Goldwyn himself—like virtually every other studio chief—was a vocal anti-Communist who supported HUAC's Hollywood inquiry. But times have changed: Indeed, the entire blacklist gala was *funded* by MGM (Metro-Goldwyn-Mayer) and most of the other major studios.

Something else has changed over the last quarter century: The need to lie about Communist Party membership seems decidedly less acute. In *Scoundrel Time,* for example, Lillian Hellman insists that she'd never joined the Party. Yet, in a document she prepared for her attorney just after she'd been subpoenaed (it was made available after his death), the popular middlebrow playwright acknowledges the fact of her formal Party ties.

Today, champions of the blacklist "victims" don't much try to dodge the communism question. To be sure, full candor has yet to burden most who treat this period. For example, in *Tender Comrades*—a just-issued collection of essays celebrating the blacklistees—the introductory piece allows that "probably, the majority of those who were blacklisted were members of the American Communist Party."

Probably, the majority? "All, or virtually all" would have been a good deal more accurate.

Ring Lardner—among the first to admit that he had been a Party member—has been joined in his candor by many other blacklist veterans. Lardner blames their long-standing collective dishonesty on the McCarthy-era political climate: "Many Americans were convinced that the Communist Party was rife with 'foreign agents' [anxious] to subvert the government." This, he explains, was a profound misperception: "Actually, we [in the Party] talked about things like union affairs in Hollywood or raising money for ambulances during the Spanish Civil War."

Pretty benign stuff, in other words. But also—sad to say—utter nonsense.

This, moreover, is an especially bizarre moment for a thinking person to advance such claims. Recently declassified Soviet wartime cables reveal that the Communist Party served as the primary recruiting ground (and vetting agency) for U.S.-based Soviet spies during the very period in question.

And other newly accessible documents (from the United States,

Russia, and the former Eastern bloc) suggest that Moscow's control over the U.S. Communist Party was even more complete than had been suspected: Party members in a position to provide the USSR with classified information were instructed to do so. Meanwhile, those whose standing in cultural life enabled them to influence public discourse were expected to serve as apologists for Stalin-style totalitarianism (including mass murder).

Requiring U.S. citizens to testify before Congress as to their political affiliations raises serious First Amendment issues—even if the group under scrutiny is the Nazi Party or the Communist Party. After all, America, unlike many European countries, permits organizations that favor totalitarianism to function legally.

This does not mean that members of such groups deserve *congratulations* for refusing to cooperate with governmental investigators. Indeed, folks who allied themselves with a foreign power and an evil cause should be *answering* questions.

A recent event in the former USSR—one that occurred at the same time as the Hollywood extravaganza, but received far less media attention—drives home the point. Last week, the Russian government reopened PERM 36, the most notorious labor camp in the Soviet gulag; it housed Natan Sharansky, Vladimir Bukovsky, and other leading dissidents.

Some eight years ago, in a fit of shame, the KGB bulldozed the entire camp—guard towers, barbed-wire fences, punishment cells, and all the rest. Now, a painstaking reconstruction effort has restored PERM 36 to its hellish former self. Tourists (and survivors) can visit, pay respects, and secure a tangible sense of the nature of the Communist state—just as tens of thousands each year travel to Auschwitz, Bergen-Belsen, Dachau, and Buchenwald.

This grim history should inform our views of HUAC's "victims."

Why haven't the movie industry Communists ever been asked what they knew about the Soviet Union and when they knew it? Why is it unreasonable to wonder when—if ever—they left the Communist Party, how they felt about the Hitler-Stalin pact, or how they viewed the 1948 Prague putsch and the subsequent Eastern bloc purge trials?

Shouldn't screenwriter Dalton Trumbo—one of the most cele-
brated of the Hollywood 10—have been questioned, at some point
before his death, about his Stalin-era claim that anti-Semitism had
been extinguished in the Soviet Union? Did those who remained
Party members *disbelieve* Khrushchev when he himself acknowledged Stalin's "crimes"? (The crimes at issue included mass murder.)

Why didn't Hollywood Communists—after taking a hard line
on their right not to be *compelled* to answer political-affiliation
questions—doff the secrecy cloak outside the hearing rooms and
publicly proclaim their faith in the Stalinist creed?

And what about that which editor and culture critic Hilton
Kramer has called "the other blacklist"—the blacklist drawn up *by*
Communists in Hollywood, on Broadway, in book publishing, and in
journalism when Stalinists dominated U.S. cultural life? Victims of
the "other blacklist" included anti-Communists and—especially—
former Communists ("renegades"). The "other blacklist," by the way,
remains operative; it's not a phenomenon of ancient history.

Boris Yeltsin couldn't reopen the Gulag *death* camps: Kolyma
and Magadan were wiped off the face of the earth after
Khrushchev's 1956 "secret speech." Written records concerning
these sites of horror, however, have survived. For example, Vice
President Henry A. Wallace visited Kolyma during World War II
and wrote admiringly about the enthusiasm for hard work manifested by those incarcerated there.

Wallace, of course, was the 1948 presidential choice of almost
everyone on the McCarthy-era Hollywood blacklist. Any second
thoughts regarding Henry Wallace?

So far, no.

THE TRUTH EMERGES

For those, like Breindel, who had been arguing the cases against accused Soviet spies Julius and Ethel Rosenberg and Alger Hiss for years against their defenders on the Left, the release of more than two thousand Soviet wartime cables that had been intercepted and translated by U.S. code breakers was a scholar's dream come true. In these columns—also the subject of a book by Breindel and Herbert Romerstein, which was completed after his death—Breindel explores the revelations of the so-called Venona papers and the devastating effect they have had on Communist apologetics.

I. F. Stone and the KGB

August 6, 1992

Let me add a bit of context to the debate over I. F. Stone's alleged KGB ties. This is a dispute that will never be resolved to the satisfaction of *all* parties. Among those who refuse to consider the possibility that I. F. Stone—a radical-Left journalistic icon—had links to the KGB are folks who still can't accept the notion that Julius and Ethel Rosenberg were Soviet agents. This group also includes people who wouldn't acknowledge the guilt of Alger Hiss even if Hiss himself were to confess.

To face the fact that the Rosenbergs engaged in espionage (a reality serious students of the case can't dispute, even if they reject the appropriateness of the death penalty) requires an intellectual reversal too painful to contemplate. The same holds for the Alger Hiss true believers.

Recognizing the guilt of the Rosenbergs means accepting the fact that the Soviets recruited spies from within the American Communist movement. Recent scholarship, of course, tells us that they did just that, turning to nonideological, paid agents only in the mid–1950s, when Moscow concluded that FBI penetration of the U.S. Communist Party rendered the old practice too dangerous to continue.

Admitting that Hiss lied and that Whittaker Chambers told the truth has long seemed to some—for reasons that grow increasingly hard to fathom—to challenge the very legitimacy of the New Deal.

Rosenberg-Hiss partisans spent years demanding that the FBI files be released. But when the files *were* opened—after passage of the Freedom of Information Act—the same people began to argue that the FBI files couldn't be trusted, that key documents had been doctored, that others had been withheld, and so forth.

Documents, first-person accounts, and other revelations from the former Soviet Union—on these and related subjects—are already receiving the same treatment.

Recently, a member of the U.S. Communist Party labeled just such a document—a receipt for $2 million signed by Gus Hall and handed to a Soviet courier—a "typical FBI forgery." The document in question had been introduced into evidence in a Moscow courtroom. It is entirely handwritten, and Hall himself hasn't denied its authenticity.

It's in this context that the I. F. Stone controversy needs to be examined.

In an article in the Washington-based weekly *Human Events,* Herbert Romerstein—a former USIA official and an authority on Soviet intelligence—reported that he'd personally followed up on a recent and intriguing claim made by General Oleg Kalugin, a retired KGB official, in a London speech.

Kalugin, who acknowledges that he served as a top-ranking Soviet operative in Washington during the late 1950s and 1960s, had spoken of "an agent—a well-known American journalist with a good reputation—who'd severed ties with us in 1956" (after the Soviet invasion of Hungary).

According to Kalugin: "I myself convinced him to resume them. But in 1968, after the invasion of Czechoslovakia, he said he would never again take money from us."

Kalugin's point—he's told the same story in public a number of times, both in London and in Washington—is that Westerners who deem contemptible everyone who took money from Moscow fail to grasp the often-nuanced character of some of these relationships.

The "American journalist," for example, was no mere mercenary, according to Kalugin; to the contrary, this was a case of the KGB helping someone do exactly what he would have done anyway—had he the resources.

Kalugin notes that the "American journalist with a good reputation" rejected the Moscow-U.S. Party line on a number of occasions.

Romerstein learned from a KGB source in Moscow that Kalugin's "American journalist" was I. F. Stone. And, in fact, Stone fits the bill. He was a firm fellow traveler, animated by sympathy for Moscow. But he wasn't afraid to break ranks with the pro-Soviet left and did so at a number of important moments.

Stone's biographer, D. D. Guttenplan, challenges Romerstein's claim in a recent article in the *Nation*. In addition to citing various points at which Stone was exceedingly critical of Moscow, Guttenplan details a conversation *he* had with Kalugin. But—as Romerstein explains in a subsequent piece published on this page—the Guttenplan-Kalugin discussion (as described by Guttenplan) actually proves nothing.

Interestingly, Guttenplan told Romerstein directly that there aren't any I. F. Stone papers. Stone's importance as a journalist makes this a genuinely bizarre circumstance. Personalities of lesser consequence—or their families—donate personal papers to university libraries, unless there is something to hide and no opportunity for them to vet the archive.

In his *Nation* article, Guttenplan doesn't discuss the fate of Stone's papers.

As it happens, we don't need an I. F. Stone archive to know whether the journalist ever met Kalugin. A 1971 Jack Anderson column (intended to disparage J. Edgar Hoover) makes reference to the fact that Stone's FBI file includes a notation of a Stone-Kalugin meeting.

Anderson saw nothing curious about the encounter—Kalugin, Anderson points out, *was* a Soviet embassy press attaché. But in light of Kalugin's actual role during the period in question, any meetings he may have had with Stone now seem a good less innocuous.

The FBI is beginning to release parts of Stone's FBI file. These documents will, in all likelihood, afford scholars information about Stone and the Soviets. It's also possible that former KGB officials who dealt with Stone will come forward and acknowledge having done so. Finally, documents confirming a Stone-KGB link may well emerge from Moscow.

Still, rest assured: Absolutely nothing will convince those who are intellectually threatened by any suggestion of a relationship between I. F. Stone and the KGB.

In the end, however, this audience doesn't much matter. Their minds are set in stone. Members of the public who are unburdened by an ideological agenda—people prepared to face the dread notion that some things are true even though Richard Nixon or Joe McCarthy said them—are the relevant audience here.

Interested observers will weigh the evidence in an honest search for the truth; they'll make up their own minds about I. F. Stone and the KGB.

Alger Hiss and the Budapest Archives

November 4, 1993

It's received wisdom by now that the few remaining Alger Hiss partisans will never accept Hiss's guilt, no matter the evidence that emerges from archives in America, the former USSR, or anywhere else. Some Hiss acolytes acknowledge that they wouldn't believe him guilty even if Hiss himself were to confess.

The Hiss case divided a generation, thereby taking on outsize significance. For some on the liberal Left, Whittaker Chambers's ability to demonstrate that Hiss wasn't just a fellow traveler, but rather a Soviet agent, seemed to threaten their grasp of global and domestic ideological currents. As the disbelieving wife of one of Hiss's State Department colleagues told the FBI during its investigation, "If Alger was a spy, then any of us could have been."

Still, evidence does continue to emerge. And the generation that's come of age in America unburdened by the ostensibly painful implications of the Hiss affair—and unafraid to examine the case on its merits—will likely conclude simply that Chambers told the truth about Hiss.

As for the new evidence, Maria Schmidt, a young Hungarian scholar researching the Hungarian Secret Police in newly available Budapest-based Interior Ministry files, encountered documents detailing information provided to the Hungarians by Noel H. Field upon his 1954 release from prison in Hungary. An ex-U.S. State Department official and close friend of Hiss, Field "disappeared" behind the Iron Curtain shortly after Chambers identified Hiss as a Communist.

Field realized that his own name would emerge in any investigation of Hiss; moreover, unlike Hiss, Field had made no special secret of his sympathy for Moscow. His ideological orientation was widely recognized when he left the State Department in the mid–1930s to work for the League of Nations, though few suspected he was transferring secret information to Moscow.

Field was correct in one respect: He was named as a Soviet agent during the Hiss trial. But he could not foresee the special hell that awaited him in the new "People's Democracies" to which he fled.

Upon his arrival in Prague, he was arrested and transported to Budapest: The Soviets and their puppets were preparing a series of Eastern bloc show trials, directed against Communists whom Stalin wanted to purge. Field became a central figure in the Czech trial of Communist Party General Secretary Rudolf Slansky and a key actor in the Hungarian version: the trial of Foreign Minister Laszlo Rajk and others.

Field's wartime work for Allen Dulles (a family friend) in the U.S. Office of Strategic Services made him a kind of Eastern bloc Typhoid Mary. For many East European Communists, merely to have had contact with Field—the "American master spy"—led to arrest and, sometimes, execution.

By 1954, however, Stalin was dead and the winds of change were sweeping the Soviet bloc. Field, who hadn't been executed—probably thanks to his U.S. passport—was debriefed by the Hungarians, undoubtedly at Moscow's behest.

According to Schmidt, Field—still a true believer—detailed the work he'd done for the Soviets. In the course of the questioning, which took place in amicable circumstances—the Hungarians, in effect, were apologizing to Field, whom they later rewarded with a villa and a generous pension—the American recounted that Hiss, too, had been a Soviet agent.

Field provided several other names and—in documents he didn't realize would ever see the light of day—actually confirmed minute details of Chambers's story. (Something of a lost soul, Field elected to remain in Hungary, where he died in 1970.)

Schmidt described her findings in a New York University lecture last month, provoking a bizarre essay in the *Nation*—a weekly long committed to Hiss's defense—by attorney Ethan Klingsberg. The author suggests that Communist archival material simply can't be trusted, a position folks who share the *Nation's* ideological disposition may well come to find increasingly useful.

Klingsberg implies that Field's 1954 testimony was coerced, a claim unsupported by evidence or logic. The article also fails to grapple with the fact that Field told the Communists something they weren't eager to hear: Notwithstanding the international Left's claims to the contrary, Hiss—according to Field—*was,* in fact, a Soviet spy.

Finally, Klingsberg fails even to confront Schmidt's discovery that a well-known letter mailed from Field to Hiss in 1957—in which Field offers to make public his "knowledge" that Hiss was convicted on the basis of perjured testimony—was but the last of several drafts of a "Field-Hiss" letter prepared by Soviet-controlled Hungarian authorities. Schmidt, who details her findings in a recent issue of the *New Republic,* located the earlier versions in the Interior Ministry files.

Is Schmidt's work nothing more than an interesting footnote to a case never to be resolved? No.

Noel Field's identification of Hiss, in secret and uncoerced circumstances, effectively seals the case against Alger Hiss.

J. Robert Oppenheimer, aka Veksel

July 27, 1995

A fair bit has been written about the release earlier this month of documents related to the Venona project—the wartime effort undertaken by the army's Signal Intelligence Service to intercept and decrypt coded cable traffic between Soviet installations in the United States (primarily the embassy in Washington and the consulate in New York) and Moscow.

The chief goal of Venona—initiated in 1943—was to learn as much as possible about Soviet espionage activities in this country. Only 2,200 intercepted messages were successfully translated—largely because the Russians used a highly sophisticated code. Early on, however, army analysts began to discover weaknesses in the Soviet encryption system.

And shortly thereafter, in 1945, the effort was advanced by a series of counterintelligence breakthroughs: the defection of Soviet cipher clerk Igor Gouzenko in Ottawa; the voluntary confession of Elizabeth Bentley, who'd served Moscow as an espionage courier; and the FBI's reinterview of *Time* editor and ex-Soviet agent Whittaker Chambers. This trio provided specific data that made the messages easier to interpret.

Venona's existence has been public information since the early 1980s. FBI special agent Robert Lamphere wrote in detail about Venona nearly ten years ago, confirming that the FBI learned about Julius Rosenberg's spy ring through the intercepts. But he was forbidden actually to quote from the documents. Similarly, no evidence gleaned from the intercepts was ever introduced in any court. As a consequence, some spies were never prosecuted. Washington deemed Venona's secrecy more important than jailing a handful of Soviet agents.

But America's dedication to secrecy in this realm became an obsession. And the fact that American scholars, after communism's demise, began to plumb Russian archives heightened the incongruity of Washington's continuing refusal to release fifty-year-old papers.

Indeed, despite mounting pressure to do so from Western researchers, the FBI and its sister agencies refused to budge. As recently as May, in fact, the late Les Aspin, a member of the President's Foreign Intelligence Advisory Board (PFIAB), asked the intelligence community whether the intercepts could be released. After receiving a pro forma negative reply, Aspin inquired about the controversial wartime role played by physicist and Manhattan Project head J. Robert Oppenheimer, the Father of the Atomic Bomb.

In a memoir published last year, an important ex-KGB general, Pavel Sudoplatov, wrote that Oppenheimer had knowingly made it possible for Soviet "moles," planted at the Los Alamos research center, to copy secret documents related to the development of the bomb. The book, written with the assistance of the general's son and two American journalists—Jerrold and Leona Schecter—didn't actually label Oppenheimer a Soviet spy. But the activities it describes bespeak a distinction without a difference.

The furor in the academic community was immense. Many charged Sudoplatov and the Schecters with posthumous character assassination. Long since dead, Oppenheimer—whose wife, mistress, brother, and sister-in-law had all been Communists—was deprived of his security clearance in 1954.

In this context, Aspin agreed to ask the FBI whether any information in its possession—from Venona or from other sources—either supported or refuted the claim that Oppenheimer had willfully assisted Moscow. FBI Director Louis Freeh replied that nothing bolstering the suggestion that Oppenheimer aided the USSR could be found. In fact, according to Freeh, a number of seemingly exculpatory documents had been discovered.

But even as detractors of Sudoplatov and the Schecters began to celebrate, a separate process—headed by U.S. Senator Daniel Patrick Moynihan—was under way on Capitol Hill. Long concerned with what he views as excessive secrecy on the part of the intelligence community, Moynihan was taking testimony from scholars protesting the continuing unavailability of the Venona intercepts.

The senator communicated his own inability to grasp the need to keep the files secret to the relevant agencies. Suddenly, the National Security Agency (NSA), the CIA, and the FBI saw fit to reconsider the issue. Thus, the set of documents released—albeit with deletions—earlier this month, as well as the promise that additional Venona files will be made available later this year.

It's not surprising that press coverage has focused on the guilt of the Rosenbergs and their compatriots. Many of the Venona documents concern the Rosenbergs directly; moreover, such doubt as may have remained about their guilt has finally been set to rest.

But it's curious that there's been virtually no discussion of what the intercepts indicate about Oppenheimer. A guide to the documents published by the NSA virtually invites inquiry in this realm; it notes that "the [espionage] role played by the person covernamed 'Veksel' remains uncertain, but troubling." It's clear "Veksel" is J. Robert Oppenheimer, although the footnotes to the actual documents suggest only that the covername may "possibly" be that of "Dr. Julius Robert Oppenheimer."

Actually, there's no room for doubt. Veksel is described as the director of "the reservation" (Los Alamos), the site of "the main practical research work" on "normous" (the Manhattan project).

It appears that a Soviet agent was dispatched to Chicago in early 1945 to "re-establish contact" with Veksel. At a minimum, therefore, Oppenheimer had been in contact with Soviet intelligence at some earlier stage. This accounts for the NSA's sense that Oppenheimer's role "remains troubling."

In all likelihood, forthcoming Venona documents will tell us more about Oppenheimer. As things stand, however, Sudoplatov and the Schecters have considerable cause for satisfaction. Not so, their critics.

The Rosenbergs and Their Apologists

August 10, 1995

Those who've long been animated by the myth that Julius and Ethel Rosenberg were victims of a McCarthy-era, FBI-orchestrated frame-up suffered a major setback last week. Walter and Miriam Schneir, the only proponents of this thesis who've ever been regarded as remotely serious, acknowledged in an article in the *Nation* that the recently released Venona intercepts had, at last, persuaded them that "Julius Rosenberg ran a spy ring composed of young fellow communists, including friends and college classmates whom he had recruited."

Thus, the release last month of the Venona files—the fifty-year-old decrypted Soviet cable traffic that first led the FBI to the Rosenbergs—has prompted the preeminent champions of the Rosenberg cause to throw in the towel.

Many who follow these matters expected the Schneirs simply to denounce the declassified cables as forgeries. After all, they had held their ground when volumes of FBI files, released under the Freedom of Information Act more than a decade ago, convinced most serious students of the case who still nurtured doubts that the frame-up thesis was ludicrous.

Similarly, the subsequent revelation that two Rosenberg confederates who'd "disappeared" around the time of the couple's arrest—Joel Barr and Alfred Sarrant—had spent their lives as military scientists in the Soviet Union also failed to faze the Schneirs.

So, why the sudden abandonment of the cause with which they've identified their professional lives? And why the acknowledgment that there's "little doubt that top CP officials were aware . . . of the party's links with the KGB"?

Let's remember: The entire point of making the Rosenberg case a cause célèbre was to deny that ordinary Communist Party members—like Julius and Ethel Rosenberg—served the USSR as spies. The Schneirs and others were determined not to allow the U.S. Communist Party to be depicted as a recruiting ground for espionage. Yes, the Venona intercepts render this position untenable—they even name the Party functionary to whom Julius Rosenberg paid his Party dues after going "underground."

But, as indicated, books, articles, and documents have, for years, made all of this plain. Indeed, if the 1950–53 legal proceedings weren't themselves sufficiently persuasive, the Rosenbergs' guilt has certainly been a settled issue since Ron Radosh and Joyce Milton published *The Rosenberg File* in 1983.

As for the Communist Party's espionage role, *The Secret World of American Communism* by Harvey Klehr, John Haynes, and Fredrik Firsov—which appeared earlier this year—uses Soviet archives to confirm what's long been clear from American sources.

The Schneirs offer an explanation for their conversion at the end of their article: "This is not a pretty story. We know that our account will be painful news for many . . . as it is for us. But the duty of a writer is to tell the truth."

Touching, perhaps. But, somehow, not entirely convincing. In fact, it seems far more likely that the Schneirs simply woke up and recognized that continuing to insist on the Rosenbergs' innocence was akin to maintaining membership in the flat-earth society.

It's important to note, however, that the article itself is by no means a mea culpa. Moreover, it's informed by a profound reluctance to acknowledge the full truth about the Rosenberg spy ring.

The Schneirs make no apologies whatever for the ugly manner in which they conducted their multidecade campaign. In a 1983 public debate in Town Hall, for example, Walter Schneir accused Radosh and Milton of writing "garbage"; Miriam Schneir called *The Rosenberg File* a "fraud." Serious charges about professional historians. But very much in line with the Schneirs' entire approach.

According to their interpretation of the case, after all, Harry Gold—the Soviet espionage agent who turned state's evidence after his arrest—was a demented, pathological liar and ordinary FBI agents were criminals who forged documents and manufactured evidence to frame an innocent couple and send them to the electric chair.

In short, the Schneirs heaped endless slander on folks who, early on, recognized truths they themselves now feel compelled to acknowledge. On a more substantive level, the *Nation* article persists in advancing a lie. The Schneirs still insist that Julius wasn't involved in atomic espionage; they claim repeatedly that he engaged primarily in "nonatomic" spying. Insofar as the government's case focused on atomic espionage, the Schneirs—by implication—are still arguing for their "unjust conviction" conclusion.

What's curious here is that the Venona intercepts make it abundantly clear that Rosenberg and his Los Alamos–based brother-in-law, David Greenglass, were deeply involved in passing Manhattan Project secrets to the Soviets. In fact, the Venona files that have been released deal only with atomic espionage. Moreover, Richard Rhodes—in his just-published study of the U.S. quest for the hydrogen bomb—uses Soviet intelligence archives to demonstrate that Rosenberg and his confederates played a highly significant role in advancing Moscow's effort to build its own A-bomb.

Rhodes explains that Greenglass—under Rosenberg's supervision—provided the Soviets with critical material on the implosion process before anyone else did so—even before Moscow received roughly the same information from agents long regarded as more important: physicist Klaus Fuchs, for example.

The Schneirs, it would seem, are either hopelessly ill informed—and unable to fathom the meaning of the new documents—or are still in the throes of a difficult relationship with the truth.

Venona and the Stalinist Remnant

October 14, 1996

Last week's two-day Venona conference at the National War College in Washington, D.C., came on the heels of the fifth and final release of declassified Venona documents. Venona was a thirty-five-year effort initiated by the U.S. Army's Signal Intelligence Service—a forerunner of today's National Security Agency. Its purpose was to decrypt and exploit intercepted Soviet "diplomatic" cables.

Thanks to extraordinary analytic work by U.S. code breakers, some 2,200 wartime messages between Moscow and its stations in this country were "translated" during the late 1940s and early 1950s. Most dealt with intelligence gathering and espionage.

The decrypted cables enabled the FBI to identify more than one hundred Soviet intelligence agents active who were in the United States. Among them: members of the spy ring directed by Julius Rosenberg, Assistant Secretary of the Treasury Harry Dexter White, Alger Hiss, and a number of other governmental officials working with the Soviets.

Many had already been linked to Moscow by Elizabeth Bentley and Whittaker Chambers, the two most prominent ex-spies who—after breaking with the Communist underground—tried to warn U.S. authorities about the scope of Moscow's espionage efforts in this country.

The Venona revelations are themselves corroborated by documents that were located, over the course of the past decade, in key Moscow archives.

Preserving the secrecy of the code break was deemed so important—by both the FBI and the NSA—that no information derived from Venona was ever introduced in an American courtroom. As a result, the government was forced to forgo a number of potentially important prosecutions.

Indeed, it was only two years ago that the FBI, the CIA, and the NSA—under heavy pressure from Senator Daniel Patrick Moynihan (D-New York), a leading critic of Washington's secrecy cult—finally agreed to the just-concluded Venona declassification project.

Last week's conference—cosponsored by the CIA, the NSA, and the D.C.-based Center for Democracy—was designed to reflect the new spirit of openness that is meant to inform life within the intelligence community. Some of the original code breakers took part, as did scholars who've long argued the essential validity of the espionage charges leveled during the early days of the cold war. (Moynihan, appropriately, delivered the introductory address.)

In a quest for balance, the conference organizers also invited convicted atom spy Morton Sobell, Michael Meeropol—the Rosenbergs' elder son—and various longtime Alger Hiss apologists.

Among the latter are left-wing activists who claim that Venona, in its entirety, is a government hoax. William Reuben, for example—the reporter for the pro-Soviet *National Guardian,* who first advanced the view that the Rosenbergs were victims of a vast Justice Department frame-up—wandered the corridors sharing his Venona-as-hoax thesis with other attendees.

Reuben also promised that he'll soon be able to "prove" the innocence of the late Klaus Fuchs, a German-born Communist and important Manhattan Project physicist. This would be quite a feat: After all, Fuchs confessed that he'd spied for Moscow and identified many of his confederates.

Fuchs settled in East Germany after serving a jail term in England and became—eventually—head of the East German nuclear research program and a member of the Communist Party's central committee. During his second life—as a leading Eastern bloc scientist-statesman—he began actually to boast about his wartime and postwar espionage role. Reuben, in short, has embarked on a difficult task.

In the end, the Venona conference produced no major revelations. The part played by the U.S. Communist Party in facilitating Soviet intelligence activities here and in identifying potential espionage recruits was recounted by historians Harvey Klehr and Ronald Radosh.

The subject is fascinating and important. It undercuts efforts by left-wing scholars to depict the U.S. Party as a legitimate—albeit radical—political party. But the relevant facts concerning the Communist Party's role aren't in dispute. They've been well documented in books and articles that have appeared over the course of the past several years.

Meanwhile, a document was distributed by the conference organizers that bolsters the credibility of the late NKVD (KGB) General Pavel Sudoplatov, whose 1994 memoir—*Unwanted Witness*—came under fierce criticism from folks dismayed by his claim that the physicist who headed the Manhattan Project, J. Robert Oppenheimer, knowingly provided secret information to Soviet espionage agents.

Sudoplatov had no choice other than to write from memory—he was barred from using Russian archives and couldn't travel to the United States. Venona, moreover, hadn't yet been released. The mere fact of his book, therefore, represents a genuine achievement.

Those who challenged the book also had to confront Sudoplatov's claim that physicists Niels Bohr and Leo Szilard, among other well-known scientists, wittingly assisted Moscow's effort to gather intelligence on the A-bomb project.

The tactic employed by many of the critics was to identify errors in the text of *Unwanted Witness*. In this context, the document handed out last week can only serve to enhance the book's reputation.

Still, few who attended the conference—most who did so know the subject well—can claim to have gleaned new insights. Nevertheless, the gathering had a decidedly compelling aspect.

Certainly, Michael Meeropol's acknowledgment that his father, Julius Rosenberg, "probably" engaged in espionage gave rise to a unique poignant moment. Meeropol, to be sure, denounced the death sentence imposed on his parents and insisted on his mother's absolute innocence. But his new position on his father marks a radical departure. Facing reality cannot have been easy for Meeropol.

Pathos of a different sort attended the encounter between Sobell, Reuben, and the Hiss acolytes, on the one hand, and the intelligence professionals on the other. Over the years, the former have had a number of opportunities to attack anti-Communist scholars like Radosh and Klehr. Never, however, have they been forced to confront members of the intelligence community—nonideological, highly patriotic professionals who chose to devote their lives to protecting U.S. security.

The presence of men like ex-FBI agent Robert Lamphere—the bureau's point man on Venona—distinguished the conference from the raucous, Left-Right "debates" that have taken place, intermittently, during the past four decades.

The most recent such event was held at Town Hall in 1983; it focused specifically on the Rosenberg case. Ronald Radosh and Joyce Milton, former leftists who'd concluded that the Rosenbergs were guilty, had just published their findings in *The Rosenberg File*. The authors squared off against true believers—Meeropol, among them—in what one pundit described as "the last event of the 1950s."

The Venona conference was different. As Lamphere and his colleagues studied Reuben, aging attorney Marshall Perlin—long a follower of the Communist Party line—and Sobell (an eighty-year-old man with a white ponytail), it was hard not to feel that the former officials thought they'd wandered into a theater of the absurd.

Sobell, for example, insisted that the fact that his own name had been misspelled in one of the Venona cables *proved* the project was a hoax. The CIA, FBI, and NSA veterans stared back in silence.

Suddenly, the ancient Stalinists seemed mad. These were not simply men whose time had passed. Once, admittedly, they may have been idealists; now—more than anything else—they seemed to be lunatics.

Paul Robeson and Soviet Jewry

July 31, 1997

In the current issue of *Common Quest*—a new magazine dedicated to improving black-Jewish relations—an article entitled "Paul Robeson's Legacy" suggests that the editors, like most who profess an interest in bettering black-Jewish ties, remain unwilling to confront the key obstacle to improved relations: facing the truth.

Having argued repeatedly in recent years that undertakings of this kind are doomed to failure, I find it difficult to view the nonsense generally evident in *Common Quest*—which is sponsored by the American Jewish Committee (AJC) in conjunction with Howard University—with surprise. After all, the ostensibly urgent need for improved dialogue—which took hold in the aftermath of the 1991 Crown Heights *pogrom*—is grounded in the premise that both groups have legitimate grievances.

This premise, however, is devoid of merit. Indeed, insofar as the American Jewish contribution to the civil rights struggle—which was animated by empathy, generosity, and a sense of social justice— has been vastly disproportionate by comparison to that of any other ethnic group, even the suggestion that mutual apologies are in order is absurd. Still, this misguided notion led to the creation of *Common Quest*—as it has to similar undertakings.

For an illustration of what such thinking produces, consider

"Paul Robeson's Legacy"—an essay on the legendary black singer and actor by his son, Paul ("Pauly") Robeson, Jr.

Paul Robeson was long an open Stalinist; Pauly, however, broke with the Party some time ago. But now, sad to say, he appears to be rethinking the candor that attended his departure from the Communist world.

During a 1949 visit to the Soviet Union, Paul Robeson—singing to a packed house in Moscow's Tchaikovsky Hall—intoned the anthem of the Jewish ghetto fighters who took up arms against the Nazis. Robeson, Pauly claims, intended his rendition of "Zog Nit Keynmol" ("Never Say That You Have Reached the Very End") as a gesture of "defiance against Stalin's infamous anti-Semitic campaign."

His father's purpose, Robeson, Jr., maintains, was to give "expression to the suffering not only of Soviet Jews, but also of the countless [other] victims of Stalin's purges." When he returned to America, the renowned artist told his son that the audience—after listening to the dramatic song both in Yiddish and in Russian—"stood and cheered and applauded and wept."

A nice story. And one that has the added virtue of being true—as far as it goes. The difficulty, however, is that it doesn't go very far.

In reality, the 1949 trip was a seminal event in Paul Robeson's life. Rumors that an unprecedented, state-sponsored anti-Semitic campaign was under way had long since reached the West. The Jewish Anti-Fascist Committee—a wartime propaganda tool created by Stalin to increase American Jewish support for the Soviet war effort—had been disbanded the previous year.

And its central personality, Solomon Mikhoels—the leading figure in the Soviet Union's Yiddish theater—had been murdered at Stalin's direct instruction only months prior to Robeson's arrival. While Mikhoels's murder was attributed to "hooligans," suspicion—heightened by the seeming disappearance of other prominent Jewish personalities—was intense.

Uncomfortable with the "official story" regarding Mikhoels, Robeson insisted on seeing another leading light in Jewish cultural life: Yitzhik Feffer, a poet and longtime Stalin acolyte. The American vocalist had hosted both Mikhoels and Feffer during their 1943–44 visit to the United States. In this context—and in view of his international stature and public pro-Soviet sympathies—Moscow couldn't easily ignore Robeson's request.

The Russians, to be sure, tried their best—Feffer was already in the Lubyanka prison. But, in the end, after fattening him up—salamis were delivered to the emaciated poet's cell and rouge was applied to his gaunt cheeks—Soviet authorities delivered him to Robeson's room at the Metropole Hotel.

The suite had obviously been bugged. Thus, even though KGB guards waited downstairs, Feffer—dressed in a new suit provided by his captors—told his American friend that all was well; tales of state-sanctioned anti-Semitism were nothing more than capitalist defamation.

It seems, however, that Feffer, using a few handwritten notes as well as body language—conveyed to Robeson the grim reality of his circumstances. Feffer, it appears, made it plain that Mikhoels had been murdered, that other prominent Jews had been arrested, that the Leningrad Party had been subjected to a major purge, and that his own likely fate was dire: "He drew his finger across his throat [as in an execution]," Robeson told his son, adding that, at the session's end, he and Feffer had embraced "like brothers." According to the American, both "had tears" in their eyes, knowing they "would never see each other again."

Robeson, like most Stalinists, was adept at lying—both to himself and to others. But the Feffer encounter appears to have imposed a heavy burden on him. After returning to New York, he told Pauly the *true* story of what had transpired—insisting, however, that it be kept under wraps until after his own death. As Paul, Jr., wrote in 1982—six years after his father had passed away and well after he himself had left the ambit of American communism—Robeson was deeply troubled by the 1949 Metropole meeting.

The singer, of course, didn't want the story used by Moscow's adversaries. As a consequence, Robeson even went so far as to tell *Soviet Russia Today* that allegations concerning anti-Semitism in the USSR were pure slander: "I met Jewish people all over the place . . . [and] I heard no word about it."

Robeson's biographer and apologist, CUNY Professor Martin

Duberman, argues that the artist's conduct was informed by the fear that speaking out might further endanger Feffer's life. This, however, is *prima facie* nonsense. (As Feffer himself had predicted, he *was* executed—in August 1952.)

Paul Robeson's silence was that of a disciplined Stalinist. Indeed, as late as 1957, after Khrushchev's "secret speech" detailed and denounced the crimes of Stalin, Robeson—American communism's leading cultural personality—was still unwilling to lend his name to a public statement of inquiry concerning the fate of Feffer, Peretz Markish, and other "disappeared" Jewish writers and artists.

All this would be of minor import—save for the fact that Robeson, Jr., has chosen to air this new version of his tale in a journal published by the American Jewish Committee. How such a piece might contribute to improved relations between blacks and Jews is a mystery. Meanwhile, the fact that the essay consists largely in half-truths renders it even more dubious. Indeed, it's hard not to wonder what persuaded David Harris—the AJC's executive director, who made his name in the Soviet Jewry movement—to lend a committee-funded journal to this exercise in revisionism.

In the last analysis, Paul Robeson, Jr.'s, piece serves as a reminder that misguided undertakings seldom produce positive results.

The Silence of the
<u>New York Times</u>

*It wasn't just crosstown, tabloid-broadsheet rivalry that led Breindel of
the* Post *to write on several occasions about the way the obituaries in the*
New York Times *sometimes distorted the life histories of those who were
either members or fellow travelers of the American Communist Party.
He was reflecting a frustration and anger common on the anti-
Communist Right that those who had worked to advance Soviet interests
in the United States were often eulogized for their commitment to
supposedly humanitarian causes—thus implicitly accepting the claim of
the American Communists in the 1930s that they were just "Democrats
in a hurry," rather than thralls to a murderous regime.*

The Case of David Goldway

August 2, 1990

Communism—Communist parties and their role in political life—
is a subject that's debated on a daily basis in every corner of the
globe.

In Eastern Europe, newly free from the shackles of Communist
rule, constant discussion over the participation of Communists and
former Communists in national politics is, quite naturally, the
order of the day.

In the USSR itself, the past misdeeds of the Communist ruling
elite are exhumed and debated with rare abandon.

Even in South Africa, home to the international community's most dynamic Communist Party, the historic fidelity of the newly "unbanned" South African CP to Stalinism has generated a national debate among blacks and whites over the appropriateness of the close ties between the Communists and Nelson Mandela's African National Congress.

But in America, where communism never held sway or even attracted a significant mass following—and where full press freedom has always been a reality—an extraordinary taboo obtains with respect to calling a Communist a Communist.

No doubt this is, in part, a legacy of the McCarthy era, when the rights of Americans to adhere to the political faith of their choosing—communism included—were trampled and when some were falsely accused of Communist ties and caused to suffer on the basis of such false charges.

No doubt the taboo is also a consequence of the Party's historical preference for a significant measure of secrecy—a view that long predates McCarthy: The CP leadership knew that ordinary Americans had been exposed to the nature of the Communist faith and to the realities of life in the Soviet Union.

Thus, the CPUSA recognized early on that few Americans would wittingly march under the Red flag or follow men they knew to be loyal to Marxism and Moscow.

In any event, whatever its roots, the taboo remains in force. It continues to encourage falsehood and to facilitate deception.

For an example of this taboo in a relatively harmless manifestation—and perhaps a harmless illustration is particularly telling in that it underscores the taboo's pervasive nature—let's look at a recent obituary in the *New York Times*.

A man called David Goldway died last week at the age of eighty-three. The nation's newspaper of record tells us a good deal about Goldway in a relatively short account.

We learn that he was chairman of the editorial board of a magazine called *Science & Society*, a journal he joined more than two decades ago. The *Times* describes *Science & Society* as "Marxist," and, indeed, the headline of the obit reports that Goldway "Led Marxist Journal."

We're told that Goldway was a teacher and administrator at the Jefferson School of Social Science in Manhattan, "a center of left-wing study," according to the *Times*.

And we're told that Goldway taught in the New York City public school system until 1941, "when he was dismissed for refusing to sign a waiver of immunity when called to testify before a New York state legislative committee investigating claims of subversive activities in the public schools."

This admirably concise obituary happens to be written in code. So, here's a translation:

David Goldway, who died last week, headed the editorial board of *Science & Society*, a journal founded and dominated by members of the American Communist Party.

He'd served as an official of the Communist Party's leading educational institution, the Jefferson School, and had previously lost his job as a public school teacher when he refused to sign an immunity waiver before testifying in front of the Rapp-Coudert Committee, which was investigating the Communist Party ties of educators employed by the City of New York.

Goldway had already been named as an active Communist Party member by several earlier witnesses.

The *Times* obit, no doubt for lack of space, failed to report that Goldway had also served as legislative representative of Local 537 of the College Teachers Union. Even if it had done so, however, the obituary certainly would not have explained that the union in question was completely controlled by the Communist Party.

Now it may be that David Goldway would have been pleased by the fact that his obituary was written in code—by the fact that the uninitiated reader would not know that ties to the American Communist movement represented the most important political commitment of his life.

Even today, most American Communists—including those who severed formal ties to the Party at one or another stage—prefer to be described to non-Communists as "Marxists" or "progressives" or "radicals."

But what cause is advanced by the cooperation of the rest of us in this insidious distortion of reality?

Isn't it important to recognize that in America, as in other democracies, a good number of serious, influential, and perhaps even well-meaning people dedicated their lives to serving a cause that has now been revealed as vile and murderous by people who were actually compelled to live under Communist rule?

It would seem so.

The Case of Millard Lampell

October 16, 1997

If the McCarthy era had a single enduring legacy, it consisted in creating and perpetuating a taboo: Since the late 1950s, it's been impossible to call a Communist a Communist—without inviting charges of Red-baiting. The fact that American Communists were allowed to masquerade as "liberals in a hurry"—as domestic political heretics, rather than as conspirators loyal to a foreign power—distorted the nature of the anti-Vietnam War movement and affected the political character of the civil rights struggle.

Folks who recognized the importance of this taboo (especially the liberal anti-Communists who were eventually ousted from the Democratic Party's elite by the McGovernite descendants of Henry A. Wallace's Progressives) found an easy way to monitor its influence: They kept an eye on the *New York Times* obituary page.

The absence in *Times* obits of any references to CP ties—save when the deceased was an actual Party functionary—made it plain that the taboo was still in force.

The result of this policy, which has had the aspect of a *Times* "style book" edict? Nearly forty years of dishonest articles on the lives of prominent citizens in America's newspaper of record.

With the Soviet empire's demise, the Berlin Wall's collapse, and, of course, the disintegration of the American Communist movement, it seemed reasonable to assume that this syndrome would itself die. Beyond the fact that the obituaries in question—as a consequence of this sin of omission—ignored the key political fact in the lives of those profiled, recent revelations have made it plain that the CPUSA was *not* an ordinary domestic political party.

As demonstrated in the just-declassified Venona cables (decrypted communiqués between Moscow and various Soviet intelligence stations in the United States) and in Comintern documents now accessible in Moscow, the CPUSA was the chief recruiting ground for Soviet espionage agents in America.

Confirmation of this reality—and of the fact that the Party had long been subsidized by the USSR—might have been expected to inform the manner in which *Times* obituaries deal with prominent personalities who belonged to the CP.

Not so.

In fact, evidence that the old line continues to hold can be seen in an obituary published just last month. The most accurate aspect of the piece—its headline—happens, also, to be meaningless: "Millard Lampell, 78, Writer and Supporter of Causes, Dies."

Actually, Lampell was a multitalented artist who devoted his creative energies to the Communist "cause." But the fact that Communism was Lampell's "cause" cannot be discerned, even from a close reading of Jon Pareles's prominently featured obituary.

According to the *Times,* Millard Lampell was a "screenwriter, novelist and songwriter"—a "socially conscious" artist who "survived blacklisting to become an award-winning television writer." Scarcely elucidated in the course of this lengthy article is the meaning of the term *blacklisting.*

The reader is told that Lampell was blacklisted in 1950. Two years later, he was subpoenaed by the Senate Internal Security Committee, but "refused to testify about his associations." The obituary, however, leaves as a mystery the question of what the Senate internal security folks actually hoped to learn from Lampell. The fact that Lampell's refusal "to testify about his associations" required him to support himself as a "ghostwriter for film and television" throughout the 1950s represents the entirety of what we're told about this interlude.

Obviously, it's hard not to wonder why this manifestly talented and seemingly well-meaning "supporter of causes" found himself, for a long period, without gainful employ. But Pareles goes no further than to note that Lampell—"who communicated [his concerns] in every medium he could"—worried about "unions, nuclear war, the Warsaw ghetto . . . and integration." (Needless to say, "associations" with folks who shared these concerns scarcely seem subversive.)

Nevertheless, the only background information Pareles provides turns on the fact that Lampell had a bird's-eye view of the New Deal–era "battles between the United Mine Workers and [the] coal companies" during his years at West Virginia University. Only the reminder that, in 1940, Lampell joined up with Woody Guthrie, Pete Seeger, and Lee Hayes to establish the Almanac Singers, "a pioneering urban folk group," enables folks familiar with the American Left to locate Lampell on the political map.

While Lampell said the Almanacs wound up "performing at union meetings [and] left-wing benefits for Spanish refugees, striking Kentucky coal miners and Alabama sharecroppers," the full truth is rather less complex: The CP created the singing group in order to advance its political line. The group's main purpose was to link up with right-wing "isolationists" (America Firsters, among others) in the battle against intervention; the Party, of course, came to this stance after the 1939 Hitler-Stalin Pact—an event that drove legions of true believers from the CP.

Lampell, however, had no difficulty singing "The Yanks Are Not Coming" and other songs that reflected the Party's new line. Absent from the obituary, meanwhile, is any comment on the fact that the Almanacs *dissolved* right after Hitler's 1941 invasion of the Soviet Union. All in all, Pareles's failure to identify Lampell as a committed Communist renders the obituary a pointless and misleading exercise.

But even *Times* obituaries that *acknowledge* their subjects' Party ties raise more questions than they answer. Consider last week's obit: "Albert Blumberg, 91, Philosopher and Communist."

Blumberg's work as CP secretary in Maryland and Washington, D.C., couldn't be ignored—nor could his labors as the Party's national legislative director. Still, the article fails to consider the bizarre fact that Blumberg ended his political career as a Democratic Party district leader in New York City. And Robert

McG. Thomas, Jr., makes no effort to assess Blumberg's ideological evolution (if any such evolution even took place).

Did Blumberg ever leave the Party? If so, when—and why? How, moreover, did he find a place in the city's Democratic leadership? How did he become an adviser to City Councilman Stanley Michaels and ex-Mayor David Dinkins, among others? These and related questions remain unanswered.

While Thomas notes that Blumberg was "hounded" by the Justice Department and various congressional committees, the writer mocks the notion that governmental authorities considered Blumberg's Party work "a cover for his role in a Stalin-directed conspiracy" against the U.S. government. To be sure, the *Times* also notes Blumberg's recent reluctance "to talk about his past." Never considered, however, is the possibility that he may well have had good reason for his silence.

Finally, it's worth examining another *Times* obit—that of ex-Representative George W. Crockett, Jr., who died last month at the age of eighty-eight. Crockett, a leader in the pro-Communist faction of the United Auto Workers, never hid his belief that only the CP—of all the elements on the U.S. political spectrum—demanded full equality for black Americans. In fact, Crockett didn't hesitate to call the Party "the conscience of America." Still, *Times*man Thomas reports that Crockett "had no interest in Communism."

This manifestly absurd claim is a telling comment on the newspaper's commitment to accuracy in this realm. What's unclear is *why* the *Times* still finds itself unable to treat honestly with communism's recent role in American life.

PART TWO
NEW YORK

The City in Decline

From the moment that Breindel took the reins of the New York Post's *editorial page in 1986, the city itself was rocked by a series of crimes and controversies that threatened to destroy it. Only with Rudolph Giuliani's election in 1993 and the subsequent dramatic drop in crime did the Spenglerian doom suffusing Breindel's writing on the city begin to abate.*

After Lisa Steinberg

April 6, 1989

Joel Steinberg, despite a last-minute bid to do his jail time here in New York City, was finally shipped off to Dannemora, near the Canadian border, this week. He'll serve out the maximum penalty for manslaughter in one of the nation's toughest prisons, a circumstance that will distress virtually no one.

Three fundamental questions attended this gruesome case—one legal, one moral, one psychological—and Steinberg's departure reminds us that the first two remain unanswered.

The psychological question—"What kind of man could do such things to his own child?"—was answered by Steinberg himself on sentencing day.

Before the judge imposes sentence, the convicted party has an opportunity to make a statement. And Joel Steinberg, who didn't testify during the trial, availed himself of the chance to address the court.

The most striking thing about his remarks was their clinical, dispassionate tone. He spoke—he informed the court—as an experienced lawyer. And, indeed, it was as if he were summing up in a case in which he was actually the defense attorney—for some stranger who happened to have retained him.

The point is not that he failed to confess and beg for mercy or even that he seemed without remorse. It's that he failed virtually to manifest any emotion at all.

In reviewing the evidence, Steinberg discussed Lisa less as his child than as the subject of an autopsy. He spoke of the absence of "hematomas" on her body and referred to the normal nature of the "fatty tissue"—all in an effort to demonstrate that Lisa hadn't, in fact, been beaten or abused.

He called the judge's attention to this and that medical document, frequently reading aloud, in an entirely normal tone of voice, from reports containing detailed descriptions of Lisa's physical state.

Steinberg suggested that Emergency Medical Service personnel might have been responsible for Lisa's death through the overzealous (albeit well-meaning) administration of CPR; this prompted Judge Harold Rothwax to an expression of astonishment at the utter brazenness of the defendant's remarks.

But the truly astonishing element wasn't brazenness or even the claim that he—Joel Steinberg—was the victim in the case.

Most astonishing was the cold, distinct, quasi-scientific tone in which Steinberg discussed his daughter's physical condition on the final night of her life. This, it suddenly seemed clear, was an altogether disconnected man.

The people in his life—his dead daughter, in particular—were but objects to him. His ability to brutalize them seemed a mystery no longer.

The legal question, of course, stems from the jury's failure to convict Steinberg of murder.

The jury determined that the defendant hadn't demonstrated the requisite "depraved indifference to human life."

Yet there was no question that Steinberg beat Lisa repeatedly over a period of months; no question that he struck the fatal blows on November 1, 1987; no question that he failed to summon help that night, choosing instead to sit by in a cocaine-induced stupor, while his daughter lay before him mortally injured.

If conduct of this sort doesn't meet the "depraved indifference" standard, it's difficult to imagine what sort of behavior would. The legal question will long linger in the minds of lay observers. For the general public, in fact, the case might have been easier to grasp had Steinberg been found not guilty by reason of insanity.

In their effort to come to terms with the verdict, many observers concluded that the jurors were protesting the fact that Hedda Nussbaum hadn't been charged.

And this, of course, points to the unanswered moral question: Should Hedda have been a codefendant?

Apart from the tactical issue—the fact that the state wanted her as a witness against Joel and granted her immunity to ensure his conviction—the real question is whether Hedda should have been regarded as a victim, like her daughter, or as an accomplice in Lisa's death.

It's clear, after all, that Hedda stood by, failing to summon outside help, while Joel Steinberg, over a period of months, beat their daughter to a pulp. As a functioning, gainfully employed adult for a good part of the period in question, Hedda had choices that Lisa didn't have.

Or did she? When she was hospitalized after her arrest, physicians determined that Hedda had been about a week away from death at the time she was apprehended.

For whatever reason, she, too, had been a captive in a house of horrors. Her inability to help Lisa reflected her inability to help herself. This was a beaten, broken woman with a broken face and a broken spirit.

Hedda Nussbaum, to be sure, was less a victim than Lisa—such distinctions remain important. But she was more a victim than an accomplice. Gluing her back together physically and emotionally simply in order to try her would have been to pervert justice, rather than serve it.

Thus, all in all, the state did well. The truly guilty party was convicted and punished (albeit with insufficient severity). The criminal justice system worked.

It's too bad the same can't be said with respect to the social service system. The failures in this realm leave a set of equally serious questions, *all* as yet unanswered.

How is it possible that Lisa wasn't identified—in school, at play, anywhere—as an abused child?

Why didn't the police, who apparently knew something of what was happening in the Steinberg household, take any action?

How did Lisa wind up in the hands of this demented couple—what happened to the adoption regulations?

There will always be Joel Steinbergs and Hedda Nussbaums in the world. But if these social service questions can be answered, with new policies and improved procedures, it may be possible to prevent such people from getting—or from keeping—children. This seems an eminently worthy goal.

A Mugger Gets $4.3 Million

March 22, 1990

The strangest thing about the award of $4.3 million by a Manhattan jury to career criminal Bernard McCummings—the money comes as compensation for injuries inflicted on McCummings by a New York City Transit Police officer seeking to apprehend him—is that the case generated remarkably little press attention and remarkably little outrage.

This suggests that ordinary people have come to accept, and perhaps even expect, utterly bizarre results—masquerading as justice—from the legal system and the courts. It's hard to imagine a surer prescription for general alienation.

Consider the case: Some six years ago, McCummings and two associates, to their surprise and dismay, were interrupted in the middle of a job. The three young men were busy beating and choking seventy-one-year-old Jerome Sandusky on a subway station platform—in the course of robbing him.

Transit cop Manuel Rodriguez and his partner arrived at the scene and intervened. Sandusky believes Officer Rodriguez saved his life. McCummings, who sought to flee, was shot in the back by Rodriguez; the officer maintains that McCummings, while trying to escape, first lunged at him, provoking the shooting.

In any event, it's clear Rodriguez used his gun to apprehend a criminal who would otherwise have escaped after committing a violent crime. The routine internal inquiry that follows any use of a weapon by a policeman found that Rodriguez had acted in accordance with police guidelines.

McCummings's substantial criminal record prompted him to accept a plea bargain in the case. The robbery, assault, and related charges were collapsed into a single guilty plea, and McCummings received a two-and-a-half-to-five-year sentence. Confined to a wheelchair—Rodriguez's bullet had struck his spinal cord—McCummings served less than three years and was released.

He thereupon hired a lawyer and sued the New York City Transit Authority, claiming himself to be the victim of excessive force. A jury found in his favor and awarded him the $4.3 million in damages.

The judge in the case refused to reduce or set aside the verdict; the Transit Authority has declared its intention to file an appeal.

Judging from the comments of one juror, he and his colleagues believed—on the basis of the instructions they received from the bench—that they had "no choice" but to find for McCummings.

It seems that the jury felt it had virtually no latitude in rendering its decision, that the U.S. Supreme Court had defined the circumstances in which police can fire their weapons to subdue fleeing suspects, and that their job—as jurors—was to assess this particular case against the high court's standards. This, in any event, appears to be the way in which the jury interpreted Justice Leonard Cohen's charge.

The jurors evidently concluded that the case failed the Supreme Court's test and that Rodriguez's conduct—notwithstanding the internal inquiry—also failed to conform to police guidelines.

They then set about to decide how much McCummings would "need" to live the rest of his life in a wheelchair.

It goes without saying, of course, that juries actually enjoy broad discretion—their real job isn't simply to apply existing case law, but to render justice, taking legal precedent into account.

Moreover, the notion of satisfying McCummings's "needs" has an absurd quality to it.

What standard did the jurors apply here? Most people who are confined to wheelchairs do not receive multi-million-dollar awards from the taxpayers, despite the fact that they generally aren't in any way responsible for their unhappy circumstances. Surely, the jurors didn't try to determine how much money McCummings would have earned had his career mugging and choking old people not been foreshortened.

Setting aside the macabre question of just how the jury arrived at the specific $4.3 million sum, the most insidious aspect of this affair consists in its likely impact on ordinary people.

What are ordinary folks to think of a system in which the criminal is awarded millions in damages for injuries sustained in the course of committing a felony?

Many will conclude that this isn't just a chaotic and frightening society—one in which a seventy-one-year-old man can't wait for a subway train without being robbed and beaten—but also a topsy-turvy one: a world in which values are turned on their head, in which right is wrong and wrong is right.

They see a society in which the victim is lucky to get away with his life, the cop is stigmatized forever, and the criminal emerges from the halls of justice—after participating in the system according in the established procedure—with millions of public money in his pocket.

It's hard to conceive of a more alienating sight. And it's difficult to imagine working people who pay taxes (to subsidize Bernard McCummings) feeling they have a stake in such a system. Or wanting a stake in such a system.

Therein—beyond the unhappy experiences of Jerome Sandusky and Officer Rodriguez—lies the tragedy.

The Wild Man of Ninety-sixth Street

August 5, 1993

There's a curious sidebar to the saga of Larry Hogue—the so-called Wild Man of Ninety-sixth Street—who's been treated for mental illness, aggravated by substance abuse, at the Creedmoor Psychiatric Center in Queens over the course of the past year.

Hogue's notoriety has made him a national symbol of the homeless street dweller, which is altogether appropriate. While most of the street homeless aren't quite as threatening as Larry Hogue, a vast number—as every New Yorker with eyes and ears knows—are mentally ill. Indeed, the Hogues of the city helped set to rest the nonsensical claim that creating more housing would, by itself, "solve" the problem of the homeless.

What's curious about the Hogue case—which is back in the news because lawyers for Hogue insist he's capable of living on his own and are demanding his release from Creedmoor—is that he's regularly described as a Vietnam veteran.

There are, of course, other curiosities here, including the apparently valid claim that Hogue has thirty thousand dollars in the bank, enough—along with an alleged disability pension—to afford him a Triple-A credit rating. Hogue, in other words, is in a position to secure a mortgage and buy a house. Thus, anyone who thinks his difficulties turn on a need for "housing, housing, housing" (as the homeless advocates used to say) need worry no more.

As for Vietnam, Hogue—it seems—was never anywhere near the place. Chris Ruddy of the *New York Guardian,* an outstanding local weekly, notes that Hogue served in the U.S. Navy from early 1963 through early 1964. Stationed at Great Lakes in Illinois and assigned to the USS *Champlain,* Hogue was honorably discharged well before the Vietnam conflict picked up steam.

Nevertheless, as Ruddy notes, Hogue has been called a Vietnam veteran at least five times during the past year by the *New York Times.* The false claim, moreover, has been repeated by the AP, UPI, and Reuters. The *Times* has been notified of its error on more than one occasion; the falsehood, however, has never been corrected.

While Hogue himself—seizing, apparently, on the national

passion for questionable "combat-induced" maladies like "Agent Orange exposure"—has, on occasion, claimed to have served in Vietnam (he once testified explicitly to suffering flashbacks caused by Agent Orange), his limited connection with reality would, ordinarily, send journalists scurrying for verification.

In this case, however, Hogue's status as a Vietnam veteran has become received wisdom. Why?

The notion that many of the mentally ill homeless are veterans of Vietnam serves a dual purpose. It promotes the impression that society at large owes this unfortunate element a special obligation. (Thus, the abundance of homeless men with handmade street signs reading, "Vietnam vet: Please help.")

It also suggests that the military—and the Vietnam War, in particular—created a generation of homeless psychotics, a useful bit of agitprop for professional foes of the military, many of whom bear a special animus toward the entire Vietnam enterprise.

Actually, the image of the Vietnam vet as a homeless psychopath is an utter fiction. A *Washington Post*-ABC poll demonstrates that Vietnam veterans are more likely than contemporaries who didn't serve to have had a college education, to own homes, and to earn more than thirty thousand dollars per year. This, of course, isn't astonishing. Military experience has always tended to enhance the skills and ultimate circumstances of those who serve.

But why let the facts spoil a good myth? The press corps prefers thinking of Vietnam veterans as Larry Hogues. And journalists are most comfortable thinking of Hogue himself as someone who, as the CBS television program *60 Minutes* put it, started having mental problems "after he was hit in the head by a propeller blade while serving in Vietnam."

Agent Orange? Propeller blade? Who cares? The point of the media elite is that Larry Hogue's problems were created by a U.S. military misadventure, not by the reckless "deinstitutionalization" policy foisted on American society by civil libertarians. Deinstitutionalization took mentally ill people out of hospitals—where they belonged and were getting actual help—and threw them into the street. Not a happy fact with which to conjure. Far better to blame Vietnam.

The Teacher from NAMBLA

October 11, 1993

We have a curious problem in New York at the moment, one that transcends entirely the question of gay rights even though it happens to involve an issue that has long plagued mainstream gay activists. Peter Melzer, until recently a physics teacher at the Bronx High School of Science—one of the nation's genuinely outstanding public high schools—turns out to be a leader of the North American Man-Boy Love Association (NAMBLA).

Melzer, in fact, is a NAMBLA officer and an editor of the NAMBLA newsletter. Thus, his name appears on the masthead of a journal that includes "how to" articles pertaining to the seduction of young boys.

Melzer's ties to NAMBLA have been known to Bronx Science officials for nearly a decade. But until his NAMBLA affiliation received wide currency—as a consequence of a television report and a spate of newspaper articles—Bronx Science took no action against him; in short, he was allowed to continue to teach.

By all accounts, moreover—this is a bit difficult to believe in view of what psychiatrists tell us about pedophilia—Melzer has never done anything untoward in his thirty-one years as a teacher. And his unblemished in-school history explains Bronx Science's reluctance to act against him.

But after Melzer's NAMBLA ties became known, pressure brought to bear by Bronx Science parents rendered the school's position untenable. Melzer was removed from his classroom and assigned to a desk job.

No formal charges have been brought against him, however. He's committed no crime, so far as anyone knows; as a consequence, his union—the United Federation of Teachers (UFT)—is arguing that his reassignment cannot be permanent. In view of the fact that he has tenure, Melzer, the UFT contends, is entitled to a disciplinary hearing. Such a hearing has now been scheduled.

Meanwhile, the Board of Education has moved to dismiss him entirely. The board contends that Melzer's "private views"—a reference to his NAMBLA activities—inhibit the proper functioning of the school system. The failure to see the board's point, and the tendency to treat this as a complicated First Amendment case, seems a comment on the disintegration of values—and on the disappearance of any sense of judgment—in important strata of American life.

Of course, Melzer has a legal right to argue the virtues of sexual relations between men and boys. And that's what he does as a NAMBLA officer. In other words, he has a legal right to advocate illegal conduct. If he incites or facilitates pedophilia, he'll doubtless find himself crossing over into the criminal realm. But let's assume, for the sake of argument—and on the basis of what's actually known—that Melzer does nothing more than extol the pleasures of "man-boy love" and edit articles about seducing minors.

Obviously, the physics teacher is acting within his legal rights. The point, however, is that teaching in a public school is a privilege, not a right. A teacher's salary is paid by the public. And living within the confines of the law doesn't entitle a teacher to keep on practicing his craft if other factors militate against the wisdom of allowing him to do so.

The Board of Education is making a rather uncomplicated point: If the school system consisted entirely of Peter Melzers—vociferous advocates of pedophilia who manage to restrain themselves while at work—the system simply couldn't function.

Suppose a teacher at a public high school writes and edits articles calling black children intellectually inferior and proposing that they be excluded entirely from the schools. Legal? Sure. Healthy for the educational system? Not exactly. Could a system composed exclusively of such teachers function? No.

Suppose a teacher champions Nazism and writes, not that the Holocaust was a hoax, but that the mass murder of Jewish children was a noble episode in mankind's history. Legal? Yes. Healthy for the schools? Not exactly.

Teachers are meant to do more than pass on information—they're supposed to serve as role models for the youngsters they encounter.

And while it's not always possible for people of goodwill to agree on whether Teacher "X" meets this standard, sometimes the case is pretty clear-cut. Sound judgment and basic discretion make the Peter Melzer case exceedingly uncomplicated. It takes a special kind of mindset not to recognize this reality.

The LIRR Killer

December 16, 1993

The guardians of political correctness seem to want to have it both ways with respect to last week's mass slaughter aboard a Long Island Rail Road rush-hour train.

On the one hand, attempts to note that Jamaican immigrant Colin Ferguson was a madman gripped by a consuming hatred of white society—an animus encouraged by aspects of the contemporary political culture—have been dismissed as ideologically inspired efforts to give a random act of insanity a racial cast.

Meanwhile, however, politically correct commentators seem oddly anxious to include Ferguson's obsessive hostility toward whites, Asians, "black conservatives," and various "racist institutions" in the general discussion of the episode.

Morris Dees—an ex-Jimmy Carter aide who founded the Southern Poverty Law Center—affords a case in point. Dees, commenting on the mass murder aboard the LIRR, notes "a rising sense of frustration among blacks that the promises of the civil rights movement are not coming to pass." Linking Ferguson to the "promises of the civil rights movement" seems a bit of a stretch. Moreover, while Dees would have it that this "sense of frustration" is "filtering down to the street," he fails to explain what role it might have played in Ferguson's imagined grievances.

Certainly, the LIRR incident was—in every relevant sense—a "hate crime." Its venue was selected so that a white suburb—rather than New York City—would be the scene of the tragedy. The victims were targeted on the basis of race; Ferguson was apparently determined to murder whites and Asians, but not blacks. And of the twenty-three commuters he shot, not one was black.

In this respect, interestingly, Ferguson's conduct reflects a national tendency: In 1992, blacks perpetrated eleven of the eighteen racially motivated homicides reported across the nation. The previous year, of course, saw the Crown Heights pogrom and the murder of Yankel Rosenbaum.

All of which suggests that someone like Morris Dees—who's made identifying *white* racism a profession—might have done well simply to ignore this episode.

Clearly, that's what the Reverend Joseph Lowery, head of the Southern Christian Leadership Conference, would have preferred. Lowery has said point-blank that Colin Ferguson's crime should not be compared to the violent antiblack racism that has long disfigured American history. "People who set out deliberately to violate the rights of blacks . . . that's a hate crime," argues Lowery, indicating an inability to recognize any other manifestation of the phenomenon.

All in all, the politically correct haven't yet figured out how to treat the LIRR massacre. The desire to call attention to the mistreatment of blacks collides with Ferguson's racist sensibility, as well as with his undeniable insanity.

The Reverend Jesse Jackson maintains that when he learned of the crime, his first instinct—after hoping no one had been hurt—was to pray that the perpetrator wouldn't turn out to be black. Jackson "knew" that a black mass killer would prompt "a rash of irrational conclusions." Such a circumstance, he believed, would "undermine progress" and embolden those "who are out for revenge."

Not surprisingly, the Reverend Al Sharpton was even more graphic: "We all know that if the person [Ferguson] is black, we are all going to be penalized."

But neither Jackson nor Sharpton can actually cite instances of a backlash in the case at hand. Indeed, the best Jackson could do was to chastise Nassau County Executive Thomas Gulotta—twice—for describing Ferguson as an "animal," even though Gulotta would likely have employed precisely the same terminology in describing a white or Asian mass killer.

Now, Jackson—who's touring New York schools to discuss the LIRR tragedy—contends that the episode had nothing to do with racial tensions. According to Jackson, Colin Ferguson wasn't on a "race rampage"—he murdered in "a fit of sickness." That's a fair stance. But in their initial effort to dictate the terms of the debate, the politically correct succeeded in spawning a measure of sheer misinformation. Thus, a black paralegal—more familiar, it would seem, with the original Jackson-Sharpton analysis than with the actual facts—maintains, according to a *New York Times* story, that "[i]f I had been on that train, wearing a business suit and carrying a briefcase, I [might] have been shot, too." After listening to Jackson, Sharpton, and Lowery, it's easy to forgive the paralegal in question for drawing this altogether erroneous conclusion. In fact, however, Ferguson was determined *not* to shoot blacks.

Before Jackson decided that race was a nonissue, he told a packed Long Island cathedral that Ferguson was "an irrational, sick man whose world was reduced to black and white"; Jackson insisted nonetheless that there would be calls for "race-baiting and retribution."

Jackson's first observation was valid: Ferguson, however demented, did manifest a proclivity for racial reductionism. But the second claim remains groundless: No one has called for revenge or "retribution." The politically correct might have preferred to see such demands. Unfortunately—at least for Al Sharpton & Co.—no one has issued them. The Long Islanders have been too busy burying their dead.

IN THE MATTER OF "BILLIE BOGGS"

The great debate over homelessness in the 1980s between Left and Right had to do with the causes of the epidemic. The Left said it was due to the lack of affordable housing and cutbacks in social programs. The Right said it was the legacy of an ill-advised decision to deinstitutionalize the mentally ill. Breindel took a particular interest in the saga of Joyce Brown, a homeless woman who made an encampment for herself on Manhattan's Upper East Side, renamed herself "Billie Boggs," and unexpectedly became a darling of leftist advocates for the homeless who took up her cause when then-Mayor Ed Koch's administration sought to commit her to Bellevue Hospital.

Justice Lippmann in Wonderland

November 19, 1987

At a time of much discussion about judges blinded by political ideology, it would be hard to find a better example than acting state Supreme Court Justice Robert Lippmann, the judge who last week ordered "Billie Boggs" released from Bellevue Hospital.

Billie, a forty-year-old former secretary, was the first person involuntarily hospitalized by mental health authorities under Mayor Koch's Project Help.

Using her as a test case, the New York Civil Liberties Union (NYCLU) challenged the legality of Koch's program to hospitalize—involuntarily, if need be—street people who display overt signs of serious mental illness.

For the moment, Billie Boggs—she named herself after a television personality; her real name is Joyce Brown—remains in Bellevue pending an appeal by the city. Commenting on the order staying her release, Billie's self-appointed NYCLU attorney—in a remarkable display of inattention to her real circumstances—remarked that Billie was disappointed because she had "expected to be able to go home [sic]." The lawyer apparently forgot that his client lives atop a hot-air vent on the corner of East Sixty-fifth Street.

But on a certain level, the NYCLU can be forgiven this inattentive disposition toward Billie. The civil liberties lawyers, after all, didn't take her on as a client out of a deep concern for her individual well-being. They made no bones about the fact that to them, she was a symbol—a tool with which to fight a program they opposed.

Justice Lippmann, on the other hand, has no such excuse. He was obliged to consider Billie Boggs as an individual—to determine whether she was likely to do serious harm either to herself or to others if released from the hospital. That's the standard for involuntary hospitalization under the state mental health law.

Given the undisputed facts in the case, the ordinary citizen might well wonder how any judge in the world could have found Billie sufficiently rational to care for herself without risk of serious harm.

If Justice Lippmann had adopted a pure libertarian stance and proclaimed Billie's right to commit slow-motion suicide in public, that would have been one thing. But he didn't, nor could he have—in this society, suicide is illegal.

Lippmann found Billie sane. Sane enough to care for herself, certainly. But sane even in a larger sense—particularly by comparison with the society that sought to hospitalize her.

Not in dispute was the fact that she lived in the street, soiled herself regularly, shouted obscenities at passersby, and burned the paper money they gave her, even though she actually survived by panhandling. The only germane fact in dispute was whether she tended to run into oncoming traffic.

Let's take a look at how Justice Lippmann deals with these various issues in his ruling. The judge acknowledges that he was impressed by Billie's demeanor on the witness stand—he notes that she was "rational, logical, [and] coherent," failing to recognize that she had by then been medicated for several days with Haldol, a powerful psychotropic drug used with considerable success in treating paranoid schizophrenia.

Lippmann accepts as entirely logical Billie's explanation—"I didn't have access to toilet facilities"—of why she relieved herself in the street and in her clothing.

The judge goes on to argue that while "seeing her . . . defecating publicly may seem deranged . . . how can anyone living in security and comfort even begin to imagine what is required to survive on the street?"

The implication is that Billie's behavior made sense in the context of her life as a street person—a context ordinary people are incapable of apprehending. It is a theme that recurs throughout the ruling.

Justice Lippmann holds that Billie's inclination to burn paper money—when she didn't like the manner in which it was given to her—"may not satisfy a society increasingly oriented to profit-making and bottom-line pragmatism, but it is consonant with safe conduct on the street."

Adding a triumphant flourish to this suggestion that only a society warped by greed could find fault with a panhandler who burns money, Lippmann asserts: "Apparently beggars can be choosers."

What about running into oncoming traffic? The city's psychiatrists reported that when they confronted Billie on the street, she insisted on her right to run into traffic; they saw in this behavior a suicidal impulse.

The NYCLU's psychiatrist countered that jaywalking is common in New York. This expert went on to contend that the mere fact that Billie hadn't yet been hurt testified to her "strong survival instincts."

This was obviously treacherous terrain for Lippmann—the whole case turned on whether Billie represented a danger to herself.

But the judge found a way out. Billie herself, when on the witness stand, had simply denied any history of running into traffic. So Lippmann chose to accept her claim over the reports of the two psychiatrists.

In a sense, this was a small-scale illustration of how the judge saw the whole case: Billie's worldview, to his mind, was far more rational and reliable than that of the authorities.

Her circumstances, Lippmann believes, are a phenomenon of social inequity, not mental illness. "Housing in New York is so expensive that in this rich city, many are driven to live in the streets," writes the judge.

Lippmann would have it that this desperate woman is an indictment of all of us.

So committed is he to this view of America as a society animated by greed and bereft of compassion that he is willing to dispatch, from a hospital into the street, a woman who relieves herself in her clothing—even over her family's plea that she be cared for in a hospital.

The judge hopes "her plight will offend the moral conscience and arouse it to action." It is he who offends the moral conscience.

Joyce Brown at Harvard

February 25, 1988

While it's not unusual for political activists to exploit the plight of unfortunate individuals in the service of larger ideological goals, there is something decidedly macabre about the ongoing "Billie Boggs" road show orchestrated by the New York Civil Liberties Union.

"Billie"—or Joyce Brown, now that she's reverted to her legal name—goes with her lawyers to the posh Windows on the World restaurant and chooses the wine for her table.

Joyce Brown goes to Harvard Law School, accompanied by her lawyers, to deliver a lecture on the homeless crisis.

Miss Brown tells her Harvard audience that she was a "political prisoner" at Bellevue Hospital—that there was absolutely nothing wrong with her other than the fact that she had no place to live. Her lawyers sit by, saying nothing.

Although she doesn't realize it, Miss Brown is a prop—a weapon being used by one side in a battle over social priorities that she doesn't even know is taking place.

It has become convenient for the NYCLU to represent Miss Brown as sane—to claim that Mayor Koch and Project Help, in a desperate effort to clear New York's streets of impoverished and unsightly people, swept an utterly sane woman into a mental hospital.

This Kafkaesque theme—a sane woman locked in insane asylum for eighty-four days—has obviously proved a good deal more accessible to the public than the NYCLU's initial, far more nuanced, stance.

The original argument, even if not persuasive, was at least honorable. The NYCLU considered the Project Help standard for involuntary hospitalization dangerously overbroad and a threat to civil liberties. Under that standard, the involuntary hospitalization of street dwellers is permissible if they—now or in the foreseeable future—represent a danger either to themselves or to others.

The part that most disturbed the civil liberties folks was the "now or in the foreseeable future" clause. This standard, they maintained, was simply too vague. It gave the authorities too much license.

For many people, the daily sight of hundreds of manifestly deranged human beings living in the streets was sufficient to undermine the NYCLU's argument—particularly since it was clear that despite the advent of winter, only a few dozen of these desperate souls could even be accommodated under Project Help.

Still, the claim that insanity alone doesn't justify involuntary hospitalization is, if nothing else, intellectually honest.

The representation that there's nothing wrong with Joyce Brown is, on the other hand, a bald-faced lie.

The NYCLU lawyers know Miss Brown has a history of mental illness that predates her appearance on the streets of New York as "Billie Boggs." They know she was hospitalized for psychiatric reasons before her recent stay in Bellevue. They know she was diagnosed as psychotic not just by three New York psychiatrists quite recently, but also by the doctors who treated her when she was hospitalized in New Jersey.

Miss Brown's lawyers know that her family believes her to be in desperate need of psychiatric help; they know her sisters maintain that she tends to be abusive, and the NYCLU attorneys know Miss Brown was convicted of assault prior to her first hospitalization.

The lawyers, moreover, must realize that the undisputed facts about Miss Brown's habits as a street dweller—from screaming aloud to soiling herself—indicate that her problems go beyond the lack of an apartment.

And they also doubtless know that even now—with a subsidized room in a hotel, a part-time job at the ACLU, and a new wardrobe from Bloomingdale's—she still reportedly mumbles to herself, using racial epithets, while walking to work. (Miss Brown denies this report: "I was just singing. Sometimes I sing the latest tunes.")

Joyce Brown, it seems, is tormented by the same demons that led her to hurl racial epithets at black men when she lived in the street. As her current roommate at the hotel notes: "She talks to herself. . . . She has a lot of anger inside."

Miss Brown insists she's the same woman she was a year ago, except that she now enjoys clean clothes and a healthier lifestyle. Unfortunately, this appears to be true. She *is* the same woman. Schizophrenia doesn't just go away.

Yet her NYCLU lawyers persist in advancing the fiction that there's nothing wrong with her—they've obviously decided that this public relations strategy is the best way to undermine the legitimacy of Project Help.

One of her attorneys even allows that Miss Brown is "too sane." The NYCLU, he says, "would have represented Joyce Brown even if she had serious problems."

Well, the fact is that she does have serious problems—it doesn't take a psychiatrist to figure this out. And in passing Joyce Brown off as sane, the NYCLU is perpetrating a hoax that calls its honor and integrity into question.

She Returns to the Streets

February 2, 1989

A year to the very week since the New York Civil Liberties Union secured her release from Bellevue Hospital, "Billie Boggs" (aka Joyce Brown) returned to the same hot-air vent in front of an Upper East Side ice cream parlor that she called home before the city took her involuntarily to Bellevue.

So, are we right back where we started from? Not really. One important factor mitigates the otherwise depressing character of this development.

No longer are there serious voices out there sounding the bizarre claim that Miss Brown is sane. Moreover, there is a consensus that the overwhelming majority of *individual* homeless—the people who, like Joyce Brown, live in the streets and public terminals of America's cities—are either mentally disturbed or substance abusers or both.

That's a major stride forward. Far fewer are the efforts to represent Miss Brown, and the thousands of other unfortunates who share her circumstances, as victims of a housing crunch.

This change is crucial—after all, the only way these desperate people are ever going to get any substantive help is if there's some agreement, first, as to the nature of their problem.

Let's remember that only a year ago, when Miss Brown was taken to Bellevue—under the terms of Mayor Koch's Project Help, she was deemed to represent a danger to herself—Norman Siegel and his NYCLU colleagues didn't simply question the constitutionality of the law authorizing the city to take citizens to mental hospitals against their will. They asserted that Miss Brown was entirely sane.

Again and again, they advanced this claim—in newspapers and on television. Despite the fact that she screamed obscenities at passersby, soiled herself publicly, and solicited money only to burn it; despite the fact that her family reported a subsequently confirmed history of mental illness requiring hospitalization.

"She's as sane as you or I," the telegenic and articulate Siegel would repeat. She "sounds like a board member of the civil liberties union," said Robert Levy, Siegel's NYCLU colleague. (This, of course, may well be true.)

And eventually, the NYCLU secured her release from the hospital. They won their victory, to be sure, on somewhat technical grounds. Failing to persuade an appellate judge of Miss Brown's sanity, the lawyers managed to get a court order preventing Bellevue from medicating her against her will. And the Bellevue psychiatrists concluded that, absent the ability to treat her psychosis with psychotropic medications, no purpose was served by her continued involuntary hospitalization.

Thus was Joyce Brown discharged—into the hands of Norman Siegel and the NYCLU.

Had the absence of a roof over her head been Miss Brown's only problem, she would have been cured immediately upon discharge: Miss Brown was provided with a city-paid-for room in the Travelers Hotel as soon as she left the hospital.

The NYCLU took her on the lecture circuit. Off she went to Harvard Law School to denounce Koch and Project Help. She likened her experience to that of Soviet dissidents—("I was a political prisoner," she told her Harvard audience)—a comparison put forward initially by Siegel.

But despite the lecture and television appearances, despite a new wardrobe purchased at Bloomingdale's (thanks to the largess of the various TV shows), despite the hotel room and a part-time job at the NYCLU itself, all was not well.

The press discovered Miss Brown shouting at passersby and soliciting money near the Port Authority Bus Terminal some two months after her discharge from Bellevue. The NYCLU lawyers explained that it was all a mixup; she'd found herself short of funds and had been embarrassed to ask Siegel & Co. for assistance.

It soon turned out, however, that this was not the first time Miss Brown had returned to the streets to panhandle. Indeed, she'd been back at it virtually from Day One. Her Travelers Hotel roommate confirmed her tendency to scream aloud at no one in particular. "She has a lot of anger inside," the roommate observed.

Not surprisingly, things got still worse. In September, Miss Brown was arrested for possession of drugs and for disorderly conduct—she pleaded guilty to the latter charge and received a conditional discharge.

And now, not surprisingly, comes news of her return to the hot-air vent in front of Swenson's Ice Cream Parlor where she first attracted the attention of the authorities.

Where's the good news in all this?

When the NYCLU's Levy was told that Miss Brown had returned to Swenson's—where she was screaming and making lewd gestures—the attorney sang a new tune. No longer did he argue that Miss Brown sounded like a NYCLU board member.

Levy merely noted, "Whether or not Joyce Brown needed help, she, like anyone, had the legal right to choose whether to accept that help, so long as she did not pose an imminent danger to herself or others."

How someone in her straits could pose anything other than a danger to herself remains an obvious question. Still, it's clear the debate has shifted to more honest terrain.

This reflects studies indicating that between 70 and 85 percent of America's "individual homeless" (the street dwellers as distinct from homeless families living in hotels) are mentally impaired and/or substance abusers. The fact that we are dealing with a mental and public health problem—not a housing crisis—is increasingly acknowledged.

If that seems manifest, let's remember that only a year ago, an acting state Supreme Court justice in New York, siding with the NYCLU, termed Joyce Brown healthy and sane, "a rugged individualist" who behaved the way she did because she knew what it took to survive in the streets of New York, streets to which she was consigned due—yes!—to a housing shortage.

The challenges ahead are enormous. Undoing the harm of deinstitutionalization by devising a working mental health care system—preferably community based—is no small task. But until almost everyone agreed that mental health was the heart of the problem, those challenges couldn't even be confronted.

THE CENTRAL PARK JOGGER

No crime in the crime-ridden city of New York provoked more anger and fear in the 1980s than the vicious rape and beating of a young stockbroker who was jogging after work in Central Park by a gang of black youths, one of whom confessed on videotape. In a manner that was becoming sadly familiar to Breindel, some leaders in the black community rallied around the mugger-rapists. In these columns, he shows how the discussion in some circles in New York came to revolve around the treatment of the criminals, while the state of the victim— one among thousands of women in New York who jogged nightly in the park—was not considered worthy of much mention.

False Compassion

June 15, 1989

The case of the Central Park jogger is back in the news.

Father Louis R. Gigante, the famed "slum priest"—a former city councilman, now a housing activist in the depressed South Bronx—propelled the Central Park affair back into the headlines by posting the $25,000 bail needed to free fourteen-year-old suspect Kevin Richardson.

The Reverend Gigante, no stranger to controversy, read that Richardson's family was poor and wouldn't be able to afford bail. Believing, according to Richardson's attorney, that "rich people and gangsters shouldn't be the only ones who are freed on high-cash bail," Father Gigante went to the bank, withdrew the sum from his own account, and posted bail. Richardson is now free.

Father Gigante's action has drawn a hugely negative response from New Yorkers in all walks of life. Even parishioners at his own St. Athanasius Church in the South Bronx—where Gigante has served as a pastor for more than twenty years—have been critical.

"Father Gigante's reputation is great, but I'm shocked that he would make a move like this," commented sixteen-year-old Tanya Oshoteco. "No one is thinking about the woman. It's absurd."

Nonparishioners were less restrained, and many have given vent to their anger in newspaper letters columns.

The well-publicized fact that Richardson has already admitted to participating in the assault (he made a videotaped confession), plus, of course, the extraordinary brutality of the crime itself, undoubtedly account for the degree of popular outrage at Father Gigante's action.

The plain truth is that it's exceedingly difficult to look on this young man as innocent until proved guilty, however technically improper any other perspective may be.

On the appropriateness of posting bail, however, Father Gigante is correct.

The purpose of bail is to ensure that the accused appears in court. The reason judges set bail to reflect the seriousness of the crime in question is that it's assumed a suspect facing a long prison term is more likely to flee than someone charged with a less serious crime.

Still, the relevant issue with regard to bail remains the likelihood that the accused will turn up in court.

The only other factor that can properly come into play is the possibility that the suspect, if freed, will commit another crime. But pretrial incarceration, based on the premise that the accused poses a danger to society, requires a ruling to this effect from a judge. And no such ruling has been handed down in this case.

Thus, insofar as Kevin Richardson has "roots in the community"—a family, a regular address, a school in which he's enrolled—he meets the standard criteria for bail.

Most people understand the purpose of bail. There's nothing particularly mysterious or esoteric about the subject. Thus, there would seem to be something inexplicable about the widespread outrage over Father Gigante's deed.

It might be possible to view Gigante's charge that this is a "society that hungers for revenge and blood" as a provocation. But both this remark, and Gigante's suggestion that he wanted to "give a boy a chance to turn his life around" (which seems a trifle premature at this stage), came in response to the initial protests.

I suspect that the anger doesn't have much to do with Father Gigante, or with the question of bail per se. The outrage reflects the fact that ordinary citizens have no confidence that justice will eventually be done in this case.

If the people of New York City believed that the joggers' attackers were likely, eventually, to be put away for a long time, they'd be far less concerned with the fact that one of the accused is now out on bail pending trial.

But the public is far from certain about this result. Indeed, many feel, along with Tanya Oshoteco, that "no one is thinking about the woman."

The fact that Richardson was cheered by dozens of his neighbors when he returned home—cheered as though "he was a freed hostage from Lebanon," according to his lawyer—cannot have encouraged the sense that justice is simply taking its course and that the posting of bail is a standard part of the criminal justice process.

The bottom line is that there's an utter absence of confidence in the system on the part of the general public. This is not a bloodthirsty society, nor is it a vengeful society; it's a scared society—scared and cynical about the notion that the rules also work to protect the victims.

Father Gigante is a compassionate man. He stood to gain nothing by involving himself in this matter. But he would do well to try to understand the broad-based feeling articulated by his own youthful parishioner that "no one is thinking about the woman."

At Trial, Still a Target

July 26, 1991

If ever there were a case designed to persuade rape victims not to report assaults to the police, the jogger trial is that case.

Rape, to be sure, is already an enormously underreported crime—estimates have it that more than half the women thus victimized never call the cops.

The reasons are plain. For starters, there's no more intimate and invasive a crime. Rape is a hideous indignity, and the ordinary human quest for privacy in this realm militates against contacting strangers—even in the form of criminal justice authorities—to inform them of a forced sexual encounter.

Then there's the fact that, for many years, women who reported rapes often came to feel that they themselves were on trial. It wasn't unusual for police and prosecutors to endeavor to assure themselves that the victim herself had done nothing to provoke the attack—and "provocation," at one time, meant anything from dressing in a less-than-conservative fashion to going to a bar alone to have a drink.

Finally, women who'd been raped were taught to regard themselves as "damaged goods."

The stigma, in short, was real and pervasive.

But heightened sensitivity—especially the advent of trained police sex-crimes units—has done much to improve the atmosphere.

Increasingly, women have been persuaded that it makes sense to try to apprehend and prosecute rapists, that society recognizes rape victims as victims, and that an effort to protect their understandable interest in privacy and confidentiality will be made.

The Central Park jogger, however—though the victim of one of most horrendous crimes in the recent memory of New York City—has not enjoyed the benefit of this sort of sympathy.

To the contrary, she has been—and continues to be—subjected to accusations and other indignities of an unspeakably cruel variety.

Strangely, the culprit in this assault on the victim's dignity is not the "system"; police and prosecutors have behaved in exemplary fashion. Ordinary citizens are to blame.

On a daily basis, a claque of demonstrators positions itself out-side the courthouse, repeatedly chanting the jogger's name, despite her public request that it not be revealed.

(That request has been violated by two newspapers aimed at black audiences, the *Amsterdam News* and the *Daily Challenge,* as well as by WLIB radio, the preeminent black-oriented station in the city.)

The demonstrators also make it their habit to shout, "The boyfriend did it," thereby suggesting that the man with whom the jogger had a normal, romantic relationship took her to Central Park, raped and tortured her, and then virtually knocked her brains out with a metal pipe.

"What was she doing in the park anyway?" is yet another "ques-tion" repeated daily by the demonstrators; it represents an effort to imply that the jogger went to Central Park that night for some nefar-ious purpose—perhaps to buy drugs—rather than simply to run.

The point of all this activity, it would seem, is not to demon-strate the innocence of the accused—their cause could be defended by the simple claim that the police arrested the wrong gang. The clear purpose is to question whether this woman—who can't walk straight, can't easily read, and has lost her sense of smell, as well as her short-term memory—was even attacked.

Why this vicious campaign against the victim of a hideous crime? There's only one answer: race.

She is white. The accused are black. Were she black—or were her attackers white—this atmosphere would not obtain.

Spectators in the courtroom would not be laughing at testi-mony concerning the crime or emitting audible gasps indicating disbelief were it not for the fact that black so-called activists discuss the case as a "legal lynching" and openly profess to wonder—as has the editor of the *Amsterdam News*—"if a rape [even] took place."

Imagine if demonstrators had stood outside the courthouse during the Yusuf Hawkins case taunting his family and expressing skepticism as to what he'd been doing in Bensonhurst the night he was killed.

In fact, there *were* daily demonstrations at the Hawkins trial.

But the message of the protesters was rather different: They insisted that the city would burn unless guilty verdicts were handed down (as they were).

These same protesters gather daily outside the jogger trial. But now they seek acquittals.

THE KOREAN BOYCOTT

In 1990, racial hostilities in Brooklyn erupted when black militants announced a boycott against small markets in black neighborhoods run by Korean families—and against one deli in particular, the Red Apple in Flatbush, where a woman had made an apparently baseless charge that she was mistreated by the owners. The boycott led to pickets and protests outside the deli—a clear effort to intimidate shoppers that went on for months without a response from city officials. Finally, the boycott came to an end after Mayor David Dinkins—largely as a result of the pressure brought by Breindel—went into the deli and bought a few items.

Where's the Outrage?

April 26, 1990

This column concerns the media—or, more precisely, a major media failure. It's also about racism. And about silence on the part of public officials in the face of something they know to be wrong. Mostly, however, it's about the media.

For the past several months, New York has witnessed an ugly, ongoing manifestation of overt racism. A group of blacks in the Flatbush section of Brooklyn has launched a boycott of Korean-owned groceries. One of the leaders of this campaign is a self-proclaimed racist—"I'm anti-white," said Sonny Carson last year, explaining that he wasn't simply anti-Semitic, a conclusion many had drawn from his previous statements.

Carson and his associates have led several campaigns against Korean merchants in different parts of the city.

The Koreans, of course, are one of urban America's most exciting success stories. They work hard, generally operating small, family-run businesses—often groceries—and their children thrive in school, achieving rare and disproportionate academic excellence even when they come from homes in which English isn't spoken. Thus, they're a natural target for those adept at exploiting resentment, as Carson and his followers obviously realize.

What's significant about this and the earlier anti-Korean campaigns (they date back to 1984) is that virtually no effort has been made to disguise their racist character.

The boycotters hold signs that read, "Don't Buy from Koreans," and pass out leaflets urging blacks not to "shop with people who don't look like us."

As in the earlier boycotts, a dispute between a merchant and a customer has been used to justify a multimonth exercise in race-baiting.

Occasionally, Koreans have been set upon in the streets. They're taunted as "monkeys" and "blood-sucking vampires" on a daily basis and told to close their stores.

This isn't an enormous or particularly well-organized undertaking. The boycott has been limited to a couple of stores in one community, and it seems to be working, in a limited way, only because many local blacks—understandably—are afraid to cross the picket lines. One neighborhood minister—a Haitian-born Protestant—proposed a compromise. He withdrew after receiving a death threat.

Still, though confined for the moment to one community, this certainly seems a big enough—and ugly enough—episode to warrant condemnation by local politicians, black and white. But the silence has been deafening. Only now—after authorities received reports that boycott organizers have been threatening other area merchants with picket lines unless these store owners pay the boycotters protection money—has Mayor Dinkins appointed a fact-finding committee to negotiate an end to the dispute.

It's hard to imagine that anyone would think there were facts to find out if, say, a Korean group or a white group were marching around with signs that read, "Don't Buy from Blacks."

Moreover, the city Human Rights Commission has already tried its hand at negotiating a settlement. After this attempt failed, a spokesman for the commission was forced to acknowledge that "[w]e don't have a good sense of what exactly the point of the boycott is."

Still, better fact-finding than nothing at all. And, let's face it, public officials are often timid in these circumstances. It's far easier not to get involved. That's a sad fact of life.

The media, however, have no such excuse. Yet the boycott has been all but ignored by newspapers, television news programs, and local magazines. Despite its duration—despite the extraordinary character of the rhetoric—it remains, essentially, an unreported event.

Save for editorials in this newspaper, there's been no consistent treatment of the anti-Korean boycott—let alone criticism—in any major media organ. Most New Yorkers have no idea that a campaign viewed by many Koreans as an effort to drive them out of the city is even taking place.

Are the media so fearful of addressing a manifestation of black racism that they're willing to ignore so grotesque an undertaking? That in itself seems racist—after all, the operative assumption has to be that coverage of the boycott will offend blacks.

Yet the vast majority of blacks obviously aren't racists. Indeed, as American racism's most persistent victims, they probably recognize the phenomenon more quickly—and are more appalled by it—than many whites.

If this were a long-term boycott of *black*-owned stores organized by a band of Ku Klux Klansmen, it would long ago have been a national story. Why should the rules change when the victims are Korean?

Where Are the Cops?

May 17, 1990

There's something especially frightening about circumstances in which chaos and anarchy reign because public authorities choose to look the other way.

Children, obviously, find violence and unprovoked aggression scary. But when they encounter the phenomenon of parents or teachers or policemen witnessing wrongdoing, yet failing—usually out of fear—to do anything about it, that becomes even more frightening.

Suddenly—in the child's view—the universe lacks any semblance of order. Suddenly, it seems conceivable that anything at all can happen, including things far worse than what the child is then witnessing.

I remember a friend of mine telling me that his son had returned from a rock concert utterly shaken. The teenager had watched a youth gang molest and rob members of the audience, while security guards—not wanting to get involved—had pretended not to see and looked the other way. The behavior of the security guards had frightened my friend's thirteen-year-old even more than that of the gang.

I understood why. And I also came to understand, even though it took me a while after first learning this bit of history, why German Jews—following the adoption of the Nuremberg Laws in 1935—tended to remark, in a genuine spirit of optimism, as though their circumstances had actually improved: "One can live under any law."

They meant that even though the decrees had disenfranchised them and deprived them of citizenship, order was better than chaos. As long as lines had been drawn, they would learn to live their lives inside those lines (unless, of course, they were fortunate enough to find refuge elsewhere), and no one would bother them.

The Jews of 1935 Germany were contrasting their new circumstances with the conditions that had obtained in Poland and Russia earlier in the century—in these places, there had been no rules within which they could keep in exchange for being left alone.

The pogroms had been constant. And not only had the public authorities refused to protect them, sometimes it was the public authorities themselves who carried out the pogroms. (The German Jews, needless to say, did not realize—how could they?—that soon "laws" would come under which they would actually be put to death.)

These points about the almost cosmic fear that an absence of order creates are occasioned by an episode that took place recently in New York.

Thanks to television, people across the nation now know of the anti-Korean boycott that's been waged for four months by black racists in the Flatbush section of Brooklyn. Some days ago, lawyers for the Korean-owned groceries that have been targeted in this ugly campaign went to court to obtain a restraining order against the picketers. Such an order was issued, and the attorneys—accompanied by heartened members of the Korean community—returned to the site and handed it to the police, fully expecting that the boycotters would be ordered away from the fronts of the groceries.

The senior police officer on hand said that the police department's legal division would "study" the order. The boycotters remained in place, shouting anti-Korean slogans and intimidating would-be customers, often with threats of violence.

For days it was possible to turn on the news at night and learn that the order was still "under study." Eventually, it was explained that the police weren't prepared to enforce a restraining order issued by a civil court. If the boycotters themselves weren't inclined to comply, the police explained, there was nothing the cops could do.

The Korean grocers were told that they'd have to return to court to obtain individual criminal-contempt citations against the picketers.

Unfortunately, there's a Catch–22 here. The grocers, obviously, don't know the names of the individual racists standing in front of their stores. So, in fact, there's nothing the Koreans can do—other than sue the police for failure to enforce the original restraining order.

Perhaps this is one of those cases in which the law is an ass, although I've yet to find a lawyer familiar with the notion that the police can't enforce civil-court restraining orders.

What I do know is how the Koreans—new Americans schooled in the faith that this is a nation of laws—view the episode. They are bewildered. And frightened. And downcast. More so, in a way, than by the boycott itself.

They weren't surprised to learn that there are bad people in America—they knew only too well that there are bad people everywhere. Nor were they astonished by their encounter with anti-Asian racism—by people carrying signs that read "Don't Buy from Koreans," by leaflets urging blacks not to "shop with the people who don't look like us."

But they are altogether perplexed by the phenomenon of police refusing to enforce the law. This they did not expect to encounter in America.

It's probably small comfort, but the Korean American grocers should know that they are not alone in their sense of bewilderment. Lots of New Yorkers are appalled and frightened by this aspect of the Flatbush episode. Lots of New Yorkers find these events more frightening even than reports of the continuing rise in violent crime.

Hitherto, no one ever doubted the determination of the police, despite their shrunken numbers, to enforce the law. Now, things seem different. And many citizens of this city feel less safe than ever before.

POGROM IN
CROWN HEIGHTS

Of all the issues taken up by Breindel in his years at the New York
Post, *there was nothing he felt more passionately about—or had more
of a role in—than calling the city to account for what he dubbed,
without irony, a pogrom in Brooklyn: Three days of rioting targeted at
Jews in Crown Heights—after a limousine driven by a Hasidic man
ran over a seven-year-old boy—went unanswered and unsuppressed by
the New York police department. The pogrom, in which eighty-one
Jews were injured, culminated in the murder of Hasidic scholar Yankel
Rosenbaum by a mob.*

Before the Riot

April 13, 1989

Early last month, in the Crown Heights section of Brooklyn, a mugger tried to rob Mrs. Shoshana Rabkim and her son. When Mrs.
Rabkim resisted, the attacker slashed her face with a razor. When her
son went to defend his mother, he too was slashed. Mrs. Rabkim
required thirty-five stitches; her son, cut behind the ear, needed seven.

Crown Heights is a racially mixed neighborhood. There have
been tensions between blacks and Jews in the area for more than a
decade. The accused, Christopher Gilyard, is black; the Rabkims
are Hasidic Jews.

Mrs. Rabkim's screams attracted a crowd; a passing black motorist was the first person to stop and give her assistance. A racially mixed crowd of Crown Heights residents raced after the mugger and roughed him up.

By the time the police arrived, Gilyard, who was out on bail from an earlier robbery charge at the time of the incident, had been injured badly enough to require—in the view of the police—overnight hospitalization.

The incident did not have a racial cast. Gilyard was not pursued because he was black; he was chased because he had slashed two people in an attempt to rob them. He would have been pursued just as vigorously if he'd been white. Moreover, he was chased, as indicated, by a racially mixed crowd.

But an attempt was made to give the incident a racial character. The Reverend Al Sharpton, who has been relatively silent since the Tawana Brawley affair, organized a motorcade through Brooklyn, culminating in a rally at which he charged that there had been repeated beatings of blacks by Hasidim.

A police investigation was mounted. It had been alleged that a certain Rabbi Shemtov and his son were part of the crowd that captured and roughed up Gilyard. The Shemtovs are neighborhood anticrime activists—Rabbi Shemtov had belonged to a neighborhood patrol group and had been involved in a street altercation once before.

Gilyard had already been indicted. Now the Brooklyn district attorney's office presented evidence against the Shemtovs to a grand jury.

Members of the crowd that chased Gilyard failed to confirm the allegations, however—and the grand jury, earlier this week, voted not to indict. Meanwhile, Gilyard is behind bars—he faces a five- to fifteen-year term.

And so ends an unhappy episode—in a not altogether unsatisfactory way (save for the fact that some neighborhood residents are distressed that the Brooklyn DA's office even tried to charge bystanders who'd helped apprehend an attacker).

It remains for us to try to come to terms with what happened in Crown Heights—not to justify the behavior of the crowd, but to try to understand it.

Needless to say, in the best of all possible worlds, bystanders would pursue armed muggers, capture them, and simply hold them—without incident—until the police arrived. But in the best of all possible worlds, a mugger, once apprehended by the police, wouldn't be promptly released on bail and left there to commit a second robbery—as happened with Gilyard.

And that, at least in part, accounts for the popular rage manifested here. Ordinary people are fed up with crime and convinced, in a profound way, that the criminal justice system doesn't work.

Violent crime is rampant. Yet in addition to the traditional criminal justice revolving door, jail overcrowding may soon require a general release of prisoners.

These are facts that people read about daily. They have frightening implications. And they give rise to genuine rage.

Many of those who are able to do so simply flee the city. People without choices feel trapped.

And in a neighborhood like Crown Heights, they endeavor to protect their community, hoping that local patrols—and, yes, perhaps even administering a beating to someone who slashes an unarmed woman with a razor—will at least persuade violent criminals to practice their trade elsewhere.

The issue here is crime, violent street crime—not race and not class. The popular sympathy for Bernhard Goetz transcended racial lines—even though he was white and the four men he shot were black—for obvious reasons: Blacks and Hispanics are the chief victims of violent crime in this city.

The Goetz case was marked by unusual circumstances. Not all that many citizens carry guns, and not all that many citizens are as overtaken by rage as was Goetz.

But there is no reason to deem the incident in Crown Heights anomalous.

Indeed, there will be more such episodes—until ordinary people are persuaded that the criminal justice system works; that it functions to protect their interests; that there's a reasonable chance the police will find a mugger or a robber; and that, at the very least, violent criminals, once apprehended, won't promptly be returned to the streets.

Kristallnacht in Brooklyn

September 5, 1991

The Jewish High Holy Days begin on Sunday night, the start of the New Year. Rosh Hashanah is followed by Ten Days of Awe, culminating in Yom Kippur—the Day of Atonement.

The Jews of New York—and of America at large—have a lot to think about during this impending period of reflection.

As in Russia during czarist days, as in Europe under Nazi occupation, the period before the High Holy Days saw a genuine pogrom: This one, like many that took place in Europe, was directed against the most visible—by virtue of dress and lifestyle—and the most defenseless Jews in New York.

Pogrom, by the way, is very much the right word for what happened; not all pogroms in the Old World were government sponsored. What they tended to have in common was the failure on the part of public authorities either to allow the police to put down the violence or even to issue condemnations.

In Crown Heights, Yankel Rosenbaum, a young Hasidic Jew—a child of Holocaust survivors who was conducting research into the mass murder of the Jews who lived in his father's village in Poland—was lynched during the three-day anti-Semitic riot. Some twenty black youths attacked him shouting, "Get the Jew."

Mobs of blacks surged through the streets of Crown Heights chanting "Heil Hitler," breaking the windows of Jewish homes, attacking Hasidic Jews—readily identifiable by their garb—in the streets and in hallways.

The Crown Heights pogrom, like most major pogroms, including the infamous Nazi Kristallnacht (the Night of Broken Glass—November 9, 1938), was whipped to a frenzy by professional agitators—some of them genuine anti-Semites; some of them black separatists, more antiwhite than anti-Semitic, but wholly aware of the incitement potential inherent in anti-Semitic rhetoric; some of them mere headline chasers, schooled—thanks to their efforts during the Tawana Brawley hoax—in Goebbels's "Big Lie" technique.

The pretext for Kristallnacht was the assassination of a German diplomat in Paris by a young Jew protesting Nazi anti-Semitic outrages. The pretext in Crown Heights was far thinner—an auto accident in which a car driven by a Hasidic Jew careened out of control, fatally injuring a black child.

Needless to say, there are many such vehicular tragedies—twenty-two took place in the past several years in Brooklyn alone. But rarely do such cases lead to indictments. And never before—certainly not in the cae two years ago when an unlicensed black driver struck and killed a Hasidic child—have riots ensued.

Ordinary people—black and white—know the difference between a car accident and a lynching. Only those who were actively interested in fomenting violence against Jews pretended that there was something special about this particular episode.

New York magazine columnist Joe Klein notes that the *Amsterdam News* wrote of the "carful of Jews" who ran young Gavin Cato down, an example of how this incident was covered in the extremist, black-oriented media. Meanwhile, mainstream media institutions, engaged in an eternal struggle to remain "evenhanded" (as between the Heil Hitler rioters and their victims), weren't much better.

Indeed, Klein wrote his column before a Sunday morning television program (on which he personally subsequently appeared) featured two reporters (both white) questioning Brooklyn district attorney Joe Hynes for half an hour about the car accident, while failing to ask him one question about the lynching of Yankel Rosenbaum.

Few in the media spoke out with honesty and clarity; Klein himself did; so, to his credit, did A. M. Rosenthal of the *New York Times*; so did former Mayor Ed Koch, Mike McAlary, and Pete Hamill, the latter three in this newspaper.

But the public officials prepared to identify this pogrom as such were even fewer.

In his public remarks and personal bearing, Mayor David Dinkins wore dignity like a cloak, refusing from the outset to recognize any moral equivalence between the accidental death of Gavin Cato and the lynching of Yankel Rosenbaum.

No doubt, in addition to pronouncing that lawlessness wouldn't be tolerated, Mayor Dinkins should have unshackled the police sooner. But it would be wrong to forget the righteous clarity of his voice that first furious night as he stood outside the Cato home while bottles and rocks flew by him.

The firm words of New York's junior U.S. senator, Alfonse D'Amato . . . also gave people of goodwill cause for comfort.

But mostly there was silence. Silence on the part of black leaders, silence on the part of white leaders—Jews included.

The silence was even more deafening than that which greeted the anti-Semitic ravings of City College professor Leonard Jeffries, who helped create the "intellectual" climate in which the pogrom took place. The race-baiters, in short, played on a virtually open field.

In the days ahead, Jews need to ask themselves some painful questions. Were they slow to react—individually and organizationally—to the violence because Hasidim somehow make assimilated Jews uncomfortable and self-conscious? Do Manhattan Jews really think Al Sharpton and Sonny Carson hate them any less than they do Lubavitcher Hasidim? Is it really appropriate to dismiss Carson and Sharpton and every other agitator as marginal? Who speaks for New York's blacks if not the Crown Heights riot inciters? Who, apart from Dinkins, took issue with the race-baiters?

Why has there been only one murder indictment in connection with the Rosenbaum lynching? (And the Hasidim are meant to have disproportionate influence!) Some twenty youths attacked and murdered this innocent young man. Where is the Civil Rights Division of the Justice Department—don't cries of "Get the Jew" and "Heil Hitler" suggest a civil rights violation?

And if we consider that the poverty and misery in which many blacks dwell somehow excuses racial bigotry and anti-Semitic violence, doesn't it make sense also to remember that the lynchings perpetrated in years past against blacks themselves by, say, the Ku Klux Klan were crimes committed by the poorest whites against the one group even less well off than they: rural blacks?

By and large, after all, Lubavitcher Hasidim are not wealthy. It's true that if they abandoned Crown Heights, the neighborhood would sink still further into an abyss of crime and poverty. It's true they work hard, have solid family structures, and find public assistance an embarrassment. Still, it remains that this pogrom was a case of the poor terrorizing the poor. Jews who read life in terms of class, rather than race, should bear this reality in mind.

As for other recent lessons, white homosexuals should remember that Leonard Jeffries has denounced their allegedly corrosive influence on contemporary culture with the same vehemence that animates his anti-Semitic pronouncements.

As the Jewish community ponders whether and where it failed in recent days, it would be wise to refrain from asking the wrong questions, such as why so many black leaders dislike Jews. After all, why did Hitler hate Jews? Why did Stalin? Why did the KKK? Who knows? Jews are always easy scapegoats for other people's problems.

Wrong questions yield incorrect answers and promote false solutions. Blacks don't spend a lot of time asking themselves what causes antiblack racism. Nor do they attempt to modify their behavior to mollify racists. Nor should they.

Blacks know that antiblack racism is wrong, and they search for ways to fight it.

Jews should know that anti-Semitism is wrong and inexcusable, whether the perpetrator is Julius Streicher or Father Coughlin or George Lincoln Rockwell or C. Vernon Mason. And they should fight it. If they fail to do so, who will?

Where Are the Leaders?

October 3, 1991

A thoughtful political essayist implied last week in his regular forum, the *Village Voice,* that I and this newspaper derive pleasure from arguing that the Crown Heights riot inciters "speak . . . for New York's blacks."

I've read Richard Goldstein's articles for years—with a sense of intellectual engagement and with admiration for the subtlety of his analysis.

Unlike various other writers who appear in the *Voice,* he is not an infantile name-caller, he doesn't engage in purely personal attacks on people with whom he disagrees, he doesn't study subjects to affect knowledge about issues with which he has no familiarity, and his politics seem entirely his own.

Yet at least one key point in his Crown Heights article makes virtually no sense. Goldstein asserts that "the failure of white progressives gave right-wingers [also described in the essay as "the *Post-Commentary* (Magazine) axis"] a chance to come out swinging." Yes, this failure on the part of "white progressives" to condemn the pogrom took place. But how does it speak to the question of who New York's "genuine" *black* leaders are?

The reluctance of white progressives to criticize blacks is—to be frank—neither new nor surprising nor particularly interesting. Moreover, there were some whites of a Left-liberal bent who seemed prepared to recognize the character of what took place: Goldstein himself calls Crown Heights "the worst outbreak of anti-Semitism in New York in my lifetime."

In any event, how would the conduct of white progressives have affected the ability of right-wingers "to come out swinging" on the issue of how blacks responded to the events in Crown Heights? White progressives are many things. But even they don't claim to be black leaders.

It was an entirely different issue—the notion that the Reverend Al Sharpton, Vernon Mason, Alton Maddox, Jr., Colin Moore, and the Reverend Herbert Daughtry were not genuine black leaders—that seemed to me absurd.

Moreover, the obvious implication is that New Yorkers somehow "know" that these men are not black leaders, that there are "responsible" black leaders who failed to make their voices heard during the Crown Heights episode, even though they regarded the lynching of Yankel Rosenbaum as wrong. The assertion is attractive. But it asks commentators to say things they can't possibly know to be true.

On what basis, for example, am I entitled to assert, say, that Representative Charles Rangel deplored the lynching of Rosenbaum? I have no idea what he thinks about what took place in Crown Heights. I know how Representative Rangel feels about lots of issues—from the coup in Haiti to Senator D'Amato's remarks about

Mayor Dinkins's South Africa trip. But as to Crown Heights, I haven't a clue.

In addition, the implication (by no means unique to Goldstein) that whites should ignore the importance of the Crown Heights agitators also asks nonblacks to strike a profoundly condescending pose—to decide who is and who is not a legitimate black community leader. This is one point on which I happen entirely to agree with Sharpton, who consistently rails against efforts by whites to read him out of New York's black leadership.

True, Mayor Dinkins condemned the lynching of Yankel Rosenbaum. Dinkins, to his credit, also condemned the ravings of CCNY professor Leonard Jeffries. But David Dinkins is both a black leader and the mayor of the entire city. His constituents include blacks and whites and Hispanics and Koreans and everyone else who lives here.

Were there other black leaders who condemned the three-day Crown Heights pogrom—which, apart from the Rosenbaum lynching, included two stabbings of Hasids and twenty-seven other bias attacks on Jews (not to mention the suicide of a Crown Heights Holocaust survivor)? Richard Goldstein doesn't cite any. And apart from Michael Meyers of the New York Civil Rights Coalition, I don't know of any.

By what standard, it seems well to ask, is it appropriate to deny the claims of Sharpton, et al., to community leadership? The fact that he denounced the "diamond merchants" in a clear effort to incite anti-Semitism doesn't disqualify him as a black leader. The fact that Colin Moore declared himself "against the Hasids" doesn't disqualify him. The fact that Herbert Daughtry warned of more violence against Jews—"I want to predict the same thing for Williamsburg"—doesn't disqualify him. And the fact that Sonny Carson said he was "proud" of Rosenbaum's killers doesn't render him a nonleader.

The standards we utilize in determining who qualifies as a white leader ought to be applied in determining who qualifies as a black leader. Do the individuals in question draw large crowds? Do they enjoy support in the black-oriented media—on WLIB, in the

City Sun, and in the *Amsterdam News*? Do they—and the views they espouse—fare well in public opinion surveys?

By all these criteria, it seems unrealistic to deem the men in question anything other than genuine black leaders.

Indeed, during the whole of the past month, the only people I encountered arguing that these were not "real" black leaders—that "responsible" leaders had been silent while Sharpton & Co. "hijacked the media"—were white public officials and white journalists.

Certainly, this is—for whites—a comforting analysis. But where is the evidence to support it?

Goldstein is wrong in believing that I'm cheered to discover rampant black anti-Semitism. Anti-Semitism doesn't cheer me. (And since he speaks of the Holocaust in Europe, which he says his parents "escaped," let me permit myself a personal note: Members of my immediate family were less fortunate.) Goldstein, moreover, is manifestly wrong in arguing that I or others who share my views hope to "locate anti-Semitism exclusively in the black community." No serious reader of this column, or of the *Post* Editorial Page or of *Commentary* magazine, could possibly draw this conclusion.

As to black leadership, note Betty Shabazz of Medgar Evers College, the widow of Malcolm X: "I am not a follower of Al Sharpton or some of the other leaders." Shabazz—who goes on to analyze Sharpton's appeal—never questions his standing as a leader. And Goldstein, it would seem, doesn't question the anti-Semitic character of Sharpton's rhetoric, which—as it happens—is less pronounced than that of, say, Mason, Carson, and so forth.

Neither Goldstein nor I nor—I suspect—Shabazz knows the breadth and depth of their following. But the fact that an effort in Albany to condemn Professor Jeffries failed to draw the signature of a single black legislator (one black assemblyman eventually signaled his support for the petition) says something important about black elected officials—people who need to be in touch with the sensibilities of their constituents.

Maybe Goldstein is right in arguing that the quest for "solidarity makes truth-telling difficult." Still, "truth-telling" is a minimal standard—neither commentators nor politicians nor community leaders have any excuse to eschew this goal.

Goldstein and I may have very different notions of how best to deal with the truths we discover. But that's a different matter. On the need to identify truth and engage in truth-telling, I'm confident we agree.

A Shocking Verdict

November 5, 1992

In the end, what do we learn from the acquittal of Lemrick Nelson, Jr., in the Yankel Rosenbaum murder case?

Some would have us conclude that the problem turns on the degree to which many blacks and Hispanics simply don't trust the police. The goal of those who advance this view is to underscore the urgency of greater ethnic and racial diversity on the police force and to emphasize the acute need for a reconfigured Civilian Complaint Review Board.

Others agree that antipathy toward cops is the problem. They argue, however, that blacks and Hispanics have been educated by the popular climate not to trust the police—so much so, in fact, that a case like the one developed against Nelson, which rested largely on police testimony, stands virtually no chance of getting a fair hearing from a predominantly nonwhite jury.

In other words, public officials and activists who encourage a popular animus toward the cops bear a measure of responsibility for this misguided finding.

The Nelson acquittal *should* awaken officials to the insidious implications of unrelenting cop bashing. Antipolice sentiment appears to have played a major role in the verdict. And such sentiment has been revved up beyond the bounds of decency—in New York and elsewhere—during the past year.

But there's another factor at work here. And it would be naive not to face up to it.

Police or no police, it's highly unlikely that a predominantly black and Hispanic jury would—in any circumstance—convict a black accused of killing a white Orthodox Jew. Not even if the defendant were apprehended carrying the blood-smeared murder weapon. Not even if he were identified by the dying victim. Not even if he actually confessed to the crime.

In other words, for Hasidic Jews victimized by blacks, New York City today is a lot like the Jim Crow South was for blacks themselves thirty years ago. Justice is all but unattainable.

This circumstance will endure until the victims refuse to put up with it. Now, if the victim in this case had been black—and if he'd been pursued by a mob of twenty or more whites yelling "get the blacks"—there's no chance whatever that only one person would have been arrested; there's also no chance that federal authorities wouldn't have been called in at the outset; and there's very little chance that a jury would have acquitted the defendant on each and every count.

But the victim *wasn't* black. Thus, as soon as word spread through the courtroom that the verdict was acquittal, the police began loosening their riot gear. The security barricades began to come down. The tension began to abate.

Why?

Because the cops knew—as did everyone else in New York— that Hasidic Jews weren't about to stage a riot. The precautions were necessary only when the possibility existed that Nelson would be found guilty. *That* might have led to a full-scale Los Angeles-style riot. But acquittal? No danger.

After the verdict was delivered, Lemrick Nelson, Sr., the defendant's father, pronounced that he had "no hatred against" Norman Rosenbaum, the victim's brother. There's something manifestly obscene about this particular remark; it's Rosenbaum, after all, who suffered the loss of a sibling. Why *should* Nelson, of all people, hate Rosenbaum? (Whether or not Rosenbaum hates Nelson seems slightly more relevant.) Yet this comment was reported without a trace of irony.

And so was Nelson Sr.'s declaration that "my son was forgiven by God." Forgiven for what? Why is it necessary for an innocent man to be forgiven by God? Was this a slip—an accidental moment of honesty—on the part of Nelson Sr.? No journalist paused to examine the implications of this odd comment.

Then again, few have paused to wonder about the appropriateness of the posttrial celebratory dinner attended by the defendant and various jury members.

The dinner was hosted by Nelson's defense lawyer, whose strategy, it's well to remember, consisted not just in attacking the credibility of the police testimony, but also in intimating that Yankel Rosenbaum—somehow—provoked his own murder.

Imagine what would have been said—by public officials and by commentators—if the Simi Valley jury had dined with the Los Angeles police officers who were acquitted of assaulting Rodney King immediately after the trial.

These are all insults: the acquittal, first and foremost; the dinner; the comments of Nelson Sr.; the suggestion by public officials (laughable in view of what was said after the Rodney King trial) that, for better or worse, citizens need simply to accept jury verdicts. They are insults aimed at the Jewish community, just as the Crown Heights pogrom itself—which saw Jews cower behind locked doors in 1991 New York as if they were back in some czarist village—represented one huge assault on Jewish lives and sensibilities.

In all likelihood, the verdict in the Rosenbaum case had as much to do with the disproportionately high rates of anti-Semitism among blacks and Hispanics—well documented in recent studies— as it did with hostility toward the New York police department.

In the end, it's all very well to parade around with placards proclaiming that "Jewish Blood Isn't Cheap." Unfortunately, Jewish blood *is* cheap in New York at the moment. Indeed, the life of Yankel Rosenbaum—a rabbinical student who came to America, ironically, to research the Holocaust—has just been declared utterly worthless.

Unless people of goodwill come to terms with the reality of what happened in Brooklyn last week—and why—there's no real reason to expect the problem to disappear.

Apologizing for the Jurors

July 29, 1993

Widely praised for his acute and thorough analysis of the August 1991 anti-Semitic riot in Crown Heights, state criminal justice director Richard Girgenti hasn't much been criticized for volume 2 of his report—a decidedly inferior study of the Lemrick Nelson trial.

True, the issues addressed in volume 1 of the report—a 400-page examination of why the city failed to control New York's worst race riot in recent memory—have far more profound implications than the question of how one trial was botched.

Incompetence, insensitivity—it would seem—dishonesty at the highest levels of city government are manifestly more compelling concerns than why the trial of Yankel Rosenbaum's accused murderer went awry.

Still, volume 2—a 140-page examination of the Rosenbaum investigation and prosecution—is replete with internal contradictions and unanswered questions. Briefly, Girgenti believes that the case against Lemrick Nelson, Jr., the black youth charged with murdering Rosenbaum, was bungled by the police and by the prosecution; that the jury acted in good faith in acquitting Nelson; and that the jury wasn't animated either by an antipolice bias or by anti-Semitism in reaching its verdict.

All this is curious in view of one key fact: Girgenti believes that Nelson took part in the attack on Rosenbaum. On page 133 of volume 2, Girgenti declares: "Based on the available information . . . it is most probable that Lemrick Nelson participated in the attack that resulted in Yankel Rosenbaum's death."

He argues, moreover, that the jury reached the same conclusion, noting on page 11 that "most jurors believed that Nelson was present at the scene of the attack and that he was probably a participant."

Indeed, Girgenti explains that if the jurors "had understood the legal principle of 'acting in concert,' they might have reached a different verdict." (The implication that Judge Edward Rappaport failed properly to instruct the jury is unmistakable.)

Lest anyone attribute base motives to the jury, Girgenti emphasizes that his probe uncovered no evidence that the jurors were animated by a mistrust of the police, by racism (the jury was predominately black), or by anti-Semitism.

Judge Rappaport is held to have caused the acquittal by failing to explain an utterly elementary legal principle to the jury. After all, "acting in concert"—or "accessorial liability"—isn't a complicated concept. In this case, it means simply that if the mob Nelson joined attacked Rosenbaum—and if the wounds Rosenbaum sustained during the attack caused his death (which wasn't in dispute)—the jury could have found Nelson guilty.

Strangely, Girgenti never explains Rappaport's failure to clarify this critical concept. Indeed, according to Girgenti, "the judge's instructions to the jury included the standard instructions on ['acting in concert']." So, what went wrong? The problem, it appears, was that "most jurors said they either did not hear or did not understand" the instruction.

It never seems to occur to Girgenti that the jurors didn't *want* to grasp the concept. Similarly, Girgenti's conclusion that the jury didn't mistrust the police is contradicted by his own observation that "several jurors . . . believed Nelson's statement [a confession] had been *fabricated* by the police." Now, if members of a jury believe the police concocted a confession, it's hard to understand the notion that they harbored no animus toward the cops. Here, in short, Girgenti's logic is difficult to follow.

Interestingly, in his response to the Girgenti report, Brooklyn district attorney Charles J. Hynes notes that a number of jurors told members of the media that they were convinced that "the testimony of . . . police officers was not believable." That, too, sounds rather like antipolice sentiment.

Finally, Girgenti's report fails to deal with the fact that, after acquitting Nelson, members of the jury attended a celebratory dinner with the defendant and his attorney. In other words, jurors who—according to Girgenti—accepted that Nelson was part of the wolf pack that attacked Yankel Rosenbaum saw fit actually to celebrate his acquittal.

Just what were they celebrating?

In his press conference, Girgenti sought to explain this unseemly episode. He argued that some jurors thought they'd been invited by Nelson's lawyer to a discussion of the trial, rather than to a celebration.

Perhaps. But the hypothesis is relatively easy to test: How many jurors left the dinner after discovering the true character of the event?

The answer is one.

In the end, it's unclear why Girgenti's analysis of the Nelson case is so much weaker than his examination of the entire Crown Heights riot. Perhaps it will take a federal probe—directed by Attorney General Janet Reno—to resolve the questions that continue to surround the lynching of Yankel Rosenbaum.

The Politics of Semantics

June 10, 1995

An unusual concern with semantics seems to have descended upon political discourse in New York. For nearly two years, both victims and commentators have referred to the 1991 anti-Semitic riot in Crown Heights as a pogrom; it remains difficult to think of a more apt term.

Of late, however, New Yorkers have been told, by Mayor Dinkins and some of his allies, that the term *pogrom* doesn't apply to Crown Heights—because the riot there wasn't "state sanctioned."

Rudolph Giuliani—Dinkins's Republican opponent—has been a particular target of the language patrol. Giuliani described Crown Heights as a pogrom in the course of wondering about the absence of a promised federal civil rights investigation into the three-day eruption of violence.

During the riot, rampaging black mobs—shouting "Heil Hitler" and "Kill the Jews"—attacked Hasidim in the streets and threw rocks and bricks at Jewish dwellings. Police, although present in force, failed for seventy-two hours to put down the violence.

The murder of one of the victims—Yankel Rosenbaum, a young scholar—has been described by Mayor Dinkins himself, among others, as a "lynching," a term with which the linguistic purists seem disinclined to quibble, even though *lynching* (more than *pogrom*) implies acquiescence on the part of the authorities.

In total, more than eighty Jews suffered physical injuries at the hands of the rioters; one frightened Hasidic woman experienced a miscarriage. A pogrom? Yes.

Historians tell us that some pogroms—the term itself dates back to the anti-Jewish rampages in Czarist Russia (and derives from the Russian word for devastation)—were spontaneous, while others were organized with state approval. The 1903 Kishinev massacre, for example, apparently enjoyed tacit governmental support. Many pogroms, however, were actually frowned on by czarist authorities and by the Holy Synod, which feared they might unleash "revolutionary" forces.

In short, the would-be experts who claim that pogroms have always been "state sanctioned" betray a brazen ignorance of modern Jewish history.

The issue itself, moreover, is unseemly. It's bad enough that an anti-Jewish riot took place in 1991 New York. That officials on whose watch it occurred would try to regulate the language used to describe it by the victims and their sympathizers bespeaks stunning audacity.

The mayor's supporters have obviously decided that his reelection effort will suffer if it becomes received wisdom that his first term saw an actual *pogrom*. Why others, who aren't animated by partisan considerations, have joined the campaign to render the term taboo in the context of Crown Heights is harder to explain.

A *New York Times* editorialist, laboring under the misapprehension that pogroms, by definition, require "government complicity," argues that calling Crown Heights a pogrom is "an insult to those who lived through the real thing." She notes that "thousands of New York Jews were not killed" in Crown Heights, unlike in 1941 Iasi (Romania), where local fascists loyal to Marshal Ion Antonescu murdered some eight thousand Jews over two days, with the help of the Wehrmacht and the Gestapo.

This illustration of "the real thing" leaves a good deal to be desired. Indeed, it's decidedly unusual to take an event that occurred within the framework of the Holocaust and dub it a pogrom. Why not cite Babi Yar?

A better example would be Kielce—the most notorious post-Holocaust pogrom. Some forty-two Jews were murdered in Kielce in July 1946: A rumor that a Polish youth had been killed by Jews sparked the violence. (A similar rumor—grounded in the accidental death of Gavin Cato, the black child who was struck by a car that veered out of control—was used by agitators to trigger the riot in Crown Heights.)

In Kielce, as in Crown Heights, the authorities eventually put down the violence, albeit a couple of days too late.

It remains that this is a bizarre discussion. If our purpose in taking care with language is not to "insult those who lived through the real thing," what about the practice of referring to black neighbors in American cities as *ghettos*?

After all, an overcrowded slum is rather different from a handful of square blocks surrounded by walls and watchtowers. Residents of real ghettos wore yellow stars; subsisted on starvation rations; and were forbidden, on pain of death, from crossing over to the "Aryan side." Those who exited did so in organized transports bound for killing centers.

No one has suggested that it insults survivors of the Warsaw and Vilna ghettos to apply the term, say, to inner-city Detroit. And that's because—for better or worse—we transfer language quite freely, especially to describe human suffering. Maybe we shouldn't. But calling the Crown Heights riot a pogrom hardly seems the most egregious example of the phenomenon.

DEMAGOGUERY AT CITY COLLEGE

The once-great City College, a division of the state-run City University of New York, had fallen into academic disrepair by the 1990s. One of the most pronounced signs of that disrepair was the conduct of Leonard Jeffries, who was, at the time, the chairman of the school's black studies department. Jeffries became a figure of controversy in the summer of 1991, when he delivered a speech laced with anti-Semitic and antiwhite comments. It transpired that these were the kinds of things Jeffries said freely in his classrooms, and efforts were made to oust him from the school—which proved impossible, owing to his academic tenure. But he was removed from his chairmanship. These columns provide a brief history of the rise and fall of Leonard Jeffries.

White Guilt

August 15, 1991

That we live in a profoundly confused and guilt-ridden society seems manifest. The Leonard Jeffries affair makes this reality unmistakable.

Jeffries is a rank anti-Semite and something of a clown. He engages in anti-Semitic hyperbole on a regular basis, often discussing subjects—the role of the Sephardic Jews in the African slave trade, for example—about which he couldn't possibly know anything, since there's nothing to know. (He would have it that Spanish

Jews played a key part in the slave trade—thanks to their leading place in Spanish mercantile life—long after the Jews were expelled from Spain.)

He argues that Jews named "Greenberg and Weisberg . . . and whatnot"—presided over a "conspiracy plotted out of Hollywood" to denigrate blacks: "Russian Jewry had a particular control over the movies, and [with] their financial partners, the Mafia, put together a financial system of destruction of black people."

He accuses particular Jews—the "debonair racist Diane Ravitch" and the "[Arthur] Schlesingers" (Schlesinger, by the way, isn't Jewish)—of leading the onslaught against Afrocentrism in education.

Now there isn't much evidence that Jeffries speaks for a whole lot of blacks. The fact that no black state Assemblyman would sign the "open letter" condemning Jeffries may prove that many blacks are unwilling to join in criticizing other blacks even when the issue at hand is gross race-baiting. But save for the case of Brooklyn Assemblyman Albert Vann, who chairs the assembly's black and Puerto Rican caucus, this reluctance doesn't demonstrate widespread anti-Semitism among black politicians. (Vann, who called for scientific proof that Jeffries had said anything erroneous about Jews, carries his own anti-Semitic baggage, dating back to the New York City teachers' strike in the late 1960s.)

Still, prominent blacks—Louis Farrakhan, Leonard Jeffries, and Gus Savage, to name a few—engage in anti-Semitism to a greater extent than they do, say, in anti-Irish or anti-WASP or anti-German polemics. Yet Jews—and this is indisputable—have marched in the front lines of the black struggle for civil rights and social justice in America. Jews and blacks, moreover, have long had common enemies: American Nazis and the Ku Klux Klan are only the most obvious.

This circumstance suggests that Jews need to ask themselves a question: Why are they—among whites, in general—*particular* targets of black bigots? What can Jews do to alter this state of affairs?

The answers aren't immediately apparent. But it *is* clear that disproportionate Jewish representation in the civil rights movement hasn't stemmed this unhappy tide—the memory of Andrew Goodman and Mickey Schwerner makes this plain. Nor has disproportionate Jewish financial support for black projects and institutions in any way served to limit manifestations of black anti-Semitism.

Does familiarity breed contempt? Is it easiest and safest to lash out at those least likely to strike back? Somewhere—as the case of Professor Jeffries demonstrates—Jews in America stumbled in dealing with this issue. While it would be foolish to exaggerate the phenomenon, it would also be folly to turn a blind eye to black anti-Semitism. This is a problem with which Jews themselves must come to terms. Pretending that it isn't there never eliminates bigotry of any sort.

Another example of the hopeless confusion that afflicts this society when dealing with issues related to race is the number of times the concept of academic freedom was invoked after news of Jeffries's Albany tirade became public.

It's long been well known—thanks to articles in the *New York Times* and the CCNY newspaper—that Jeffries uses his college classroom (when he bothers to show up) for diatribes akin to the one of which he delivered himself in Albany last month. At CCNY, in fact, his bigotry extends to blacks who marry white women and to "faggots." It has been reported that he called the space shuttle catastrophe "the best thing to happen to America in a long time." Jeffries believed the shuttle accident might slow the space program and prevent whites from "spreading their filth through the universe."

On one occasion, when asked what should be "done" about white people, he explained that, "If I had my way, I'd wipe them from the face of the earth."

Jeffries is paid $71,000 per year by the taxpayers. Would "academic freedom" protect from censure a white professor who used his classroom—when he bothered to appear—to suggest that blacks be wiped "from the face of the earth" or to decry "faggots"?

Those who resort to the academic-freedom argument for inaction on the Jeffries matter; who fail to realize that teaching nonsense amounts to consumer fraud perpetrated against students; who don't note that heading a department is an honor, not a "right"; and who don't recognize that calling for mass murder based on race is not a practice that can lightly be ignored, have lost anything resembling a moral compass.

Long after Jeffries's views were widely known, he was actually tendered a reward—via his appointment to the commission convened by state education commissioner Thomas Sobol to rewrite the American history and social studies curriculum in New York's public schools.

Some would have it that this appointment, more than anything else, is a comment on Sobol, who has since emerged as something of a national laughingstock—a white male engaged in a ridiculous attempt to play up to the black radical elite.

But the relative hesitancy with which public officials and university educators have grappled with the Jeffries matter, particularly in recent days, demonstrates that Sobol, in all likelihood, merely typifies an insidious syndrome: Excuses, apologia, and ostrichlike conduct are very much the order of the day when white leaders are compelled to confront black racism.

This is nothing other than an affliction experienced by many whites in high places. But it's dangerous. It poses a genuine threat to the social fabric, a fact to which ordinary people—at long last—are beginning to awaken.

Leonard Jeffries: The Untold Story

November 14, 1991

Last Saturday, the *Washington Post* introduced its readers to the Leonard Jeffries affair, a tale that's been familiar to New Yorkers since the middle of the summer.

Dr. Jeffries, chairman of the black studies department at the City College of New York, achieved a measure of notoriety at a state-sponsored black arts and culture festival in Albany this past July—by delivering himself of a rambling tirade aimed at "the Jews who controlled Hollywood" (folks named "Weisberg and Greenberg . . . and whatnot") and their Mafia-linked Italian American "financial partners."

According to Jeffries, Jews and Italians used the motion picture industry "to put together a system for the destruction of black people."

In the same talk, Jeffries accused Jews of financing the African slave trade and referred to Assistant Secretary of Education Diane Ravitch as a "sophisticated Texas Jew."

Jeffries, to be sure, was already known in New York as the author of theories defining blacks as "sun people" (humanistic and kind and communal) and whites as "ice people" (implication obvious.) He also received attention as a chief draftsman of state education commissioner Thomas Sobol's discredited report on multiculturalism.

But the furor over Jeffries's (televised) performance in Albany led the City University of New York trustees (CCNY is a CUNY campus) to debate removing him from his department chairmanship. Chairing a department, needless to say, is an honor bestowed by the university—it has nothing to do with tenure.

The trustees last week decided to defer their decision on Jeffries, fearing—as CCNY President Bernard Harleston later explained—campus and community "unrest" (riots, building takeovers, and so forth). The basis for the trustees' decision is a bit perplexing in view of the fact that "unrest" is, in any event, an annual feature of CUNY life. But that's a separate matter.

The point here is that Jeffries, as a result of recent developments, is now a national story. Thus, the front-page treatment in the *Washington Post*.

The *Washington Post* article, however, is nothing short of bizarre. For one thing, it links Jeffries with CCNY philosophy professor Michael Levin, a man who argues that blacks are intellectually inferior to whites. But the article, though highly specific in many respects, never notes that Levin, unlike Jeffries, refrains from using his classroom to teach race theory. And this is a central point as regards the academic freedom question. (The *Washington Post* headline reads: "Racial Beliefs Collide: Testing Speech Limits at CCNY.")

Punishing Levin for statements he makes outside his classroom would, indeed, be a dicey proposition. Acting against Jeffries for what he "teaches" in class, on the other hand, would be far less difficult. The latter's reiteration of utter falsehoods, for example, virtually invites a review focusing on his basic professional competence.

The *Washington Post* story also fails to discuss Jeffries's hostility toward homosexuals. In particular, it neglects Jeffries's recent renewal of his assertion that whites "introduced" homosexuality—which he sees as alien and insidious—into black life. Yet from a news stand-point, this issue, too, couldn't be more timely; indeed, Jeffries's latest pronouncement on this theme has prompted gay-led demonstrations against Jeffries, including one at Columbia University, timed to coin-cide with a Jeffries speech to Columbia's Black Student Organization.

In another strangely glancing reference, the *Washington Post* piece barely acknowledges a new and central allegation concerning Jeffries: The professor allegedly threatened to kill a black reporter from the *Harvard Crimson* who came to CCNY to interview him.

In the *Crimson* interview, Jeffries, as always, denounced Jews; he also referred to Harvard Professor Henry Louis Gates, Jr.—the chairman of the African American studies department at Harvard—as a "punk and a faggot."

While such remarks, in themselves, are standard fare for Jeffries, he seems, for some reason, to have had second thoughts about having made them to the *Crimson.* He allegedly instructed his bodyguard—Jeffries complains constantly that *he's* in physical danger—to seize *Crimson* reporter Eliot Morgan's tape of the inter-view; when Morgan refused to surrender the tape, Jeffries threat-ened him with death, according to Morgan.

As things stand, Manhattan district attorney Robert Morgenthau's office has said it will investigate the complaint as soon as Morgan pro-vides a full account of the episode. Morgan intends to return to New York to do just that.

Curiously, the *Washington Post*—even in the course of a lengthy story on Jeffries—deemed this episode worthy only of a single sen-tence. Indeed, the entire piece—which describes Jeffries as an "embattled black man"—has a strangely sympathetic aspect.

And while a failure to treat any one of the elements discussed here—Jeffries's hostility to gays, his comments to Morgan about Professor Gates (a nationally recognized scholar), the implications of the threat he issued to Morgan, the manner in which he uses his classroom—might easily be overlooked, the notion that all this escaped the notice of a reporter for one of the finest newspapers in the land is genuinely hard to fathom.

The real story is that the truth about Leonard Jeffries, at long last, is emerging. He's a racist, an anti-Semite, a homophobe, and a thug. The department he chairs—at a public university—is a racially exclusive club. And even the president of CCNY has acknowledged that he deems Jeffries a racist. Notwithstanding tendentious news stories in prestigious papers, the scam isn't likely to go on much longer.

Filling a Quota

May 13, 1993

Professor Leonard Jeffries and the City College of New York (CCNY) agree that Jeffries was removed as chairman of the school's black studies department after a 1991 speech he delivered in Albany.

Jeffries and CCNY also agree that in the course of the Albany tirade, the professor denounced "the Jews" for various alleged crimes, including the African slave trade, which Jeffries says was organized by Jews.

But Jeffries charged that the college had no right to terminate his chairmanship on the basis of a speech its administrators didn't like. He sued the City University of New York (CUNY)—CCNY's parent—demanding back the chairmanship, alleging harm to his reputation, and accusing the university of violating his academic freedom and free-speech rights.

CCNY argued that the Albany speech was merely the straw that broke the camel's back; the college contended that Jeffries's conduct had long dismayed university officials.

CCNY administrators, however, proved unable to produce a paper trail supporting this claim. As a consequence, the jury agreed with Jeffries. Damages have yet to be awarded.

The result is curious in at least one respect. It is by no means clear that "academic freedom" has anything to do with the administrative tasks—and the honor—associated with a department chairmanship. Jeffries, after all, had retained his tenure and his salary throughout. He was never fired.

And no one—in theory, at least—should enjoy the right to serve as a chairman for life. Thus, if the CUNY trustees felt Jeffries had disgraced City College by indulging himself in an unabashedly racist diatribe at a major (televised) public event, it's hard to grasp why the university shouldn't have the authority to remove him. The verdict, in short, doesn't make a whole lot of sense.

But this doesn't absolve CCNY with regard to the manner in which it actually dealt with Jeffries over the years. The professor's rank anti-Semitism had manifested itself regularly prior to the Albany speech. In fact, Jeffries has long used his classroom to spout racist nonsense about Jews—whom he routinely describes as "dogs"—and about white people in general. (He maintains that whites are "ice people," capable of great evil owing to their alleged shortage of melanin—a brownish black pigment found in the skin.)

Jeffries made no secret of his views on race. He also failed frequently to show up at his own classes and produced no scholarly work whatever. In the last analysis, his original appointment to the CCNY faculty, his tenure award, and his appointment as head of black studies all indicate a profound disregard for elementary academic standards.

The Jeffries affair reminds us that black racism is tolerated on the campuses of major universities. An ongoing episode at Wellesley College offers another illustration of the same phenomenon.

At Wellesley, a black professor named Tony Martin has been using a bizarre and paranoid text entitled "The Secret Relationship Between Blacks and Jews"—a "study" produced by Louis Farrakhan's Nation of Islam Historical Research Department—to inculcate in his students many of the anti-Semitic lies embraced by Jeffries and other Afrocentrists.

Professor Martin has been criticized by a handful of Wellesleyites—students and faculty—for *abusing* his right to "academic freedom." But no one has challenged his prerogative to assign the text in class, notwithstanding the fact that it purveys a series of lies about Jewish historical responsibility for black prostitution, about age-old "Jewish warmongering," and about the authenticity of the "Protocols of the Elders of Zion."

Academic freedom, it would seem, includes the right to propagate outright lies—especially when the falsehoods are advanced by black radicals. It should be noted that a white professor interested in teaching, say, black intellectual inferiority would have a hard time finding an academic home.

And this brings us to the real lesson of the Jeffries affair. Instructors like Leonard Jeffries (and Tony Martin) are tolerated by white-dominated institutions because they are black, because they teach black studies, and because most of their students are black. A kind word for the attitude that informs CCNY's thinking in this realm (and that of Wellesley) is condescension.

Leonard Jeffries fills a quota. He is no more qualified to teach at a major university than the quasi-crackpots who hawk political pamphlets in the street. But CCNY was concerned with creating the appearance of a thriving black studies program. It wasn't interested in judging black studies according to conventional standards. And cowardice in the face of prospective campus unrest prevented the college's administrators from dismissing Jeffries—despite his manifestly substandard performance.

White condescension toward blacks is a form of racism. Thus, a search for racism at CCNY might well begin by examining not Leonard Jeffries's removal from the black studies chairmanship, but the circumstances surrounding his initial appointment and subsequent promotions.

Lies About the Slave Trade

May 27, 1993

The provost of the City University of New York (CUNY), Basil Wilson, unwittingly demonstrated the essence of what's dangerous about places like City College—a CUNY subsidiary—granting tenure, titles, and honors to bigoted pseudo-scholars of the Leonard Jeffries variety.

Wilson—speaking last week at yet another conference on improving black-Jewish relations—decried an alleged absence of scholarly research aimed at refuting Professor Jeffries's assertions about Jews.

In particular, Wilson noted that while Jeffries's claims about Jewish hegemony in the slave trade were made some two years ago, "there is not yet a comprehensive body of evidence to refute" the CCNY professor.

As it happens, Wilson's contention is false in every respect. Jeffries's assertions about the dominant role played by Jews in the slave trade—which, by the way, long predate his notorious 1991 Albany speech—stand utterly refuted by a massive body of scholarship.

Wilson might do well to consult David B. Davis's *The Problem of Slavery in Western Culture* (1966), Salo Baron's *The Social and Religious History of the Jews* (1952), Elyahu Ashtor's *The Jews of Moslem Spain* (1973), Roger Sawyer's *Slavery in the 20th Century* (1986), and literally scores of other books and articles. The CUNY provost would discover that Jeffries's rantings in this sphere amount to a tissue of lies.

If Wilson means that no summary of existing scholarship has been compiled for the express purpose of challenging Jeffries, there, too, he's dead wrong. A UCLA-trained scholar, Dr. Harold Brackman, published a monograph last year that makes short shrift of the various anti-Semitic claims—including the slavery myth—advanced by Afrocentrists like Jeffries.

Also worth noting is Wilson's failure to mention the fact that Jeffries himself has done no scholarship of any sort in this realm. The provost, in short, is calling for scholarly refutation of claims that were advanced without scholarly support of any kind. Why the double standard?

Still, let's consider the larger implications of the CUNY provost's argument. Wilson would have it that even malicious slander—entirely at odds with existing scholarship, entirely unsupported by any evidence—has to be refuted directly if it is advanced by someone in a position of authority.

In other words, if Professor Earl Butz of Northwestern University—who, unlike Jeffries, happens *not* to use his classroom to spew his anti-Semitic venom—contends in pseudo-scholarly articles that the Holocaust was a gigantic hoax, it's incumbent on Holocaust scholars to drop whatever they're doing and devote themselves to refuting Butz.

Wilson, presumably, wouldn't deem the thousands of books, photographs, films, and archival documents—not to speak of testimony from survivors—adequate refutation of Butz and his ilk. The provost would prefer it if, say, Professor Yehuda Bauer of the Hebrew University or Dr. Martin Gilbert of Oxford and Tel Aviv abandoned ongoing projects in order to demonstrate that Jews, in fact, *were* gassed at Auschwitz.

Well, what if some professor at a school with even lower standards for tenure than CCNY declares that the earth is flat? Does Wilson think the nation's leading physicists should convene a conference to produce a refutation?

What about the case of Chicago mayoral aide Steven Cokely, who declared in 1988 that the AIDS epidemic is the result of a governmental conspiracy to murder blacks? Cokely, who believes that "doctors, especially Jewish ones, . . . inject AIDS into blacks," now works for Minister Louis Farrakhan.

Does Wilson believe there should be a specific governmental response to Steven Cokely, insofar as he held appointive office in a major city when he discovered the "truth" about the AIDS epidemic? Does Wilson deem the existing scientific and lay literature on AIDS inadequate?

How about scholars who've endeavored for years to demonstrate that blacks—by nature—are less intelligent than whites? Does Wilson worry that there's been no recent effort to refute such claims, despite new studies—grounded in IQ tests—advancing this thesis? Does he feel that black scholars have fallen down on the job?

I'd like to think there would be something inherently undignified about a conference of black scholars convened for the purpose of producing papers demonstrating that blacks are not less intelligent than whites. I suspect that Wilson—who is black—might agree. But it seems equally plain that a conference of Jews convened to deny Jewish hegemony in the slave trade would also be undignified. And that's a point Wilson doesn't seem to grasp.

CUOMO, PÈRE ET FILS

Breindel's capacity for largehearted support and friendship across ideological lines was never clearer than in the way he wrote about the Cuomo family. Despite his editorial page's harsh criticism of the policies undertaken by former New York governor Mario Cuomo, Breindel understood and appreciated the role Cuomo played to save the New York Post—*the newspaper that was so critical of him. And Breindel became a close friend of Andrew Cuomo, son of Mario, whose innovative efforts to aid the homeless won Breindel's support as well.*

Andrew's HELPing Hand

July 6, 1989

There are those who talk, and there are those who act. Andrew Cuomo belongs to the latter category.

Rather than simply bewail the plight of the homeless and level charges at the government for failing adequately to assist this beleaguered population, Cuomo—a young attorney and the son of New York Governor Mario Cuomo—decided to do something himself.

Project HELP is his creation. (He abandoned a flourishing and lucrative law practice in order to run it himself.) HELP is a nonprofit company that—combining the expertise of private firms (which provide services on a pro bono basis) with available public monies—builds and runs transitional housing for homeless families.

Cuomo has discovered that he can place these families in facilities that offer on-site social services—and thereby ready them to live on their own—for less money than it costs to maintain such families in rat-ridden, crack-filled welfare hotels.

This is not a small-scale experiment of the sort that—while relatively successful—doesn't really tell us all that much.

The initial HELP facility, known as HELP 1, is a two hundred-unit complex in the East New York section of Brooklyn that houses between seven hundred and eight hundred people. There are other HELP facilities already operating or under construction throughout the state of New York—in Westchester County, Suffolk County, Albany, and elsewhere in New York City.

Moreover, local governments from around the nation are asking HELP for guidance in replicating the experiment.

HELP's method is to take a family—this tends to mean a mother and one or more children—out of a welfare hotel and into a HELP facility. During a period of several months, this family is taught to live on its own. When on-site social service workers deem a family ready, assistance in locating an apartment is provided. The average length of stay in a HELP facility has turned out to be just about six months.

Efforts are made to monitor a family's success in living on its own during the post-HELP period. And by all available indices, the results have been good.

Why does HELP work? Because it represents an honest attempt to come to terms with the nature of the homeless program.

Unlike other "homeless advocates," Andrew Cuomo doesn't run around town declaring of the homeless families that they are "people just like you and me, save for the fact that they've lost their jobs or experienced a fire."

He doesn't pretend that the problems of the homeless are attributable solely, or even largely, to a housing shortage. To the contrary, Cuomo argues that these are not people just like you and me. He believes they lack the rudimentary skills necessary to survive in the real world. And he says that to build housing, and then simply hand these families the keys to their new apartments, will accomplish nothing.

Cuomo points out that some of these mothers spent their own

childhoods in welfare hotels. They have never experienced normal life—and they have no notion of how to deal with contemporary society.

HELP tries to teach them to function. It doesn't just provide beds and a couple of rooms for six months.

Mothers are taught how to buy clothes for their children, and what foods to purchase in the course of the week. They are taught how to keep an apartment clean.

They are expected to know where their children are—whether in the HELP-run day care program or with the HELP-sponsored Little League team or in school—at every moment of the day.

Project HELP is a tight ship. The HELP 1 rules and regulations run to more than four single-spaced pages, including curfew hours for children under fourteen.

There are on-premises drug programs aimed at terminating addiction to crack and other street drugs—Cuomo estimates that at least 50 percent of the mothers and older children who are placed in HELP facilities have drug problems. But this statistic doesn't even come close to illustrating the condition these families are in when they arrive at HELP's doorstep. Even the oft-used term *underclass* doesn't fully explicate the degree to which they dwell in a world apart.

Sometimes an anecdote makes the point better than any set of statistics. When Andrew Cuomo was holding Little League tryouts at HELP 1, he noticed a young boy, ten or eleven years old, who would extend his glove to receive a toss, yet wind up—again and again—with the ball hitting him square in the chest.

When the boy came up to bat, he would stand in position properly, waiting for the pitch. But he would swing only after the catcher had already caught the ball. Again and again.

Something was clearly amiss. Cuomo walked the young man over to the health center—where a cursory test established that he was legally blind.

How, railed the HELP founder, could this have gone undetected? How could the mother not know? How—Cuomo finally asked—could the child have been promoted in school? The answer to that question came quickly: "He's never been to school."

Such is the nature of this population. Not all of their problems, needless to say, are solved by the time they leave HELP—not by a long shot. Indeed, for many of the mothers, it may already be too late.

But at least these families have a fighting chance at making it—and affording them this fighting chance costs the taxpayer less than subsidizing their stay in a welfare hotel, a point worth emphasizing because it underscores a critical fact: With Project HELP, no one loses.

Mario and the *New York Post*

January 29, 1993

Over the course of the last week, I found myself actively engaged in the effort to prevent the *New York Post* from shutting its doors. The battle turned on the need to buy time.

Bankers Trust Co. has long been the *Post*'s chief lending institution. And the bank—determined to end its financial exposure—was dead set on terminating the *Post*'s line of credit. Banks are currently besieged by regulators—all blessed with twenty-twenty hindsight—searching for ill-advised loans. Thus, from its perspective, Bankers Trust's position—if less than sympathetic—was at least understandable.

The *Post*'s executives (of whom I'm one) pleaded for a few extra weeks' time to find a buyer. We believed that a 20 percent across-the-board temporary wage cut—as well as an increase in the newsstand price of the paper (within New York's five boroughs)—would create a four-week period during which the company might, at a minimum, keep itself on an even keel.

Potential buyers were in the process of reviewing our financial records. Expressions of interest from parties with the means to purchase the newspaper were coming in at a rapid clip. The *Post*, however, needed time.

Bankers Trust took the view that it would not risk assuming responsibility for one more nickel. The bank wanted the rough equivalent of a security deposit—a $1 million to $3 million security deposit.

And no one with whom we spoke was ready, at a moment's notice, to put cash of that magnitude on the table.

Certainly, the *Post* should have initiated the search for a buyer/investor at an earlier juncture. (The paper failed to do so for complicated reasons—reasons that need to be discussed in detail elsewhere.)

Perhaps the bank should have been a bit less rigid. A new owner, needless to say, would have served Bankers Trust's financial interests far better than closing down the paper. But the bank's officials were set in their position.

Where we saw the loss of more than seven hundred jobs, the death of the nation's oldest daily, and the loss of a distinct voice in New York life, the bank saw an end to a seemingly interminable flow of red ink.

Eventually, of course, a prospective buyer willing to offer up-front cash *did* emerge—in a manner so improbable as to defy reality. Just as *Post* publisher Peter Kalikow was telling his senior staff that publication of the newspaper would be suspended, financier Steve Hoffenberg telephoned to inform both the *Post* and Bankers Trust that he wanted to buy the paper.

Hoffenberg declared his willingness to put money on the table immediately. And the very next day, he did just what he said he would do, providing Bankers Trust with a $2.5 million letter of credit.

The *Post* survived. Hoffenberg is advancing in his effort to buy the newspaper.

I, meanwhile, learned a lot in the course of the week. Not just about banking and matters financial. But about people.

All of us expected that public officials and prominent citizens would speak out on our behalf. And many did so—from John Cardinal O'Connor to Senator Alfonse D'Amato to City Council Speaker Peter Vallone. The *Post,* after all, is a New York institution—a piece of the city's history and an element in its daily life. In addition, needless to say, seven hundred jobs—in a ravaged economy—are just that: seven hundred jobs.

But these particular individuals are, in a sense, political allies of the *Post*. True, all of them, at one time or another, have been unhappy with news stories and/or editorials. That goes with the territory. Still, it remains that these are men who, by and large, identify with the *New York Post*'s ideological sensibility. (I suspect they would have spoken out in any event, but they *are* old friends.)

One New Yorker, however, threw himself into the fray with a determination so fierce that untutored outsiders might have thought *his* job was somehow in jeopardy: Governor Mario Cuomo. The governor called the bank—again and again. He called *Post* executives just to get progress reports. He asked his top economic aide, Vincent Tese, to return from vacation and actually help structure the rescue effort.

Cuomo, in short, worked as hard as we did.

All of which is a bit curious in at least one respect. On the political level, the *Post* and the governor have long had what might be described as a mixed relationship. We endorsed his candidacy for reelection in 1990, but supported his opponent four years earlier.

We've backed many Cuomo administration initiatives, but we've also criticized the state's tax and fiscal policies. While we think we've been fair, Cuomo has had his share of grievances (and then some). It's hard to imagine that in the state of New York, the *Post* is his favorite media organ.

Yet in the past week—and this is the key point—none of that mattered. The governor did what he thought was right. He tried to save a newspaper. He went about the task without any expectation of reward. His goal was to ensure that pressmen and reporters and mailers and drivers—and all the other people who labor to publish a newspaper—didn't lose their jobs.

From the standpoint of someone who watched the drama from what might be called a ringside seat—and who's disagreed with the governor on more than one occasion and expects to do so again—the episode admits but one conclusion: Mario Cuomo is an honorable man.

PART THREE

THE FATE OF
THE JEWS

THE HOLOCAUST

The son of parents who narrowly escaped the Holocaust, Breindel was never more passionate as a writer than when taking up the subject of the murder of the six million. It was his self-appointed mission to reject efforts to thrust the Shoah into the historical past, even though it had taken place in our time—to keep the memory of the genocide and its lessons alive. The Shoah was the subject to which he returned most frequently during his ten years as a columnist for the New York Post.

A New Horror for Elie Wiesel

June 13, 1987

Elie Wiesel went to Lyons last week. The Nobel peace laureate—an Auschwitz survivor whose literary gifts have made him a voice for Holocaust survivors in general—was invited by the Lyons Jewish community to testify at the trial of Klaus Barbie.

As Gestapo chief in that French city during the German occupation, Barbie dispatched several thousand Jews to Auschwitz. And the Lyons Jewish community hoped Wiesel could somehow do the impossible—describe for the court the indescribable, evoke Auschwitz.

Wiesel's further mission was to give the Holocaust moral and historical dimension—to identify the uniqueness of the crime.

It was clear that Wiesel would be cross-examined by Barbie's attorney. But it wasn't clear beforehand that he would actually be attacked. Indeed, it seemed likely that even Barbie's strident attorney, Jacques Verges—though a stranger to self-restraint—would take on a somewhat subdued aspect.

Not because he was cross-examining a Nobel laureate. But because the witness was an Auschwitz survivor, testifying in a courtroom that had just heard of how Verges's client "emptied out" the Jewish children's home at nearby Izieu, of forty-four children tossed into trucks "like sacks of potatoes" on the first leg of the journey to the Auschwitz gas chambers.

But this background did not give Verges pause. The defense attorney—whose client is "boycotting" the trial—assaulted Wiesel, reportedly in a voice that shook with anger.

Shouting questions that sounded like accusations, Barbie's lawyer demanded that the witness address himself to "other atrocities" comparable to the Holocaust. What about the French war in Algeria? Verges wanted to know. What about the massacre of Vietnamese civilians by American troops at My Lai? What about— as Verges put it—"Jewish atrocities against Arabs?"

Hadn't these deeds also taken place in the twentieth century? And hadn't they gone largely unpunished? Weren't they just as terrible as what had happened to the Jews at the hands of the Nazis?

Wiesel replied that he was "against all brutality no matter where it comes from." But he went on to note the fundamental difference between the events to which Verges referred and the Holocaust. The latter was a wholly unparalleled phenomenon—a unique effort to wipe an entire people off the face of the earth.

In the Nazi war against the Jews, every Jew was guilty—simply by virtue of being alive.

Not because the Jews represented an impediment to German political hegemony in a particular place—as did some Algerians to the French colonists.

Nor was the My Lai comparison any more apt. It takes willful ignorance not to grasp the difference between atrocities committed by isolated military units in wartime and a state policy of mass murder aimed at a particular civilian group.

As for "Jewish atrocities"—a revealing construction that may help explain the personal affinity between the lawyer and his client—Verges could cite but one forty-year-old incident: the killing of some two hundred civilians during an Israeli attack on the Arab village of Deir Yassin, a base for Arab irregulars, during Israel's 1948 War of Independence.

The distinction between that event and the Nazi Holocaust is self-evident. And it seems clear that Verges included Deir Yassin in his catalog of horrors only to realize a perverse thrill. Charging Jewish Holocaust survivors with atrocities at the trial of a Gestapo officer apparently pleased Barbie's lawyer.

But what is the tactical purpose of Verges's line of argument—why challenge the Holocaust's uniqueness?

Verges can't prove Barbie's innocence. But he can try to mitigate the horror of the crime—by suggesting that many, if not all, governments do these terrible things. It's happened before, and it'll happen again, Verges is saying, so get off your high horse about Klaus Barbie.

There's also the unspoken implication: If everyone is guilty, then—in a sense—no one is guilty. Not even Barbie.

Barbie's lawyer is in the process of demonstrating the manner in which history can be distorted by what Jeane Kirkpatrick has called the moral-equivalence syndrome. In contemporary terms, moral equivalence is the tendency to equate, say, the U.S. military action in Grenada—where American troops rescued U.S. citizens in danger and promptly went home—with the brutal nine-year Soviet occupation of Afghanistan. Both are cases of superpowers using their soldiers to invade nearby smaller countries.

Therefore, Grenada equals Afghanistan. Or, according to Jacques Verges, the Holocaust equals My Lai equals Algeria, etc., etc.

There are those who see an anomaly in the emergence of Verges, very much a man of the Left, as an advocate for Klaus Barbie, a Nazi who tortured and murdered Communists.

But Verges and Barbie are not strange bedfellows. The lawyer's dexterity with the moral-equivalence argument—which, at its essence, is always an effort to defend totalitarian regimes by attacking free societies—makes him a natural for Barbie. Each atrocity tale hurled at Wiesel by Verges incriminated a democratic country—the United States, France, and Israel.

Elie Wiesel—after testifying—told reporters that Verges was

"full of hatred, hatred for me personally, hatred for the Jewish people, and hatred for the victims." Wiesel might have added free societies to the list. It is this last hatred that brought Verges and Klaus Barbie together.

Kurds, Jews, and the "Experts"

April 11, 1991

As I listened this week to American officials explain, privately and publicly, why it was impossible for Washington to halt the massacre of the Kurds in Iraq, I realized I'd finally encountered the answer to a perplexing question.

When I was studying in England some years back, I did research in declassified British Foreign Office documents—and later in the U.S. National Archives—on questions pertaining to the failure of the Allied governments to take measures to rescue the Jews of Europe or even to slow the slaughter.

There were no Soviet documents available at the time. But that didn't much matter; no one had ever expected Moscow to take humanitarian measures in behalf of the doomed Jews or anyone else. The manifest Soviet goal was to defeat Hitler and to impose Communist rule on as much of Europe as possible.

The British and the Americans, on the other hand, were constantly beseeched by Jewish, particularly Zionist, groups to take active steps toward rescue.

Proposals ranged from bombing the railway lines leading to Auschwitz—just to disrupt the flow of human cargo to the gas chambers—to feigning an interest in negotiating *Blut gegen Wahre* (blood for goods).

The phrase, and proposal (which concerned the Jews of Hungary), were Adolf Eichmann's, and it's conceivable that if London and/or Washington had indeed feigned an interest, the mass murder of the Hungarian Jews—which continued through to September 1944—would have been halted temporarily. Hundreds of thousands—literally—might have been saved. Nothing would have been sacrificed by the Allies.

But the diplomats in Whitehall and in Foggy Bottom always had complicated reasons for passivity in the face of genocide. Bombing the railway lines was simply impractical, it was said. And even if it could be done, the breaks in the lines would immediately be repaired.

Moreover, taking direct steps of this sort in behalf of the Jews might well, according to Assistant Secretary of War John J. McCloy, prompt the Germans to adopt "even more vindictive" anti-Jewish measures. (What John McCloy believed could be more "vindictive" than mass murder in gas chambers remained a closely held secret.)

As for actually rescuing people, one Foreign Office diplomat, upon hearing of the Eichmann offer, wondered aloud what the British "would do with a million Jews."

"Where," he asked, "would we put them?"

All this took place after eyewitness reports, aerial photographs, and human espionage confirmed the hitherto inconceivable notion that the Nazis were actually endeavoring to murder all the Jews in occupied Europe.

While it was ugly and devoid of compassion, the Anglo-American unresponsiveness during the late 1930s, when refugee ships like the *St. Louis* weren't allowed to dock—and the unresponsiveness that marked even the early years of the war—seem to me the product, at least in part, of an understandable failure of imagination.

Who, in the twentieth century, could believe that Hitler actually meant to murder—by means of modern technology—all the Jews he could lay his hands on?

But by 1944, the specific fate of these people was no secret. And yet British and American officials could always think of ten reasons for doing nothing.

Was anti-Semitism the chief factor here? Somehow, it seemed not. Yes, I encountered a few callous marginal notes penned by men who later rose to prominence. ("More from the wailing Jews," wrote one British diplomat after learning new details about the Nazi murder apparatus from a Zionist delegation pleading for some sort of action.)

But, in the end, it was simply easier to construct elaborate justifications for passivity—Step A would lead to Step B, which would lead
to Step C, which would inevitably lead to an unacceptable Step D.

The riddle, from my standpoint, was that here were England
and America, engaged, at that very moment, in an unimaginably
complex enterprise—waging a world war. Bold and creative thinking was a daily necessity.

How, in this context, could trying out a few simple measures—
destroying the railway lines, bombing the gas chambers, issuing
detailed short-wave radio warnings—have seemed too complicated
to consider?

I didn't know.

But consider the justifications for failing to help the Kurds,
while American forces are occupying a tenth of Iraq, while the
United States is capable of dominating its skies:

We would have to occupy all of Iraq to prevent the slaughter. If
we'd ordered Saddam to ground his entire air force and to break up his
large armored formations, he'd almost certainly have felt compelled to
do so; thousands of Kurds and Shiites would have been saved.

We're told we'd have to accept the creation of a Kurdish state in
the north—which Turkey opposes—and a Shiite state in the south,
which would likely ally itself with Iran. Nonsense; this sort of pro-
jection bears no resemblance to the goals of those under assault.
Nor is there evidence to support the view that this outcome would
likely take place.

Moreover, "forward thinking" of this sort by diplomats and
strategists might well have kept us even from going to war—think
of the number of "experts" who told George Bush the Arab "street"
would rise and fracture the coalition as soon as the first American
bombs hit Iraq. How many "strategists" assured the president that a
ground war would take months and would cost America dearly?

The experts—the professional strategists—can always come up
with reasons to do nothing. Therein lies the heart of the matter.

Elected officials—presidents and prime ministers—learn that
to get things accomplished, the folks who think "ten steps ahead"
have to be ignored; when necessary, the bureaucrats must simply be
ordered to act.

When a president wants to do something—liberate Kuwait, for example—he learns quickly that direct orders produce results. When he isn't sure he wants to act, the forward thinkers seize the day. The result is passivity.

If George Bush had ordered U.S. diplomats and military men to halt the ongoing slaughter in Iraq—without invading the rest of the country, within the context of the cease-fire pact—the slaughter would have been halted or at least slowed. If Franklin Delano Roosevelt had wanted to save Jewish lives and defeat Hitler, both goals could have been accomplished.

The Full Story Behind Bitburg

April 25, 1991

A little over two years ago, knowing that former President Reagan was in the process of preparing his memoirs, Kalman Sultanik, a member of the U.S. Holocaust Memorial Council during Ronald Reagan's two terms in the White House, took it upon himself—in a dignified and respectful manner—to write Reagan concerning the 1985 Bitburg Affair.

The Reagan-Sultanik correspondence was released last week; it makes for extraordinary reading.

Sultanik's purpose was to ask Reagan to reevaluate, in his memoirs, the decision to visit the German military cemetery at Bitburg—a decision the White House had refused to reconsider even after it was revealed that members of the SS, not just ordinary Wehrmacht soldiers, were buried there.

Saluting Reagan on behalf of the American Jewish community leadership for advancing "the cause of freedom and democracy, including the integrity of the State of Israel and the rights of the Soviet Jewish community," Sultanik hoped the former president, aided by the passage of time, might see why visiting such a site would so pain Holocaust survivors—like Sultanik himself—and others who endeavor to perpetuate the memory of the Nazi slaughter.

He also sought to persuade Reagan that the visit served to give aid and comfort to historical "revisionists" whose goal has been to liken Nazi—and even SS—conduct during the Second World War to the normal behavior of armies at war.

Sultanik noted that before the 1980s, the fact of Nazi atrocities was never a matter of dispute, that only among fringe historians of the far Right and the far Left was there ever an effort to liken Nazi crimes against unarmed civilians to wartime measures taken by civilized societies.

Most Americans remember Bitburg in the context of a promise the president made to German Chancellor Helmut Kohl to visit a German military cemetery as an ultimate gesture of German-American reconciliation—a promise the president felt he could not rescind, even after it was revealed that SS men were buried there, even after Nobel Peace Laureate Elie Wiesel, the conscience and voice of Holocaust survivors, pleaded publicly with the president, before a hushed audience in the dome of the U.S. Capitol, to change his official itinerary.

"That place is not your place, Mr. President; your place is with the victims, not [at the gravesides of] the S.S.," Wiesel told Ronald Reagan.

The trip, of course, went forward. Its larger purpose was to underscore the solidity of the NATO alliance, and Kohl characterized the visit to Bitburg as an essential component. Reagan, according to more than one participant in the various advance discussions, was deeply torn: He wanted to honor his promise to Kohl without betraying a personal commitment to ensure that the memory of the Holocaust—and the recognition of its historically unique character—endured.

Many believed at the time that close aides—in particular White House chief of staff Donald Regan—played key roles in persuading the president not to ask the Germans to shift his schedule.

Now, it seems, there was another factor at work. The former president, in his May 1989 reply to Sultanik, penned the following extraordinary sentence: "As for Bitburg itself, I did some research on my own and learned that, yes, there were some S.S. troopers there, but a number of them were buried in prisoner uniforms. They had been executed for trying to shield inmates from torture and the ovens."

Sultanik—masking his shock at this extraordinary claim in an effort to keep the tone of the exchange appropriately correct—wrote back to Reagan, reporting that he'd never encountered any such information and asking for documentation. Subsequently, Sultanik wrote the former president that the Jerusalem-based Holocaust research center, Yad Vashem, had conducted an exhaustive inquiry in an effort to verify the claim and had been unable to do so.

Suffice it to say here that this is no surprise. While Yad Vashem and various other groups regularly honor European non-Jews, or their descendants, who aided Jews during the Nazi era—painstaking inquiries are undertaken based on both written scholarship, contemporary documents, and survivors' testimonies in the course of identifying worthy recipients—the number of actual SS men who fit this bill in any way is somewhere between minuscule and nonexistent.

And the notion that such folk, had they existed, would have been buried in German military cemeteries, albeit "in prisoner uniforms," is—frankly—absurd.

Wherefrom, then, did the president of the United States acquire this insidious "historical" tidbit? Eventually, in yet another letter, Reagan tells Sultanik: "I'm sorry there is no documented evidence regarding the S.S. troopers buried in prisoners uniforms that I know of . . . German officials having to do with my visit were the source of this information." Reagan insists that he remains "satisfied" with the information, although he later notes that "S.S. guards who gave such help were few in number."

Now, if any German official involved in preparing the Reagan visit to the Bitburg cemetery—or anyone else for that matter—can produce the name of even one SS man buried there in a "prisoner uniform" for the crime of having shielded "inmates from torture and the ovens," this official, to say the least, has a major scoop on his hands.

If not, a great American president was seduced by outright lies into making a trip that did him dishonor—no small matter.

Judeo-Centric?

June 21, 1991

Much has been written about the effort of the New York State Board of Regents to rewrite the public school educational curriculum—part of an ongoing campaign led by state education commissioner Thomas Sobol to combat the alleged Euro-centric bias informing the existing social studies and history program.

But relatively little attention has been paid to a sidebar (a special "annex," actually) that accompanies the "Syllabus Review Committee's" most recent report.

In a way, the absence of excitement over the annex is entirely understandable. The report itself, after all, is a highly dubious proposition—an effort to substitute ethnic cheerleading for traditional teaching.

It is animated, in part, by the view that schools should concern themselves with inculcating in students a sense of self-esteem—self-esteem grounded, not in personal achievement, but in cultural heritage; and it promotes an approach that can only have the effect of heightening general Balkanization at the expense of social cohesion.

In the context of so insidious a report—which, to be sure, follows an even more insidious, and semiliterate, initial draft (the so-called Sobol report)—it's not surprising that one bizarre appendix, signed by just one member of the twenty-three-person panel, hasn't given rise to special alarm.

Still, there's a lot to be learned from the "annex"—particularly as it regards the concerns, prejudices, and priorities of at least one of the report's star authors, Dr. Ali Mazrui, a political scientist and Africanist who holds the lucrative Albert Schweitzer Chair at SUNY Binghamton.

Professor Mazrui's comment focuses on the generally accepted meaning of the term "Holocaust." He deplores as *"Judeo-centric"* [his italics] the tendency to use it solely to refer to what he describes as "the 12-year experience of the Jews under Nazi intolerance."

In Mazrui's view, it's critical that this term *not* be "reserved exclusively for the Jewish experience." According to the professor, "American children need to know that genocide was part of the birth of *this* [again his italics] nation."

He insists, in short, that "the holocaust began at home. . . ."

Some may note an immediate flaw in Mazrui's argument. Obviously, there's another readily available term that serves the professor's purpose—the one he uses initially: *genocide.*

Thus, whether or not it's appropriate to teach schoolchildren that genocide was integral to America's birth (it's doubtful that New York parents actually want this notion handed down to their children as accepted wisdom), Mazrui himself demonstrates that it isn't necessary, educationally or semantically, to broaden the meaning of the term *Holocaust* by depriving it of its "Judeo-centric" character. Why, then, is Mazrui dead-set on fighting this battle? Why is he so disturbed by the fact that *Holocaust* has come to describe the mass murder of six million Jews by Hitler and his collaborators? Wherefrom this obsession—an obsession so pronounced as to provoke him into submitting a separate "annex" to a long public document?

As it happens, Jewish scholars and essayists came rather late (the second half of the 1950s) to the view that one specific term— *Holocaust* (or, in Hebrew, *sho'ah*)—should be used to refer to the Nazi slaughter.

Elie Wiesel was among the first to argue that the Nazi attempt to destroy an entire people solely on alleged "racial" grounds—a people with whom Germany had no real conflict of a territorial or ideological nature—required an altogether distinct term.

The historic definitions of *Holocaust* include "burnt offering" and "total destruction of life, especially by fire."

Thus, the argument that *Holocaust* was, indeed, the most appropriate term to describe the Nazi annihilation of European Jewry made considerable sense. And most present-day American dictionaries add the definition: "systematic destruction of over six million Jews by the Nazis."

What's interesting here, of course, is Mazrui's notion that the term itself has, somehow, been stolen. The view that the Holocaust was a unique historical event—that for the reasons identified above, the Jewish tragedy differed even from the Ukrainian famine under Stalin, the destruction of the American Indians, the Cambodian autogenocide, and other mass explosions of cruelty—animates those who deem it necessary to reserve a distinct term for the Jewish ordeal in Nazi Europe.

The few who object are, by and large, easy to locate. They are found in the precincts of the far Right and on the far Left. In both cases (consider Mazrui's use of the term *Judeo-centric*), they tend to be, to put it charitably, less than fond of Jews.

Among those who object, "Holocaust revisionists"—flat-earth types who deny that the Holocaust even took place—predominate on the Right. Anti-Israel activists—prompted by the link between the creation of a Jewish state and the Nazi attempt to annihilate the Jewish people—enjoy parallel primacy on the Left.

Ali Mazrui belongs to the latter sect. That he has played a key part in proposing a new social studies/American history curriculum for New York state's public schools is profoundly disturbing.

Acquiescence in Evil

May 21, 1992

The Chairman, journalist Kai Bird's impressive new biography of John J. McCloy—World Bank president, high commissioner for Germany, and deacon of the American Establishment—teaches an important lesson. From a moral standpoint, powerful men come in vastly different forms.

There are those who willingly permit great harm: sometimes by blocking the right course of action, sometimes simply by failing to act.

There are those who deliberately look the other way—to avoid facing the issue at hand and doing that which they know to be right.

And there are men who do what's right and moral, come what may.

Three types. And examples of each emerge in just one chapter of this compelling book. McCloy—sometimes called "America's most influential private citizen" because he spent so much of his career outside government—was an illustration of the first.

Acquiescence in evil—as documented by Bird—will forever tarnish McCloy's reputation. True, McCloy—as Franklin D. Roosevelt's assistant secretary of war—occasionally did more than just acquiesce. For example, he bears principal responsibility for the indefensible 1942 policy of rounding up and interning the *nisei*; manifesting the same efficiency and zeal that guided him to success as a Wall Street lawyer and as chairman of the Chase financial empire, McCloy organized the creation of internment camps for Japanese Americans.

But equally striking is Bird's examination of McCloy's studied refusal, during the war years, to approve any attempt to rescue the doomed Jews of Europe. Whenever a rescue plan was broached— from stalling for time through fake negotiations with the Nazis to bombing the railway lines leading to the death camps—McCloy found a reason to block it. Sometimes, he used logistics as an excuse, sometimes domestic political considerations, sometimes geostrategic concerns.

But the answer was always the same: No.

McCloy knew details of the Nazi mass murder program by mid–1943. A subscriber to the thesis that nothing could be done to assist Europe Jewry apart from winning the war as quickly as possible, McCloy—also afflicted with a mild case of social anti-Semitism—vetoed every proposal that crossed his desk.

In August 1944, after D-Day and while the Jews of Hungary were being gassed at Auschwitz at a rate of some six thousand per day, McCloy—who'd already read a detailed report on the killing factory prepared by two Auschwitz escapees—was called on to review a plan to bomb the gas chambers there.

He told a World Jewish Congress official—repeating a claim he'd deploy again and again during the final two years of the war— that such a bombing run would require the "diversion of considerable air support." This was a lie—oil refineries only miles from Auschwitz were bombed regularly during this precise period. But McCloy's reply carried an implicit threat: "You Jews are asking us to slow the war effort."

He then added a priceless, even funny (in a macabre sort of way) observation: "[S]uch an effort [bombing the gas chambers], even if practicable, might provoke . . . more vindictive action by the Germans."

It would be interesting to know what John J. McCloy believed could be "more vindictive" than the daily gassing of thousands of men, women, and children.

My guess is that McCloy had nothing whatever in mind; indeed, he probably gave the entire matter very little thought. Thus, this bizarre observation from a man who—if nothing else—was always cautious and thorough, in word and deed. The issue didn't interest him.

Type 2—the man who looks the other way—emerges in the pages of Bird's book in the form of Supreme Court Justice Felix Frankfurter. In one extraordinary scene, Frankfurter—a leader of the American Jewish community—listens to a firsthand report on the gassing of Jews at the Belzec death camp delivered to him in late 1943 by Jan Karski, a Catholic courier working for the Polish government-in-exile.

Karski—at great personal risk—had smuggled himself into Belzec. After hearing him out, Frankfurter tells the courier: "I am unable to believe you."

The Polish ambassador protests that there's no justification for accusing Karski of lying. The eminent jurist thereupon offers a nuanced distinction: "Mr. Ambassador, I did not say [he] is lying. I said I am unable to believe him. There is a difference." Then Frankfurter—waving both his hands and murmuring "No, no"—executes an about-face and leaves the room.

Interpretation? Felix Frankfurter *couldn't* accept Karski's report. Had he done so, the justice's conscience would have required him actually to do something—in view of his exalted status in FDR's Washington. And Frankfurter lacked the stomach to take on an explicitly Jewish cause—even that of his dying brethren in Europe—in a less-than-sympathetic climate. "Disbelief" served him well.

Type 3—the man who speaks out—appears in the same chapter of Bird's study. Henry Morgenthau, Jr., FDR's treasury secretary, might well have behaved in the manner of Frankfurter.

Morgenthau, however, was made of different stuff. A proud Jew, he would not let the issue of European Jewry rest. Nor the question of rescue. He commissioned a report on *The Acquiescence of this Government in the Murder of the Jews.* At one point, he called McCloy an "oppressor of the Jews" at a cabinet meeting. Eventually, he forced the creation of the War Refugee Board and saved tens of thousands of lives.

A man of conscience, it turns out, can do a great deal in a position of power. True, Morgenthau paid a price. McCloy and others who resented the treasury secretary's personal war on Nazism conspired against him. After FDR died, they succeeded in ousting him.

But the final victory belongs to Henry Morgenthau, Jr. History—as exemplified by Kai Bird's biography of McCloy—records all: McCloy's sublime indifference to the Holocaust, Frankfurter's cowardly refusal to accept its reality, Morgenthau's stubborn and heroic determination to thwart Hitler's design.

This book has a timeless message. Those who, even today, find themselves in positions of power would do well to take note.

Nazi Doctor Without Remorse

February 18, 1993

Hans-Joachim Sewering, a German physician who still practices medicine in the Bavarian town of Dachau, reached the pinnacle of his highly successful career last year when he was elected president of the World Medical Association. Sewering, who was meant to take office this fall, had no reason to believe he would face any difficulties.

True, he'd been a member of both the SS and the Nazi Party; true, he was responsible for sending Babette Froeweiss, a fourteen-year-old girl suffering from tuberculosis and epilepsy, to a "euthanasia" clinic in 1943. (Froeweiss was given a fatal overdose of barbiturates after Sewering determined that she was "no longer suitable" for Schoenbrunn, the TB hospital at which he worked.)

But this information had been in the public domain for fifteen years. In fact, the news magazine *Der Spiegel* published documents recounting Sewering's role in the Froeweiss case in 1978.

And Sewering's rise in German medical politics had continued unimpeded. He'd gone on to serve as president of the Federal Physicians' Chamber and as the World Medical Association's treasurer.

Questions about Sewering's untidy history *were* raised at various points. But he always managed to have powerful friends in the right places. Inquiries were fended off. The German Medical Association was firmly in his corner. And, with his election last fall, it appeared he had finally overcome any obstacle his Nazi past might ever pose.

Not so.

An uproar ensued within weeks after his electoral triumph was announced. Protests from within and without began to overwhelm both the World and German medical associations. Some one hundred German doctors published a petition decrying Sewering's participation in the euthanasia program.

Not surprisingly, new information began to surface about Schoenbrunn, the hospital at which he'd been stationed during the war years. It quickly became apparent that Babette Froeweiss was but one of many "euthanasia" victims dispatched to their deaths from Schoenbrunn.

An Israeli delegation filed a formal protest. And Sewering— even though he'd initially secured the support of fifty-one out of sixty-three World Medical Association organizations—found himself the target of a campaign waged by physicians in Canada, the United States, Israel, and Germany itself.

Eventually, Sewering gave up the fight and tendered his resignation. The decision afforded him a rare opportunity for utter candor. Sewering blamed "world Jewry" for his downfall.

Actually, he was merely echoing a charge leveled by his most prominent German champion, the current head of the Federal Physicians' Chamber, Dr. Karsten Vilmar-Vilmar, who holds the "World Jewish Congress" responsible for Sewering's downfall.

What's important to remember about the Sewering episode is that this wasn't a debate about whether or not to place an aging physician on trial. The issue at hand was his *elevation*—to the presidency of the most influential body in international medical politics.

It's also well to recall that few facts about Sewering's personal history were even in dispute. The doctor acknowledges his SS membership, although—shades of Kurt Waldheim—he insists that he joined the Nazi criminal elite in order to belong to a "riding group." (Sewering implies that participation in an SS cavalry unit was the only way for a young man to develop his equestrian skills during the period in question.)

As for the Nazi Party, Sewering has made no effort whatever to justify his membership.

Only with respect to his role in the "euthanasia" program did Sewering endeavor to dissemble. He says he didn't know that sending Babette Froeweiss to "the responsible healing institution at Eglfing-Haar" meant dispatching the disabled teenager to her death.

But there is ample evidence demonstrating that the fate of the 909 patients sent to Eglfing-Haar from Schoenbrunn was no secret. The former was a notorious murder facility. Indeed, Catholic nuns who worked at Schoenbrunn have testified that lay workers at the hospital—and even the victims themselves—knew that a transfer to "Haar" meant death. That the doctors also knew goes without saying.

The lessons inherent in this episode are worth considering. Many accomplished physicians (Germans and non-Germans) have indicated that they view Sewering's "mistakes" as errors of a sort to which a young man is entitled. This is a decidedly benign attitude to strike regarding a colleague who facilitated the "medical murder" of a child.

It's plain that some people are inclined to oppose any effort at all to "dredge up" unpleasant memories. The need to "put the past to rest" continues to inform the thinking of many altogether decent West European professionals—men who have nothing whatever to hide.

Finally, there's the oft-cited Konrad Lorenz illustration: If a man [Lorenz] who publicly endorsed "euthanasia" during the Nazi period can go on to enjoy a career marked by rare honors—even including a Nobel Prize—how can lesser figures be penalized for their acquiescence in the very same undertaking?

The Lorenz argument doesn't seem highly compelling. But, curiously, it has even been used by a Sewering defender who himself spent time in Nazi concentration camps.

No one seems to have noted that one factor never even entered the Sewering debate: remorse.

How does Dr. Sewering himself feel about his past? Is he inclined to apologize for his wartime role? Does he nurture any sense of moral ambiguity?

To all of the above, the answer, it seems plain, is no. By his lights, Sewering is himself a victim—a victim of "world Jewry."

Truth be told, it may well be that Sewering has suffered. Yes, he prospered in postwar Germany. But who can know to what heights he might have risen had Hitler won the war?

The Warsaw Ghetto Uprising, Fifty Years Later

April 8, 1993

Fifty years ago this month—Passover 1943—the last Jews still alive in the Warsaw Ghetto rose up in armed revolt against their German oppressors. Of the nearly half a million souls who'd been herded into the sealed thousand-acre ghetto in the autumn of 1940, fewer than fifty thousand remained. All the rest had perished. Some had died of starvation. Most had been deported to Treblinka.

The uprising in the ghetto, planned for months by the tiny Jewish Fighting Organization, was triggered by the final Nazi effort to render Warsaw *Judenrein* (Jew-free). The Germans were determined to enter the ghetto on the night of the first Seder and dispatch the haggard, skeletal remnant to the gas chambers.

They anticipated no resistance—and with good reason. The Jews were weary, they had few weapons, they were utterly untrained, and they lacked any means of contacting the outside world.

Nevertheless, a battle took place; indeed, fighting raged for nineteen days. Again and again, SS troops were repelled. Eventually, the Germans—resorting to tanks, heavy artillery, and flamethrowers—conquered the ghetto in house-to-house combat.

The Jewish survivors of the uprising numbered no more than a few hundred; all the rest fell in battle, perished—literally—in the flames, or were herded onto the Treblinka-bound transports.

German casualties were relatively light. And on May 8, 1943, SS General Jurgen Stroop ordered the ghetto razed to the ground. Stroop even blew up the Great Synagogue; he then declared triumphantly—in a bound, photo-illustrated volume presented to Heinrich Himmler—that "the Jewish residential district in Warsaw has ceased to exist."

Despite its marginal military implications, the Warsaw Ghetto uprising represents the most sublime moment—along with the establishment of the State of Israel—in the modern history of the Jewish people. The revolt was a ray of sunshine, and it appeared at the Jewish people's darkest hour.

The establishment of the Jewish state, of course, was an affirmation of life—the enduring life of the very people Hitler had sought to eradicate from the face of the earth.

The uprising, on the other hand, was about death. The course of the battle in the Warsaw Ghetto was never in doubt. The decision to resist was purely a gesture for posterity—an effort by doomed men and women to choose for themselves the manner in which they would die. The surviving remnant of an ancient community had decided to make itself the master of its last moments.

In honoring the ghetto fighters half a century later, it isn't necessary to exaggerate their military achievements. The mere fact that this meager and tormented band of idealists—armed only with a few malfunctioning revolvers—found the will to resist is something of a miracle.

The Jewish fighters of Warsaw left behind well-hidden documents. These papers, which were discovered after the war and include their call to arms, make it plain that they grasped the desperate nature of their circumstance.

The resistance organization harbored no illusion that outside forces—the Polish Home Army, the government-in-exile in London, the Allied powers—would come to its aid. Its members fought with one goal in mind—to redeem their national honor by refusing to go as sheep to the slaughter.

This is not to say that heroism during the dark days of the Holocaust didn't express itself in other ways. Dr. Janusz Korchak (Henryk Goldschmidt), the famed pediatrician who doubled as the

"Polish Dr. Seuss," conducted himself just as heroically as any ghetto fighter by insisting on escorting "his" children—he ran an orphanage in the ghetto—to Treblinka. To soothe the children in their final hours, Korchak rejected the well-intentioned entreaties of admiring Poles who'd sought to rescue a famous man.

Heroism can also be ascribed to ordinary mothers who remained with and calmed their own children, to rabbis who stayed with their congregations, to brothers who wouldn't abandon their sisters. Still, the ghetto fighters who took up arms in Warsaw fifty years ago—rather than climb through the sewers and make a run for the woods—have a special place in Jewish history. In their quest to die with dignity, they inspired future generations to *live* with dignity.

When men and women who know they are doomed manage, somehow, to seize control of their own collective destiny, they provide proof positive of the human spirit's indomitability.

It's no coincidence that the ghetto resistance broke out on the first night of Passover. The Germans invariably conducted major raids on major Jewish holidays. In this instance, however, because their intended victims fought back, the Nazis unintentionally added a new dimension to an ancient celebration.

The exodus from Pharaoh's Egypt saw Jews liberate themselves from physical bondage. The uprising in Warsaw represented an end to spiritual bondage: The ghetto fighters cast aside the passivity that had defined Jewish life in the Diaspora and opted for the path of armed resistance.

Their choice has informed Jewish national life—in Israel and in the Diaspora—ever since.

François Mitterrand's Curious Paean

May 18, 1995

French President François Mitterrand appears to have designed the manner of his departure from public life with the precision of a choreographer. Seriously ill with prostate cancer, Mitterrand—who turned over his office to Jacques Chirac yesterday—has been careful and deliberate about where he appears and what he says. This circumstance, naturally, endows his words with special resonance.

If ever there's been an opportunity to look behind the mask and see the real François Mitterrand, this is it. Thus, Mitterrand's speech in Berlin last week—delivered on the eve of the fiftieth anniversary of the Nazi surrender—cries out for scrutiny and explication.

In a stunning gesture, the French president took it upon himself to administer to Germany an act of absolution. Beyond his message, even his phraseology was striking:

"This [V-E Day appearance] is one of my last official acts and I am proud to be here with you," Mitterrand said, adding that coming to Berlin represented "the least I owe to Germany." The news that Mitterrand recognizes a special personal debt to Germany is in itself noteworthy.

True, he was a prisoner of war there. True, he collaborated with the Nazi puppet regime in Vichy until the tide of the war turned against Germany—a fact that he long took pains to conceal. But these experiences wouldn't likely induce a sense of personal obligation. To the contrary, most European public personalities with such a background would seek to avoid discussion of the period in question.

Not so, Mitterrand.

Indeed, consider the rest of his remarks—which are hard to view as anything other than bizarre: ". . . my country, which was at first defeated and occupied, shared victory with its allies. . . .

"I have not come to celebrate the victory. I rejoiced for my country in 1945. I have not come to underline the defeat, because I knew how much strength there was in the German people, its qualities, its courage, never mind what uniform it wore or even what motivated the soldiers who were about to die in such great numbers. They were courageous. They were prepared to die. For a bad cause, but what they did had nothing to do with that. They loved their country."

It might be comforting to dismiss this ode to German courage as an exercise in rambling nonsense—the ill-considered thoughts of an old, sick man. But Mitterrand's speech can't easily be written off. Nor can it be likened to President Reagan's 1985 attempt to explain his visit to the German military cemetery at Bitburg, a site where Waffen-SS members were buried alongside ordinary Wehrmacht soldiers.

The propensity toward moral equivalence that informed Reagan's comments about dead German teenagers who'd been pressed into military service can be seen as a reflection of thoughtlessness. The motives of the men who wore German uniforms during the Second World War never kept Ronald Reagan awake at night—the issue isn't central to the modern American experience, nor was it crucial to Reagan's personal political odyssey.

Mitterrand's tribute to German valor is another matter entirely. The purpose of the soldiers who fought for Hitler points to questions critical to the history of Europe in this century: How did Nazism seize the German imagination? How did the land of Goethe and Ludwig van Beethoven produce Auschwitz and Bergen-Belsen?

Mitterrand, moreover, contradicts himself: At the outset, he asserts that it doesn't matter why these ostensibly courageous young men took up arms; later, he suggests that their cause was "bad"; finally, he concludes that love of country—generally regarded as a virtue—animated the German struggle.

For obvious reasons, Mitterrand's remarks caused something of a stir in France. While it's often noted—accurately—that the French have failed to confront the real implications of their conduct during the war years, it remains that a "correct" national position has evolved. As Mitterrand's friend and adviser Jacques Attali put it—after insisting on his "complete disagreement" with the president of the Republic—"The only German soldiers whose courage I respect are those who deserted or rose up in revolt."

The political scientist Alfred Grosser, an architect of postwar Franco-German reconciliation, echoes Attali, albeit in a milder tone: "The president did not distinguish sufficiently between Germans who were responsible for the atrocities and those who tried to resist." Grosser deems this distinction central to the reconciliation itself.

To believe either that Mitterrand was confused or that he failed accurately to express his personal sentiments is altogether implausible. It's far more likely that age and illness have afforded him a special sense of license. No longer does he feel called upon to pretend to a sensibility that isn't his.

The real François Mitterrand respects the German soldiers who occupied France in 1940. The real François Mitterrand granted journalist Pierre Pean access to his personal papers—knowing that they'd reveal the hidden truth about his collaborationist past—because he isn't ashamed of his decision to cast his lot with Marshal Philippe Pétain. Maybe Mitterrand intends to end his days by telling the truth about himself.

We need to bear in mind, moreover, that this is a man with political antennae as sophisticated as any in Europe. He may well know that, in these pronouncements, he's speaking for France's silent majority.

Zion and Zionism

A passionate Zionist, Breindel believed that in the wake of the Holocaust it was a sacred duty of all Jews to defend the state of Israel and to fight those who attack it militarily, with terrorism, or ideologically. While his ideological views went through an evolution from the 1970s to the 1990s, his hard-line views on Israel's security never changed. He was as skeptical of the Israel-PLO Oslo peace process in the 1990s as he was of the Nixon-Carter-Reagan Middle East peace processes that preceded it. He viewed the PLO and its chief, Yasser Arafat, as a successor to the Nazis in their determination to wipe the Jewish state off the face of the earth. That perspective became increasingly rarely heard in the mainstream media in the years Breindel was writing his column. Hundreds of letters of condolence poured in to the New York Post *after his death, and nearly every letter mentioned Breindel's staunch defense of Israel as the key reason for their fondness and enthusiasm for Breindel's work.*

The Shame of the United Nations

November 12, 1987

Twelve years ago this week, the United Nations General Assembly passed its resolution declaring Zionism to be a form of racism. It was a deed as widely known as anything the UN has ever done.

Daniel Patrick Moynihan, the U.S. ambassador to the UN at the time, told the General Assembly it was committing an "infamous act." Moynihan warned—to no avail—that the UN would come to be known as "a place where lies are told."

Chaim Herzog was Israel's ambassador to the UN back then. Herzog rose to the podium to denounce the resolution. Declaring it "no more than a piece of paper," he tore the document in two.

Three weeks earlier, in late October 1975, the Israeli ambassador had told the UN's Third Committee, from whence the resolution emerged: "You have degraded this world organization by introducing this anti-Semitic element, and in doing so you may destroy it ultimately."

Herzog is back in America this week. As president of Israel, he is making the first state visit to the United States by an Israeli head of state.

As if to greet his comrade-in-arms from that lonely period, Moynihan—now Senator Moynihan—shepherded a joint resolution through both houses of Congress. It declares the UN's Zionism resolution "inconsistent with the Charter of the United Nations" and "unacceptable as a misrepresentation of Zionism." And it urges that the U.S. government "lend support to efforts to overturn UN General Assembly Resolution 3379."

Moynihan wasn't seeking merely to mark an unhappy anniversary, although there was special poignancy in the fact that the House passed his resolution on the exact date of the UN vote twelve years ago. This effort on Capitol Hill is actually the first stage in an international diplomatic campaign. The joint resolution itself is identical to one that passed the Australian federal parliament a year ago.

Moynihan's idea is to take the "Australian resolution," now that it's been passed by Congress, to all the world's democracies and would-be democracies—to see it passed by as many legislatures as possible.

Then, bearing the Free World's imprimatur, the resolution will be presented to the General Assembly in September of next year— and the UN will be asked to undo the harm it did in 1975.

There's something compelling about Moynihan's plan to send the same resolution "round robin . . . from one democratic institution to another."

But if the body that suffered the greatest harm from the General Assembly's "infamous act" was the UN itself—as Moynihan and

Herzog predicted—why not let those responsible take the initiative in undoing it?

The Zionism resolution, after all, was passed by a Soviet-Arab-Third World coalition, the same bloc that dominates the world body today. And the resolution did, in fact, do abiding damage to the UN.

It heightened the sense among the *peoples* of the Free World—not just among their governments—that the UN is nothing more than a forum in which insignificant countries let off steam, an unserious place where nations posture and playact, animated by the knowledge that no real consequences attach to what they say or do.

That this perception came to be far more widely held in the aftermath of the Zionism resolution is hard to contest. Even Javier Pérez de Cuéllar, the UN secretary general, apparently believes that the 1975 resolution weakened the UN.

Why then should those who fought this slander at the time—many of whom care relatively little for the world body—lead the campaign to repeal the resolution?

The fact is that the Zionism resolution—for all the damage it did to the UN—also gave strength to the Soviet-Arab effort to delegitimize Zionism and Israel.

I was a graduate student in England in the late 1970s, and I watched in amazement as Left-dominated student unions, in university after university throughout the country, barred Israeli representatives from speaking on campuses.

The method used was always the same. Resolutions would be passed denying campus podiums to "racists." It would then be asserted—on the basis of the UN's Zionism resolution—that the ban applied automatically to Zionists, that is, Israelis.

This syndrome manifested itself not just in England, but throughout Western Europe.

Moreover, there are other countries in the world—mostly less developed countries—where international politics is actually taught in school through UN activities and resolutions. Children grow up accepting, as a matter of received wisdom, that Zionism is a form of racism.

Thus, the importance of the effort to repeal this ugly lie. In addition, forcing each UN member-government to declare itself on this issue at the next session of the General Assembly will provide an interesting lesson in where the forces of freedom stand thirteen years later. Whether the news is good or bad, the lesson is worth having.

Saving the Falashas

May 30, 1991

On November 10, 1975—in what then-UN Ambassador Daniel Patrick Moynihan termed an "infamous act"—the United Nations General Assembly passed an odious resolution declaring Zionism "a form of racism." This weekend, the world had an opportunity to see for itself just what Zionism is all about.

The government of Israel, having managed to gather Ethiopian Jews from all around that country into the Addis Ababa vicinity over the past ten or so months, airlifted virtually the entire Ethiopian Jewish community to safety in Israel.

The operation took place in utter secrecy. More than fourteen thousand Ethiopian Jews—called Falashas (outsiders)—were transported, in the course of a three-day period, to a land they had never seen. They flew aboard Israeli Air Force C–130 transport planes and El Al 727, 747, and 757 jets.

The Ethiopian government—long pro-Soviet and not itself particularly well disposed toward the Falashas—was collapsing. Rebel forces were eight miles from Addis Ababa when the airlift began.

Ethiopian Jews, of course, are black—as black as other Ethiopians. (And most Israelis, needless to say, are Caucasian.) But the Falashas, because they identify themselves as Jews, were likely—in the view of outside analysts, including State Department officials—to be "very vulnerable" in turbulent political circumstances.

This condition, historically, is nothing new for Jews. Many times throughout their history, Jews have been—to say the least—"vulnerable." And they've had no safe haven to which to flee.

What's different now?

Zionism: the existence of a Jewish state.

Jerusalem decided last week—as it has on many occasions since 1948—to ensure that what had happened to "vulnerable" Jews in the days before there was a Jewish state would not happen again.

An agreement was negotiated with the collapsing Ethiopian government, an agreement brokered—to his eternal credit—by President Bush himself.

The Israelis evidently paid small cash ransoms to individual interim Ethiopian officials. Armed Israelis—soldiers in plainclothes and members of the security services—entered Ethiopia; organized the Jewish community; prepared it for the impending mass departure; and drove the stunned and overjoyed men, women, and children to waiting aircraft in buses.

The planes ferried the fourteen thousand Jews on their one thousand, eight hundred-mile journey and landed at Ben Gurion airport near Tel Aviv. Prime Minister Shamir was there to welcome them, as were thousands of other Israelis.

As one Ethiopian Jew put it: "Isaiah's prophecy has finally been fulfilled. . . . All Israelites can now return . . . to the land of our forefathers."

The planes took off at the rate of two to three per hour. The aircraft were desperately overcrowded. There were special planes for newcomers suffering from tuberculosis. A number of the new immigrants were orphans whose parents had succumbed to famine.

In 1984, some twelve thousand Falashas were transported to Israel—again thanks to the intercession of Washington—before Ethiopia's military dictator, under pressure from the Arab states, halted the evacuation (which was code-named Operation Moses). That enterprise was sparked primarily by the general famine ravaging Ethiopia.

This airlift—Operation Solomon—was prompted by the concern that impending political instability might well create a climate in which hostilities aimed at Jews could not be countered.

Again, the airlift was a near-total success. And earlier this week, Shamir—after calling President Bush to thank him for facilitating the exodus—vowed that the two thousand or so Jews who still remain in Ethiopia would also soon be rescued.

They remain, in part, because the now-departed Marxist dictator, Colonel Mengistu, slowed the mass flight in hopes that he
could hustle the Israelis—desperate to rescue Ethiopian Jewry—
into providing him with arms with which to thwart the rebels
(many of whom are also Marxists). Once Mengistu himself fled,
realistic negotiations with the interim government resumed.

In the end, the Ethiopian Jews—"black Jews" who trace their
lineage to King Solomon—were saved by brethren they had never
seen, some of whom risked their lives to bring the Falashas to a land
of which they had only dreamed.

There's only one word that describes this extraordinary
endeavor: Zionism.

Read the news reports, look at the photos, watch the film
footage—one fact is plain: Notwithstanding any UN resolutions,
Zionism—whatever else it may or may not be—is not "a form of
racism."

Three Days with Menachem Begin

March 12, 1992

I interviewed Menachem Begin over the course of three days when I
was twenty-two years old and just out of college. Begin had just
emerged from a twenty-seven-year Churchillian wilderness period
as a Knesset backbencher; his ascendance to the post of prime minister was still being greeted in the United States, in Western Europe,
and in half of Israel as a frightening political earthquake.

Begin, the "ex-terrorist," was now Israel's leader. *Time* magazine
assisted uninitiated readers by explaining—to the new prime minister's fury—how to pronounce his surname: "Begin," *Time* noted,
"rhymes with (Charles Dickens') Fagin."

Needless to say, Begin at that juncture was less than well disposed toward the Western media. As a consequence, he'd declared a
"no more interviews" policy. (There would be a number of "no
interviews" interludes in the years to come.)

But it happened that he'd liked an essay I'd written in the *New*

Republic just after his surprise electoral victory. The piece endeavored to explain the distinction between urban guerrilla warfare as practiced by Begin's Irgun Zvai Leumi and PLO-style terrorism.

Begin had believed in targeting official installations, and he even favored issuing advance warnings in order to avert civilian casualties. He also opposed sending his men on suicide missions.

The PLO, of course, specialized in airplane hijackings, in attacks on ordinary Jews at prayer in synagogues throughout the world, in the murder of Israeli Olympic athletes. Arafat & Co., moreover, deliberately targeted defenseless civilians—in Israel and elsewhere.

The prime minister read the *New Republic* article and granted an interview (which was published in *Rolling Stone* magazine).

For me, Begin was already a figure out of the history books. I had no idea, when we met in the late summer of 1977, that preparations for Anwar Sadat's historic visit to Jerusalem were just then under way; talks between Begin's foreign minister, Moshe Dayan, and Dayan's Egyptian counterpart had been held in Morocco a month earlier under the auspices of King Hassan.

And, in fact, in the middle of our discussions, Begin flew briefly to Bucharest to meet with Romania's Nicolae Ceaucescu—to hammer out final details related to the impending summit with Sadat.

Of this, I knew nothing. Begin's immediate goal, it seemed to me, was to solidify his base at home: to persuade Israelis that he was not an antidemocratic demagogue and to demonstrate that he could represent Israel effectively in the international community. The notion that he was already preparing to negotiate a peace treaty with Israel's most formidable Arab foe would have seemed exceedingly far-fetched.

Our talks consisted of an effort by Begin to teach me the essence of Zionism—the Zionism of his revered mentor, Ze'ev Jabotinsky.

The prime minister explained that the image of his own father and brother—marched to a riverbank and shot, along with thousands of other Jews, directly after the Germans entered his Polish hometown of Brest-Litovsk—was constantly in his mind. (His mother was murdered in the city hospital, as were the other Jewish patients there.)

In Begin's view, the slaughter of his family—like the Holocaust itself—was a direct consequence of the Jewish national condition: "Homelessness led to helplessness and defenselessness." The latter, Begin maintained, actually provoked the murderers (to whom Begin would refer as the "German two-legged animals" and their collaborators).

The answer to the Holocaust? The surest path to avoiding any repetition? Jewish national sovereignty in a secure Jewish state.

If Menachem Begin was animated by a single core belief, it was this fundamental faith in the justice and necessity of the Zionist endeavor.

When he ordered the 1981 bombing of the Iraqi nuclear facility at Osirak, Begin was convinced that Baghdad was developing nuclear weapons (history, of course, has confirmed his assessment). Understandably, the prime minister believed that Iraq wouldn't hesitate to use such weapons against Israel.

Moral suasion, in Begin's view, was a vastly overrated diplomatic commodity. If Israel wanted to spare itself a second Holocaust, Jerusalem would have to act against Saddam Hussein—decisively, forcefully, and alone.

Begin knew that condemnation of Israel's assault on the Iraqi reactor would be swift and furious. But he made no secret of the fact that he preferred condemnation of this sort to the perennial expressions of heartfelt sympathy that had been tendered Jews by the international community throughout the centuries—always in the wake of huge calamities.

Begin is often compared, appropriately, to Charles de Gaulle. Just as De Gaulle enabled France to come to terms with Algerian independence, Begin's credentials as an unyielding nationalist made it possible to return the Sinai to Egypt—in exchange, of course, for a full and formal peace agreement.

But it also occurs that Begin can be likened to Ronald Reagan. True, there were differences: Begin was a genuine intellectual, widely read, fluent in several languages. In the end, however, both men were guided by a few core principles—from which flowed their politics.

The passing of Menachem Begin reminds us that political change has come to Israel. Yitzhak Shamir, Begin's comrade in the underground struggle against British rule (actually, Shamir left the Irgun for the even more radical Stern group), will likely be Israel's last non-native-born prime minister. The torch has been passed.

For Israel, Begin's death represents the demise of a genuine Founding Father. His accomplishments, of course, are legion: From surviving Hitler and Stalin to hastening the end of the British mandate as Irgun commander (he was, at one time, the "most wanted man" in the British empire) to assuming, late in life, the office of prime minister and negotiating a peace treaty with Egypt, Begin left an indelible imprint on history.

Indeed, he *lived* the history of the mid-twentieth century. In the last analysis, he embodied Ze'ev Jabotinsky's vision—a vision of Jewish men and women unburdened by the stigma of exile. Jabotinsky defined his vision when he penned the anthem of his own youth movement, Betar. Begin was the pre-Second World War Betar commander in Poland.

The anthem envisages "the rise of a people" willing to sacrifice "blood and flesh" to emerge "proud and generous and strong." In Jabotinsky's view, the duty of Begin's generation was plain: "To die or to conquer the mountain."

Menachem Begin conquered the mountain. But as he himself would often note: "Oh, how numerous are the graves on the slope."

The "Purity of Arms"

September 29, 1995

Even as the negotiations between Israel and the PLO occupy center stage in the politics of the Middle East, a bizarre sideshow—one that threatens to poison the Israeli-Egyptian relationship—continues to draw unusual attention.

Late last month, a retired Israeli brigadier general unburdened himself of what he depicted as a painful forty-year-old secret: Arieh Biroh told interviewers that he and another soldier had murdered forty-nine Egyptian prisoners of war in cold blood during the 1956 Sinai campaign.

As if on cue, an Israeli historian reported *his* "finding" that some three hundred unarmed Egyptians—prisoners of war and civilians—had been murdered: some during the Sinai campaign, others at the initial stage of the 1967 Six-Day War.

In response, the state-regulated Egyptian press, including the quasi-official daily *Al Ahram,* launched a vituperative rhetorical assault on Israel and all things Israeli.

One newspaper insisted repeatedly that Israel's ambassador to Cairo, David Sultan, was personally responsible for killing one hundred Egyptian prisoners of war in 1967. The frenzied attacks on Sultan—who was a high-school student during the Six-Day War—reverberated throughout the Egyptian media, eventually forcing the diplomat to request reassignment.

Egypt's President Hosni Mubarak adopted an above-the-fray posture, implying that he had no interest in using the controversy to heighten tensions between Cairo and Jerusalem. Mubarak regularly reminded Western reporters that Israelis had raised the issue first—not Egyptians. Had he wished to do so, of course, Mubarak might easily have put out the fire. Instead—probably in an effort to impress pro-fundamentalist elements—the Egyptian leader fanned the flames.

Indeed, any doubt about Cairo's interest in prolonging the controversy should have been dispelled when the Egyptians staged a Katyn-like discovery of two "mass graves" in the Sinai near El Arish. A number of Bedouin "witnesses" were produced who claimed to remember seeing Israeli troops kill Egyptian soldiers after the latter surrendered on June 6 and 7, 1967.

Conspiracy theorists are doubtless having a field day trying to explain who stands to benefit from this bizarre episode. It seems sufficient, however, simply to consider the hard facts.

The controversy *did* originate in Israel with General Biroh's account. Is Biroh telling the truth? Did Israelis kill Egyptian prisoners? Possibly.

To be sure, no independent evidence has emerged, and many veterans of the 1956 paratroop drop at the Mitla Pass—the operation in which Biroh took part—insist that he's either lying or imagining events that never took place. But at several moments in October 1956, the fighting at Mitla took the form of hand-to-hand combat. It's at least conceivable that Egyptian prisoners were shot—both then and in 1967. No combat army in history has been utterly free of troop misconduct.

True, the Israel Defense Forces (IDF) have a more developed code of honor and discipline than any other army in recent memory. The "purity of arms" concept, which continues to guide the IDF, has its roots in prestate Zionist doctrine. According to this principle, a military force retains its "purity" only if it restricts the use of weaponry to moments of utter necessity.

In short, Biroh's claims represent an assault on Israel's national psyche and a challenge to the moral legitimacy of Zionism. This is why a set of allegations concerning a few isolated events—events that may or may not have even taken place thirty and forty years ago—has been a feature of public discourse in Israel for nearly a month.

It's worth noting, moreover, that it's hard to imagine an Egyptian veteran coming forward with a parallel story. It's even harder to imagine an Egyptian newspaper covering such claims. And it's impossible to imagine ordinary Egyptians caring about whether Israeli prisoners of war were shot in cold blood four decades ago.

Yet the Egyptian track record in this realm—while less bestial than that of the Syrians—leaves much to be desired. Israel, for example, notified the Red Cross just after the Yom Kippur War that twenty-eight of its own soldiers had been murdered in Egyptian captivity. The Israelis learned later that many more had been killed, some after having been tortured. In addition, it's been reported widely that after Egyptian troops stormed across the Suez Canal in 1973, they bayoneted wounded Israeli soldiers in several of the bunkers of the Bar Lev line.

Egypt, in other words, is in no position to claim the moral high ground on this front.

Israel's Fault Lines

November 17, 1995

A dual chasm—long a relatively subdued feature of Israeli life—has come increasingly to inform national discourse in the Jewish state. Separately, each fault line has had a long history. But an alliance between two elements on one side of the chasm—secular nationalists and religious Zionist hard-liners—is a phenomenon of fairly recent vintage.

One component of the larger rift is the split that divides the Labor Zionist Left and the militant Right; it has been a fact of Zionist history virtually since the onset of the post–World War I British mandate for Palestine. Today, this essentially political split expresses itself in the context of the peace process.

The other schism—that which divides the religious and the secular—is even older. Indeed, it can be traced to the very birth of political Zionism, which—as a decidedly secular movement—found itself either ignored or opposed by most of Orthodox Jewry. Only after the Holocaust vindicated the Zionist creed did most surviving Orthodox Jews reconcile themselves to the need for a sovereign Jewish state.

Notwithstanding the apparent fusion within Israel between Orthodoxy and ultranationalism, it's well to note that not all Orthodox Jews identify with the Israeli Right.

Certainly, however, the alliance exists. It cemented itself in the aftermath of the Six-Day War, a momentous period in the life of the state. And in recent years, its importance has grown by leaps and bounds.

Needless to say, times that are fraught with tension often afford political paranoids the opportunity to slip inside the fence and insinuate themselves into the mainstream debate. It's in this context that Yigal Amir and his coconspirators appear on the Israeli landscape.

Cells of Orthodox nationalists began to use unusually violent rhetoric just after the 1982 war in Lebanon (a period, let's remember, during which Menachem Begin and Ariel Sharon were routinely decried as "fascists" and "Judeo-Nazis" by mainstream voices from within the "Peace Now" camp). But the current debate over the peace process has given rise to a level of tension and demagogy unprecedented in Israel's national experience.

This should not surprise: After all, prior to his assassination, Yitzhak Rabin's policies—on the preeminent issue of the day—enjoyed the support of little more than 50 percent of the population. Yet Rabin's certainty that a unique opportunity had presented itself—a chance for peace that could not be squandered—caused him to press forward without securing anything resembling a national consensus.

The fact that Rabin and Shimon Peres were prepared to transfer the West Bank to alien rule on the basis of a razor-thin 61–59 majority in the Knesset is a comment on their willingness to test the very fiber of Israeli democracy.

Such a path—in light of the Oslo agreements' implications for Israel's security and for the entire Zionist enterprise—served virtually to invite fanatics like Yigal Amir to "protest" their sense of disenfranchisement.

Since Israel's birth in 1948, few in any sector of Israeli life had doubted the determination of the Jewish state's enemies to destroy it; and few Israelis believed that anything other than eternal vigilance could ensure the state's survival.

But all of this started to change. First came Israel's withdrawal from Sinai—in the context of the peace with Egypt; then came the Lebanon war, which shook the nation to its core and gave rise to a powerful pro-peace movement; next came the Palestinian intifada, which encouraged new thinking about Israel's security needs, while fostering a searing national debate over the Israel Defense Force and the "occupation"; finally came the ascendance of Yitzhak Rabin and the signing of the Oslo agreements.

Suddenly, the siege has begun to lift. Israel has signed full peace treaties with two of its neighbors—Jordan and Egypt—and is negotiating with the PLO. The Jewish state—long an international pariah—has established diplomatic relations with China and the Vatican. Its new commercial ties stretch from the Gulf states to Japan.

Meanwhile, the combination of the Soviet Union's demise and

the development by Israel of an independent nuclear capability has produced a circumstance in which Israel's permanence, for the first time, seems axiomatic. At long last, the Jewish state is becoming the "normal" society envisaged by Theodor Herzl, the father of political Zionism.

In response to all of this, the Israeli Right—secular nationalists and religious Zionists—launched security-related protests. They focused on Arafat's manifest inability to halt Arab terror and agitated about the centrality of territory to the Zionist idea.

Meanwhile, Amir and his coconspirators—a bizarre, aberrant cell within the nationalist camp—found themselves terrified by the prospect of normalization. In their view, Jews are meant to be—in the words of the prophet—"a people that dwells alone." Amir and his ilk are *comforted* by the necessity of living in a fortress—they have no desire to leave it. The Israel they see about them is a society in thrall to materialism. They yearn, not for the peace and prosperity Shimon Peres envisages, but for a Manichean climate of confrontation.

It's easy to see the Amir group as violence-prone Sephardic Jews, haunted by fearful memories of life in the Islamic Diaspora. But while many are Sephardim, many are not. It's easy to classify them as Kahane-style "American refuse." But while American emigrants are prominent on the extreme Right, Rabin's assassin and his collaborators are not Americans. Nor, in fact, are they West Bank settlers.

These are ordinary Israelis who happen to be frightened by the prospect of modernity. The fact that they consider themselves Orthodox Jews—and apparently sought rabbinical approval for their deed—doesn't demonstrate that they reflect a deep, endemic rift in Israeli life. The conspirators are a meager lot. And they rely—as Martin Peretz puts it in the *New Republic*—on "theological recklessness in times of change."

Six Days Plus Thirty Years

June 6, 1997

Thirty years ago this week—after nearly a month of threats from Egypt's Gamal Abdel Nasser and his Pan-Arab allies—the Israel Defense Forces launched a lightning three-front military campaign; six days later, the map of the Middle East had been changed irrevocably. Nasser's vaunted Moscow-built air force was a heap of smoldering rubble. Also in ashes was the Egyptian ruler's endlessly repeated pledge to "drive the Jews into the sea."

Silenced, too, were the hate-filled voices—broadcasting from Cairo and Damascus—that had for weeks dominated the international airwaves, promising the imminent destruction of "the Zionist entity." Fighting alone, Israel had escaped a direct threat to its survival. By June 11, 1967, its hour of peril was over.

In early May 1967, Nasser—emboldened, subsequently, by global acquiescence—had ordered United Nations Secretary-General U Thant to withdraw UN peacekeeping forces from the Sinai peninsula. The UN troops had been stationed in the Sinai for more than a decade; their arrival had taken place in the context of Israel's 1957 Sinai pullback. By serving as a buffer in a territory that had otherwise been rendered demilitarized, the peacekeepers had quieted the region's most volatile front.

Nasser's expulsion edict—which was attended by an order to Egypt's military to bar Israeli commercial vessels from the Straits of Tiran—effectively re-created the conditions that had triggered the 1956 Sinai campaign.

Israel's 1967 response—a preemptive strike during which its army also drove King Hussein from the Jordanian-occupied West Bank, reunited Jerusalem, and chased the Syrian military from its shelling perch atop the Golan Heights—was virtually inevitable. The series of provocations staged by Nasser invited a military reply.

The Six-Day War enabled Israel to forge a new identity. No longer was the Jewish state a mere haven for the oppressed—that is, an essentially humanitarian undertaking. By virtue of its stunning victory, Israel had assumed the status of a regional superpower.

In the years to come—even after the near-catastrophe of the

1973 Yom Kippur War (Egypt's surprise attack nearly led to an Israeli military debacle)—the state that had been built on the ashes of the Holocaust would come to be depicted, especially by the Soviets and their Eastern bloc–Third World allies, as an international pariah. Indeed, in 1975, the UN General Assembly (after shelving plans to expel Israel from the world body) adopted a resolution declaring Zionism—the national liberation movement of the Jewish people—"a species of racism."

The current debate over the future of the "peace process" makes it appropriate to use the anniversary of the Six-Day War in an effort to attain a fuller understanding of the concerns that animate Israeli policy makers. This process, after all, is grounded in the premise that Israel—by surrendering specific territories and facilitating the establishment of a West Bank–Gaza Palestinian state—can normalize its relations with its Arab neighbors.

In this context, the fact that the territories in question weren't even in Israel's hands prior to the 1967 war explains the skepticism of many Israeli officials regarding the notion that this approach represents a pathway to lasting peace. During the Jewish state's first nineteen years, the countries that surround Israel never wavered in their express determination to destroy the Jewish state.

For obvious reasons, neither the Sinai nor the West Bank nor Gaza nor the Golan contributed to this pan-Arab resolve. Nor, needless to say, did the nonexistence of a Palestinian state.

The West Bank, recall, had been annexed by Jordan in 1948— along with East Jerusalem. Gaza residents were living under Egyptian military rule—under a regime far more repressive than that eventually imposed by Israel. The Sinai, of course, was an actual part of Egypt. And the Golan Heights had been in Syrian hands since the 1949 Rhodes armistice ended Israel's War of Independence.

Israel, in other words—during its first two decades—was in no position to prevent the establishment of a Gaza–West Bank Palestinian state; nor could the Jewish state have blocked a mass ingathering of Palestinian refugees from the camps in which the latter languished.

True, much can change in thirty years. But it's hard not to wonder about the validity of the contemporary view that genuine peace can be attained only if Israel surrenders the territories it occupied in 1967. Although this analysis has taken on the aspect of received wisdom, its fundamentally ahistorical character is difficult to ignore.

What, after all, impeded diplomatic recognition of Israel by its frontline Arab neighbors during the nineteen years prior to the Six-Day War?

Some would argue that the ruling elites in the Arab world still deem the establishment of a Jewish state in the Middle East a violation of the natural order. In the view of many, in fact, this perspective enjoys greater currency today—in light of the advent of Islamic fundamentalism—than it did thirty years ago.

True, the peace Anwar Sadat negotiated with Israel in 1979 endures. And in Sadat's case, a land-for-peace formula defined the terms of the eventual treaty. Sadat, however, is dead—in large part *because* he pursued peace. Meanwhile, relations between Israel and Egypt—the most powerful and populous Arab state—are less warm today than could have been envisaged even during the Camp David meetings' least promising moments. Indeed, to describe the existing Cairo-Jerusalem relationship in terms of a "cold peace" significantly understates the unhappy nature of the ties now in place.

All in all, Israel—as it observes the thirtieth anniversary of the Six-Day War—needs to decide whether the general factors that gave rise to that conflict remain relevant. It may be comforting to note that the world has turned over many times in the past three decades; moreover, the specific issues that produced the 1967 war can legitimately be consigned to the past.

But PLO Chairman Yasser Arafat's continuing unwillingness even to comply with his Oslo obligation to delete from the Palestinian National Covenant its various, ringing calls for Israel's destruction cannot but heighten the concerns of those who fear that precious little has changed.

Blaming the Victim

August 7, 1997

If there's a phrase that might easily be banished from the contemporary diplomatic lexicon, it's "enemies of peace"—a term of art that seems to be reserved for Palestinian terrorists who murder Israelis.

For one thing, it's inaccurate. The bombers who killed thirteen civilians in a Jerusalem market last week had no doctrinal hostility to peace per se. The terrorists in question are enemies of *Israel*. Eliminate what they view as a violation of the natural order—the existence in the Middle East of a Jewish state—and most will abandon the path of violence. Only a handful would likely persist in waging war against the secular, authoritarian regimes in, say, Cairo, Damascus, and Amman. And those who did so would, almost certainly, be crushed—by Hosni Mubarak, Hafez al-Assad, and King Hussein.

The second problem with the "enemies of peace" formulation—which is aired, along with pro forma condolences, by official spokesmen in Washington, at the UN, and throughout Western Europe every time terrorists strike at Israel—is that it consists of a coded message. Attended by implicit warnings from Western statesmen about the importance of returning to the negotiating table, the message is that Israel shouldn't even think about halting talks with those who seek its destruction.

Last week, for example, after offering up a ritualistic "enemies of peace" denunciation, Robin Cook, Great Britain's new foreign secretary, noted that the Jerusalem bombing "reinforces the urgency of a return to dialogue and negotiation." Another way of putting the matter? Hurry up, bury your dead, and get back to the "peace process."

Now, were there some validity to the notion that talks with Arafat might actually bring about an end to the violence, such suggestions would be worthy of consideration. But there's no evidence whatever that negotiating with the PLO will cause terrorism to abate. Indeed, whereas it was once possible to argue that the PLO chief *couldn't* halt the carnage, it's been apparent for some time that

Arafat's strategy turns on creating leverage for himself by providing—or withholding—the security cooperation to which the PLO committed itself at Oslo.

The mere fact that 259 Israelis have been killed by terrorists since the 1993 accords were signed—more than in any comparable period in the Jewish state's fifty-year history—would seem sufficient to prove the PLO's noncompliance. But a number of other factors confirm this unhappy reality.

In Gaza and in the parts of the West Bank now under Palestinian Authority (that is, PLO) control, the Islamic militants who carry out the attacks have established a terror infrastructure, which includes training bases and weaponry-supply centers. Hamas's state-within-a-state couldn't exist without Arafat's acquiescence.

And much of the actual violence—according to U.S. and Israeli intelligence—is encouraged by the Palestinian Authority. On some occasions, PA officials—at Arafat's instruction—simply look the other way.

Even if this disposition didn't serve the PLO leader's larger strategy, Arafat's inclination to adopt it wouldn't surprise. Recall: Some 98 percent of the West Bank–Gaza Palestinian population lives under PA rule. And, as indicated in a poll conducted just after the March café massacre in Tel Aviv, nearly 50 percent support the terrorists; only 38 percent oppose them.

Arafat's terrorism policy, in short, reflects the sensibility of his constituents. This is why—even since the Jerusalem bombing—the PA-controlled Voice of Palestine has engaged in business-as-usual anti-Israel incitement, broadcasting false stories alleging that Israel shut down two hundred infirmaries, as well as various mosques, throughout the West Bank.

Only hours after last week's bombing, the Voice of Palestine aired an interview with Jibril Rajoub, Arafat's West Bank security chief, who charged that "the Israeli government is responsible for the attack because of its crazy and irresponsible policies."

In view of the fact that all of this comes not from the "enemies of peace," but from the very folks with whom Israel is meant to *make* peace, it seems reasonable to wonder about Washington's current (postbombing) policy orientation. Has the United States decided to reduce the pressure on Netanyahu & Co., pending an enhanced measure of compliance with Oslo on the part of the PLO?

No.

In fact, as Dennis Ross, the Clinton administration's special envoy, departs for Israel this weekend, there's no indication that he'll stray from the State Department's tendency to demand—as the Jewish communal leader Malcolm Hoenlein puts it—"new quids for old quos."

The "new quids," of course, are unilateral concessions by Israel: a freeze on the enlargement of existing West Bank settlements, an end to housing construction in Jerusalem's Har Homa neighborhood, and so forth. Such steps, Washington believes, will produce energy sufficient to restart the peace talks while firming up Arafat's ostensibly precarious circumstances.

As for the "old quos," the PLO will be pressed merely to comply with the terms of existing agreements—by "renewing" (yet again) its commitment to combat terror and by honoring its Oslo pledge to repeal the articles in the Palestine National Covenant that call for Israel's destruction.

Lest anyone think that last week's carnage has caused the United States to reconsider its approach, the State Department declared Tuesday that Israel's decision to withhold $70 million in funds promised to the PA was "counterproductive." While professing sympathy with Israel's security concerns, the department's spokesman, James Foley, acknowledged that Washington had asked Jerusalem to reverse its decision. This warning shot—while unlikely to impress the Netanyahu government—points up a dual irony.

Thus far, Israel *has* honored the financial obligations it took on in the 1994 post-Oslo economic protocol; last year, in fact, the Israelis transferred some $339 million to Arafat.

Netanyahu's reward? Recent events speak for themselves.

Meanwhile, it's curious to consider the fact that the administration won't be able to meet its own financial obligations vis-à-vis the PA. In recessing Friday without extending the legislation that governs U.S. relations with the Palestinians, Congress—in an unmistakable comment on the PLO's continuing noncompliance—caused an automatic suspension of U.S. aid. The funds in question cannot be reinstated until both houses of Congress return in September.

Not surprisingly, the administration refrained from any last-minute attempt to high-pressure the relevant senators and congressmen.

Israel, presumably, is an easier target. Or, as President Clinton put it yesterday: "[Despite] the . . . bombs [detonated] by the enemies of peace . . . Israel has a responsibility to carry its end of the load."

ON BLACK
ANTI-SEMITISM

Breindel believed that, in the 1980s, a new strain of anti-Semitism had begun to make itself known—an anti-Semitism specific to the extremist black community—and that it was not being answered effectively or appropriately either by mainstream black leaders or by the established media. In 1984, the heretofore obscure demagogue Louis Farrakhan became a national figure because, even as he denounced Jews for their "wickedness" and praised Hitler as a "great man," he was supplying security to the presidential candidacy of the Reverend Jesse Jackson. Jackson seemed to reflect Farrakhan's views when, in the company of a black reporter from the Washington Post, *he called New York City "Hymietown." Notwithstanding the controversy this caused, Jackson was given a prime-time speaking slot at the Democratic National Convention that year and became an important American politician.*

Breindel wrote often about black anti-Semitism, especially as it affected New York City. The four columns that follow concern other, less well-known incidents that reveal Breindel's ability to be both light of touch and absolutely straightforward at the same time.

Meaningless Apologies

May 18, 1988

The most interesting thing about the controversy over Chicago mayoral aide Steve Cokely's tape-recorded lectures—which focused on international Jewish conspiracies, the sinister implications of the crucifix, and the Jewish effort to inject black babies with AIDS—isn't their bizarre content. There are lots of cranks around, some of whom sometimes manage to secure political appointments.

More striking than Cokely's demented worldview is Chicago Mayor Eugene Sawyer's response. The mayor thought that disassociating himself from his protégé's views and telling Cokely to "tone down his rhetoric" would take care of the problem.

When these "measures" proved inadequate, Mayor Sawyer decided on a more radical course of action: The mayor's office, purportedly speaking for Cokely, issued an apology (which Sawyer himself accepted in the same press release).

Only when it became clear that the dust simply hadn't settled did Sawyer—responding to what he termed "tender times" and the need to "reconcile differences"—accept his aide's resignation.

The key point here is the notion that apologizing can take care of virtually anything.

Cokely's lectures, distributed by Louis Farrakhan's Nation of Islam bookstore, posit the existence of an international "secret society" that seeks to oppress blacks and create a Jewish-controlled world government.

In one lecture, Cokely charges that the "AIDS epidemic is a result of doctors, especially Jewish ones," injecting black babies with the AIDS virus.

Yet another theme in the former mayoral aide's rhetorical repertoire is the claim that Christopher Columbus was just "a Hispanic Jewboy." Cokely also holds that the crucifix is "a symbol of white supremacy." He's unhappy with the Reverend Jesse Jackson for employing "Jewish advisers" and with former football great Walter Payton for associating with a Jewish businessman.

Certainly it's distressing that someone with views of this sort should ever have been appointed to public office, particularly in light of the fact that Cokely was on Sawyer's small aldermanic payroll when the lectures were delivered.

The mayor, in other words, had reason to be aware of his aide's bizarre ideological sensibilities when he named Cokely to citywide office. But it's at lest conceivable that Sawyer was not aware of the lectures. And finding a crackpot in the ranks of a new administration—Sawyer became mayor upon Harold Washington's death six months ago—isn't all that unusual.

More distressing is the possibility that the mayor's initial failure to act on Cokely stemmed from political considerations. After news about Cokely's lectures hit the press, Sawyer's choice to head the city's Commission on Human Relations—the Reverend B. Herbert Martin—allowed that Cokely's observations about the international Jewish conspiracy had "a ring of truth."

And a local political activist, one Lu Palmer, asked rhetorically: "Why should I be surprised at doctors injecting AIDS in black children?"

If Sawyer, who is black, felt he would be injured in the eyes of the black community by dismissing Cokely, it's reasonable to worry that Cokely's views have a wider cachet than one would wish. Even so, it remains likely that Sawyer is simply a coward, an easily intimidated politician unburdened by moral or political principles.

And this brings us back to the question of apologies. Sawyer clearly thought that a mea culpa from Cokely would settle the matter, especially if attended by a mayoral disavowal—not of Cokely, to be sure, but of his views.

After transcripts of Cokely's lunatic lectures were published, the mayor announced: "I spoke with this young man and he indicated that he did not feel this way in his heart."

What in the world does this comment mean? Cokely doesn't "in his heart" believe Jewish doctors injected the AIDS virus into black babies? Did the thirty-seven-year-old mayoral aide somehow misspeak?

At a later juncture, Sawyer declared: "I've talked to Mr. Cokely and he indicated that he's not anti-Semitic." Here, too, the mayor's meaning is a mystery. How does it matter whether Cokely deems himself an anti-Semite? Perhaps he only dislikes Jews who belong to the international "secret society."

The point is that Cokely's pernicious conspiracy theories have to come from somewhere. They aren't accidental. And while an apology for an isolated off-color remark may be appropriate—Spiro Agnew's reference to a "fat Jap," Jesse Jackson's reference to New York as "Hymietown"—what does it mean to apologize for the suggestion that Jewish doctors are spreading AIDS?

Absolutely nothing.

Giving Sanction to Bigotry

October 6, 1988

The Reverend Leon Sullivan is a Philadelphia clergyman who came to wide renown as the author of the "Sullivan Principles," an anti-apartheid code of conduct for multinational corporations doing business in South Africa.

In order not to be boycotted by foes of apartheid here in the United States, companies were asked to pledge compliance with a set of guidelines drawn up by Sullivan; they included "nonsegregation of the races in all eating, comfort, locker-room, and work facilities"; "equal and fair employment practices"; and "equal pay for all employees doing equal or comparable work," among several other conditions.

Sullivan's efforts won him many admirers and allies among whites. In view of the fact that his entire approach to the antiapartheid struggle was predicated on the cooperation of white-dominated corporations, this isn't at all surprising.

And for this very reason, it came as perplexing and disturbing news that last May, at Sullivan's invitation, Louis Farrakhan preached from the podium of the Zion Baptist Church in Philadelphia, Sullivan's own parish.

About Farrakhan—admirer of Hitler, champion of the view that Judaism is a "gutter religion"—little needs to be said. His status as a vulgar racist in the tradition of the Ku Klux Klan (and P. W. Botha and Dr. Goebbels) isn't in dispute.

When Murray Friedman, the Philadelphia-based regional director of the American Jewish Committee—and a longtime comrade-in-arms of Sullivan—learned of Farrakhan's impending visit to the church, he promptly wrote Sullivan expressing his disquiet:

> Dear Leon:
>
> I am looking forward to celebrating with you on June 24th your retirement party. As I wrote you earlier, this brings back warm memories, including the Great March on Washington in 1963 in which we participated together.
>
> Leon, I must mention something I just learned that is deeply disturbing both to me and other leaders of the Jewish community. I understand Louis Farrakhan is coming to Zion Baptist Church this Friday. Farrakhan's message of anti-Semitism is well documented. . . .
>
> I am deeply troubled by the legitimacy provided for his anti-Jewish views by his association with a mainstream church such as your own.

Friedman went on to note that the principle of freedom of expression doesn't require "us to make our platform available" to bigots. "Let him hire his own hall," Friedman suggested. He enclosed background material on Farrakhan, "lest there be any doubt about his views."

Sullivan responded promptly, the following day, in fact. Not surprisingly, he needed no instruction as to Farrakhan's views. Sullivan also made it plain that his invitation to Farrakhan wasn't prompted by First Amendment considerations.

Farrakhan was preaching at the Zion Baptist Church because Sullivan, having "known Mr. Louis Farrakhan for a number of years, [has] very high regard for him."

Sullivan told Friedman that Farrakhan's "message . . . is very much needed in Philadelphia."

He cited Farrakhan's call for black self-help, "strengthening the Black male, uniting the Black family and fighting drugs," but failed even to address—let alone disavow—Farrakhan's history of overt and violent anti-Semitism.

Sullivan closed by expressing to Friedman his sorrow that we "do not agree on this particular matter."

When a Philadelphia-based official of the B'nai B'rith Anti-

Defamation League wrote to Sullivan protesting the Farrakhan visit, Sullivan responded by sending the ADL man his reply to Friedman.

Earlier this month, New York City Mayor Edward I. Koch also wrote Sullivan concerning the Farrakhan invitation. Koch pointed out that Farrakhan's recent activities have included the distribution of tapes advancing the allegation that Jewish doctors injected the AIDS virus into black children in Chicago.

Although Koch and Sullivan had met on a number of occasions in connection with anti-apartheid protests, Sullivan failed even to respond to Koch's letter.

What are we to make of this episode?

The easy—and therefore tempting—conclusion is that Sullivan is an ugly anomaly: a man who cries out when injustice is done to one of his own, but who falls deaf when one of his own does injustice to others—and is willing even to embrace the bigot.

The trouble, of course, is that Sullivan isn't alone among mainstream black leaders in his attitude toward Farrakhan. Since Farrakhan burst onto the national scene in 1984, Jews have had enormous difficulties persuading black leaders to repudiate him.

Bewildered and even frightened by this experience, Jewish leaders have been disinclined even to discuss it. But from Los Angeles to Chicago to Philadelphia, the experience has been constant.

It took considerable prodding to persuade even Los Angeles Mayor Tom Bradley to issue a statement condemning a local Farrakhan rally. Bradley, to be sure, was chided for doing so by a number of black elected officials, one of whom—City Councilman Robert Farrell—has since been appointed to the Democratic National Committee.

And this points to one possible interpretation of the reluctance to criticize Farrakhan: Black officials are *afraid* to do so, lest they be attacked for breaking ranks.

This explanation, by itself, would afford considerable cause for concern. But it is manifestly incomplete.

Leon Sullivan—and there's no reason to doubt his word—*admires* Louis Farrakhan. Sullivan is well aware of Farrakhan's views on Jews, Hitler, and all the rest. Yet Farrakhan will continue "to be welcome to speak at Zion."

So—once again—what are we to make of all this?

The answer seems plain: In view of the fact that Sullivan is a mainstream actor in the civil rights movement, Jews and other whites who still aspire to a common front with blacks against bigotry—in the tradition of Dr. Martin Luther King, Jr.—have a great deal to worry about. And little cause for optimism.

What Jesse Jackson Didn't Say

July 14, 1992

It was surprising to discover, on returning to the United States last week, that the Reverend Jesse Jackson's speech in Brussels at a World Jewish Congress Conference on Anti-Semitism was received by many here as a significant step forward on Jackson's part. His declaration that Zionism is a genuine "liberation movement" was the focus of most press accounts, and Jackson was portrayed as having extended a warm hand of friendship to the Jewish community.

Most of those who took part in the Brussels conference and actually listened to Jackson's address—I was one—had a decidedly less enthusiastic reaction. Jackson didn't discuss black anti-Semitism—not the rap culture, not the Farrakhan movement, not the Leonard Jeffries affair, and not the Crown Heights pogrom. Nor did he speak to any evolution in his own view of Jews.

His comments about black-Jewish relations, while welcome, were far from expansive. He made reference to the black-Jewish alliance that obtained in the Martin Luther King, Jr., era. He took note of the murders by the Ku Klux Klan of Andrew Goodman and Mickey Schwerner, Student Non-Violent Coordinating Committee volunteers brutally killed—along with James Cheney, who was black—while trying to register black voters in 1964 Mississippi.

Jackson also made mention of the leadership role played by Jews in groups like the NAACP. But, all in all, it was pretty slender stuff. At no point, moreover, did Jackson endeavor to come to terms with what went *wrong*. Never, in short, did he seek to grapple with the bizarre phenomenon of black hostility toward Jews: American

Jews, after all, were preeminent among white ethnics in the extent of their support for black social and political advancement. Yet Jews became the focus of black hostility toward whites, not, say, Italian Americans or Irish Americans or WASPs.

Lots of commentators and scholars—blacks, Jews, and others—have sought to explain this paradoxical circumstance. Some would have it that "more" has always been expected of Jews.

Some favor a simpler explanation of black anti-Semitism: Familiarity breeds contempt.

Jackson, however, offered no thoughts at all on the cause of the phenomenon. Indeed, he urged that "closed scars . . . not be turned into open wounds in the name of . . . candor." This amounted to an injunction *not* to try to focus on just how and where things went amiss—a strange way to go about building a foundation for a new black-Jewish alliance, Jackson's ostensible goal.

Jackson's comments on Israel seemed tentative and highly partisan. He commended "Rabin's wisdom in freezing settlements" and called the Rabin electoral victory "a breath of fresh air," thereby identifying himself with those who embrace the view that "Israeli intransigence" has been the central obstacle to a regional peace settlement.

True, Jackson mentioned—if briefly—the darkest moment in the history of the Jewish people, alluding to the Holocaust by reminding his audience of Washington's 1939 refusal to admit the German Jewish refugees aboard the *St. Louis.*

But even this reference was couched in the context of moral equivalence. After mentioning the *St. Louis,* for example, Jackson took note of Washington's decision to incarcerate Japanese Americans during the Second World War. (He did not, however, observe that the vast majority of those aboard the *St. Louis* perished in Nazi death camps, while virtually none of the Nisei—notwithstanding the unforgivable treatment meted out to them—died in captivity as a consequence of maltreatment.)

In the end, Jackson's speech offered a firm condemnation of anti-Semitism—along with equally strong criticism of every other form of discrimination. Had anyone else delivered it, the talk would have fallen into the nonnews "dog-bites-man" category; after all, general condemnations of bigotry don't make for high controversy these days.

The fact that the speaker was Jesse Jackson, however, seems to have turned these relatively bland remarks into front-page news—in the *New York Times* and the *Washington Post.* Whether this circumstance is something to celebrate—for Jews or for Jackson—has to be regarded as an open question.

Jackson, to be sure, had no trouble identifying specific manifestations of what he deemed to be anti-Semitism—when they were evident in the precincts of the Right: He was outspoken in attacking former President Reagan's 1985 visit to the SS cemetery in Bitburg. Likewise, he had harsh words for a distant and isolated episode in Fred Malek's career under Richard Nixon. (Malek, a George Bush campaign chairman and one of Israel's leading friends in the American business community, once provided President Nixon with a list of Jewish employees in the Labor Department.)

But it's hard to take seriously a speech that condemns Fred Malek for a single two-decade-old misdeed—ignoring the strong and appropriate contemporary friendship between Malek and the Jewish community—while failing to mention Louis Farrakhan or Leonard Jeffries or ex-Chicago mayoral aide Steve Cokely, a man who contends that Jewish physicians invented AIDS as part of a genocidal antiblack conspiracy.

I remain convinced that Edgar Bronfman, the president of the World Jewish Congress, was right to extend an invitation to Jesse Jackson. If Jackson's remarks serve, in any measure, to reduce the legitimacy that anti-Semitism enjoys in black America—especially among the elites—it will have been well worth having invited him to Brussels, despite the fact that he seized the opportunity to rehearse the standard Rainbow Coalition demands for improving America; despite the fact that he declaimed at length to a puzzled audience about the "unacceptable" number of blacks behind prison bars without referring to the phenomenon of rampant urban crime.

Jackson *did*—in his way—extend his hand. He *did* evidence a measure of familiarity with Jewish fears and Jewish suffering. If his words, somehow, trickle down—or if, more important, he chooses to deliver his speech to black, not Jewish, audiences—Bronfman will have been vindicated as to his controversial decision to invite Jackson to Brussels.

This is not to say that the Reverend Jackson made any case whatever for renewing the shattered alliance between blacks and Jews. There's too much out there in the way of hard-core black anti-Semitism—from Farrakhan to the rap culture to the orientation of black media outlets—for Jews to plunge back into a world in which they're less than welcome.

Dialogue? With Farrakhan?

October 26, 1995

In a fantastically funny coda to Louis Farrakhan's Million Man March, some Jewish leaders found it necessary actually to respond to the Nation of Islam leader's call for dialogue between "us" (in context, this was a royal "we") and "the Jews."

Farrakhan, of course, told his largely middle-class mass audience that while he doesn't like "this quarrel" with "the Jews"—implying that there's some sort of two-way argument in progress—he'll sit down to talk only if no preconditions obtain.

Even as his bow-tied Fruit of Islam storm troopers hawked copies of the *Protocols of the Elders of Zion* and like texts, Farrakhan affected an inability to fathom the unwillingness of the "bloodsuckers" to break bread with him.

Happily, the Jewish communal leaders and commentators who confronted his proposal seem to have concluded that entering into a dialogue with an unrepentant Hitler admirer doesn't make much sense.

Dissecting Farrakhan's offer, some noted that his point about the Jews' willingness to treat with Yasser Arafat doesn't stand up under scrutiny. True, virtually no one commented on Farrakhan's curious suggestion that "the Jews"—rather than the State of Israel—had entered into talks with the PLO. Meanwhile, his claim that rivers of blood separate Jews and Palestinians, while no blood separates Jews and blacks, didn't prompt anyone to note that this rendition of reality ignores the Crown Heights pogrom. (It also ignores the Nation of Islam view that Jewish doctors invented the AIDS virus in order to annihilate blacks.)

Still, commentators tended to note the contrast between Arafat's agreement—prior to the PLO's talks with Israel—to renounce terrorism and Farrakhan's absolute refusal to disown his blanket condemnation of Judaism as a "gutter religion."

Thus—for the moment, at least—the dialogue he pretends to seek with "the Jews" seems unlikely to interest any "bloodsuckers" of stature.

But the suggestion that discussions with Farrakhan will likely prove unproductive is consistently attended by the observation—rendered in the manner of a loyalty oath—that enhanced black-Jewish dialogue is welcome and necessary.

Why, actually, is this notion accepted as received wisdom? Because there's disproportionate black anti-Semitism? Because surveys tell us that blacks—especially educated, middle-class blacks—dislike Jews more than they do other white groups?

Certainly, proponents of dialogue are animated by these concerns. But should this be the case?

Forgive the heresy, but wouldn't Jews be far wiser to conduct an intracommunal conversation informed by the very same questions? Maybe, in other words, Jews need to begin asking *themselves* why they arouse more hostility among blacks than do, say, Irish Americans or Italian Americans or WASPs.

Farrakhan says blacks need to talk to other blacks. Well, perhaps it's time for Jews to talk to other Jews. Such an internal discussion might yield interesting conclusions. Could it be, for example, that black anti-Semitism is directly related to the historically disproportionate Jewish engagement in the civil rights movement? Jewish representation in the battle against American racism has, indeed, been enormous and disproportionate. As a consequence, in the late 1960s, when Black Power advocates called for the expulsion of whites from civil rights organizations, Jews experienced the brunt of the impact.

In their internal dialogue, Jews may want to consider the uncomplicated proposition that familiarity breeds contempt. For another potential topic, how about the adage that people who are engaged in protest tend to shoot at their friends, rather than at their enemies, knowing with some certainty that their friends aren't likely to shoot back?

It's past time for Jews to try to come to terms with the phenomenon of black anti-Semitism. The emergence of Farrakhan—a classic, European-style anti-Semite—as a black leader with vastly enhanced national stature only serves to underscore the urgency.

Let's note, moreover, that for all the hot air about separating the message from the messenger—and all the hollow words about the laudable "goals" of the agenda-free march—a *Washington Post* survey indicates that nine out of ten participants said they had a favorable view of both Farrakhan and the Nation of Islam in the aftermath of the rally.

Insofar as the demonstrators were considerably wealthier and considerably better educated than black America as a whole, Jews would do well to hurry up and "dialogue"—with themselves.

CULTURAL HOSTILITIES

It was Breindel's greatest fear that the dark treatment of Jews in the twentieth century would somehow become obscured and forgotten in the battles over current cultural issues. In these six columns, he took up efforts to distort and politicize recent Jewish history—and, in another example of his willingness to ignore calls for ideological solidarity— took on one of the country's most prominent conservative cultural voices, John Simon, when he believed Simon guilty of "dredging up a Nazi anti-Semitic stereotype."

The Nazi Conductor

February 23, 1989

Herbert von Karajan visits New York this week for a series of concerts that may represent the renowned conductor's final appearance on an American concert stage. Karajan is eighty years old and in frail health. His Carnegie Hall appearances with the Vienna Philharmonic were almost canceled.

The news that he would conduct was greeted with relief and enthusiasm in American music circles, a reminder of the esteem in which he is held. The eagerness with which he has been awaited is a reminder, also, of the fact that Karajan's controversial political past has not been an issue for a very long time.

Yet there is no more prominent former Nazi active on the international scene. (Even Kurt Waldheim wasn't actually a Nazi Party member, unlike Karajan.)

How did the Austrian conductor manage to escape the obloquy that might have been expected to descend upon him after the Second World War?

The answer, ironically, is that Karajan put the question of his past to rest by pleading blind ambition—he became a Nazi, he claimed, because failing to join the party would have prevented him from advancing professionally.

He treasured his career above all else, Karajan maintained, relying on the belief that his worshipful fans would sympathize with his sense of priorities. By and large, he was right: The careerism explanation proved satisfactory.

The trouble is that it doesn't stand up under scrutiny.

It's true that some leading German and Austrian performers became Nazis in order to advance their careers. This is the context for Karajan's claim that he joined the party in 1935, to qualify as music director of the Aachen Opera in Germany.

But records at the Allied Document Center in West Berlin show that Herbert von Karajan actually joined the Nazi Party in Salzburg, Austria, on April 8, 1933. His party membership number was 607525.

Shortly thereafter, the Austrian Nazi Party was banned—and there was no professional advantage to be gained from signing on with the Nazis in 1933 Austria. Karajan appears to have joined not to advance himself, but—on the contrary—at some risk. Hitler, after all, had come to power only nine weeks earlier—and that was on the other side of the frontier.

Less than a month after he joined the Austrian party, according to the documents, Karajan became music director at Ulm in Germany. There, on May 1, 1933, he joined the German Nazi Party.

It might be argued that Karajan was preparing himself for a successful career in Germany all along, even while still in his native Salzburg, and that his decision to join the Austrian party was part of a grand design.

But West German music historian Fred K. Prieberg points out that Nazi membership was "not a precondition" either for the job in Ulm or—if one assumes that Allied records are lying and Karajan is telling the truth—for the post in Aachen.

Karajan, moreover, claims that he left the party in 1942 when he married a woman of partial Jewish ancestry. But documents make it clear he was still a party member as late as May 1944. And there is, in fact, no evidence that he ever left the Nazi Party.

It doesn't appear that Karajan did anything criminal during his years as a Nazi. But it is well to remember that he and the other artists who backed Hitler served the Nazi cause well, lending the regime a certain moral legitimacy.

The Nazis needed the Richard Strausses and the Herbert von Karajans to rebut charges of barbarism hurled at them during the 1930s. That's why these men were courted—Karajan was a particular protégé of Herman Goering.

And, indeed, by remaining in Germany and affiliating with the Nazis, they helped blind the world to the realities of Nazism at a crucial historical moment.

It may be that Karajan was an early Nazi enthusiast who underwent ideological disillusionment and actually became the mere opportunist he claims to have been. Still, by remaining silent, he acquiesced in the persecution of Jewish artists and in the banning of masterpieces written by Jewish composers.

His swift postwar "denazification" came about despite the documentary evidence demonstrating an absence of candor—we are dealing with someone very good at landing on his feet. Since then, of course, his career has been the stuff of legends.

Whether he sold his soul to the devil or gave it willingly, believing in the devil's cause, Herbert von Karajan has escaped moral reckoning. Nothing can be done about this unhappy fact. But if those who hold tickets to his concerts were to remain at home, instead of heading out to cheer him, they will have found a way to register a sense of moral indignation at the free ride he has enjoyed.

The Mean-spirited Critic

April 20, 1989

A dispute over a well-known theater critic's tendency to mock the physical characteristics of performers whose ethnicity—in his view—renders them unsuited to the parts they play has turned into a major cultural controversy.

Colleen Dewhurst, the president of Actors Equity, impresario Joe Papp, and Hazel Dukes of the NAACP are just a few among many who have called for the dismissal or chastisement of *New York* magazine theater critic John Simon—in response to a recent review by Simon of a Papp production.

In his review of Shakespeare's *The Winter's Tale,* Simon rides his ethnic-casting hobby horse with particular vigor. He maintains that the production is marred by "perverse casting" and argues that the "chief disaster" is allowing actor Mandy Patinkin to play King Leontes.

According to Simon, Patinkin's "bulky, hulking head, further swelled by a mass of raven hair, makes him look rather like a caricature in the notorious Nazi publication Der Stürmer." Simon's message: This obvious Jew has no business playing anything in Shakespeare's repertoire, save, perhaps, for Shylock and kindred Jewish roles. Certainly, Patinkin, given his appearance, shouldn't be on stage as King Leontes, Simon would have it.

In the same review, a couple of paragraphs later, Simon also takes issue with the casting of black actress Alfre Woodard as Paulina. He says she looks like "a cross between Topsy [of *Uncle Tom's Cabin*] and the Medusa."

Simon goes on to term Woodard a "pretty fair impersonation of Butterfly McQueen." (McQueen, of course, was best known for her portrayal of Scarlett O'Hara's excitable slave nanny in *Gone with the Wind.*)

This is clearly mean-spirited and ugly stuff. Papp's response— "I'm really disgusted by this"—seems just about right, although the impresario's added suggestion that Simon "look in the mirror" because he's "hardly the ideal Aryan . . . and may be a denying, self-hating Jew" goes a bit far. In fact, it drags Papp down to Simon's level. Who, after all, cares *why* the European-born Simon is so repelled by Mandy Patinkin's Semitic features that he can't focus on the play?

The calls for Simon's dismissal were rejected by *New York* magazine's able publisher and editor Edward Kosner, who views the question largely in free-speech terms. Kosner, in an Editor's Note published in response to Dewhurst's letter, defends Simon's right to hold an "unpopular view" on an "esthetic issue on which thoughtful people may legitimately disagree."

Surely, Kosner is correct in affirming Simon's right to argue that ethnic considerations—and, indeed, physical characteristics—should play a role in casting. In fact, this isn't a particularly radical stance—hunchbacks, after all, aren't often cast as leading men.

Simon, to be sure, takes a rather absolutist view. But the real issue, in any event, isn't Simon's right to advance this point of view. The question is whether it is appropriate for him to express it by likening a Jewish performer's appearance to the caricatures that appeared in Julius Streicher's newspaper.

The caricatures in question were a key feature of Der *Stürmer,* a quasi-pornographic, high-circulation, Nuremberg-based scandal sheet that depicted Jews—often on its front page—as misshapen, hook-nosed, reptilian creatures engaged in defiling Aryan women.

Streicher was a demented pervert and an embarrassment even to the Nazi elite; he was half-crazed by the time he was put on trial after the Second World War.

But the caricatures he published in *Der Stürmer* were important: They set the tone for a central element in the Nazi propaganda onslaught against the Jews and were widely imitated in other Nazi publications, on stage and even in films—chiefly because they served the purpose of dehumanizing the Jew by likening him to an animal. They rendered concrete, in other words, the Nazi concept of the Jew as a "subhuma'" (*Untermensch*) and thus helped pave the way, by contributing to the necessary mass psychological reconditioning, to the Final Solution.

This isn't irrelevant historical background. Simon's description of Patinkin as looking like a *Der Stürmer* caricature involves a highly specific historical reference; it's important, therefore, to identify the reference and to spell out what it evokes for those familiar with it.

The question for the public isn't whether Simon should be dismissed by *New York* magazine—that's between the critic and his editors. Nor is the issue—to reiterate—Simon's right to argue his views on casting, ethnicity, and physical appearance.

The real question—again—is whether Simon, in the course of making his case, crosses over into the realm of the inappropriate.

What's appropriate and what's not is invariably a judgment call. And it's true Simon uses the word "notorious" to describe *Der Stürmer*—a device intended to protect him from charges that he condones the caricatures. But this transparent effort doesn't change the bottom line.

In the last analysis, Simon, introducing from nowhere a Nazi reference in order to enliven his point, compares the physical appearance of a Jewish performer to a *Der Stürmer* caricature. If that's not inappropriate, it's hard to imagine what is.

The Lie Behind *Days of Rage*

September 14, 1989

When the New York affiliate of the Public Broadcasting Service (PBS) aired the film *Days of Rage* last week, it was presenting a work that had, in important ways, already been discredited.

An article in the *New Republic,* subsequently cited in the *New York Times* and elsewhere, had revealed that filmmaker Jo Franklin-Trout—in apparent violation of PBS guidelines—had received funding from "interested parties" (i.e., the Washington-based Arab American Cultural Foundation). To avoid broadcasting out-and-out propaganda, PBS rejects films subsidized by interested parties.

Despite the filmmaker's claim that she had merely purchased rebroadcast rights and copies, it seems plain the foundation—which is itself funded by Kuwait, other Arab governments, and Middle Eastern corporations—wasn't lying when it claimed actual sponsorship of the film in material circulated to its own members and backers.

Indeed, the system of agreeing to pay Franklin-Trout after the fact for the various remaining rights seems to have been designed precisely to enable her to claim that she'd made the film with her own money—a practice rare even among independent filmmakers. Actually, the agreement was concluded before the film was shot.

PBS maintained that it had been unable, as of the broadcast date, to confirm the covert-subsidy charges. But in a mysterious announcement that accompanied the broadcast, it refused to reject the allegations, noting only that "[PBS] . . . at this time has found no basis for canceling the broadcast."

PBS did not mention a revealing sidebar to the larger controversy. An individual featured in the film, New York attorney Michael Posner—the executive director of the Lawyers Committee for Human Rights and an outspoken critic of Israeli policies in the occupied territories—had written to the filmmaker "expressing [his] profound disappointment with 'Days of Rage'" and formally disassociating himself from the film.

Posner, who is recognized and respected for his willingness to take unpopular stands—and who has, in the past, come under criticism for publishing condemnatory findings concerning Israel—had agreed to be interviewed, he reminds Franklin-Trout in the letter, "after you assured me that you intended to present an impartial and balanced examination of various human rights problems in the occupied territories."

The film does no such thing, Posner notes; he also takes exception to the manner in which the interview with him was edited.

PBS would have done well to take note of this development—because Posner is one of the film's fig leaves: part of the effort to pretend that *Days of Rage* is, in fact, an honest, objective examination of life in the territories during the uprising, rather than a mere diatribe against Israel.

And this goes to the heart of what's wrong here, to a point PBS seems, as yet, unable to grasp. There is nothing objectionable about honest reportage informed by a readily recognizable, clearly identified point of view.

Deception, however, is another matter. When journalism that attempts to put forward a specific point of view pretends that it is offering an objective portrait of the issues at hand, it becomes rank propaganda: The critical fact is that the reader or viewer is being deceived.

Whether PBS wants to broadcast advocacy journalism is, of course, up to PBS. Clearly, it does so—on a regular basis. An entire PBS series—*Frontline*—was journalism with a defined and unmistakable point of view. But there was never any attempt to hide the point of view. And that makes all the difference in the world.

PBS should not be in the business of airing propaganda—it should not be deceiving its viewers as to what they are seeing (certainly not in view of the fact that public and tax-exempt funds are involved).

That PBS knew there was something wrong with this film is plain—that's why the network's New York affiliate, WNET, was asked to present "wraparound" material immediately before and after *Days of Rage* (curiously, PBS refused to let Posner take part in the postfilm discussion).

But PBS doesn't yet seem to grasp *what* exactly was wrong with Franklin-Trout's effort. In the end, it's not all that complicated. If she and they had said, in effect, "This is a film about the intifada as it is viewed by many—though not all—Palestinians on the West Bank and in Gaza," there might well have been a case for airing *Days of Rage*.

Even in this context, the film's numerous misrepresentations—as to the allegedly nonviolent nature of the uprising and with regard to the history of the Middle East conflict—would have required some editing.

But the network and the filmmaker did not acknowledge that *Days of Rage* is an effort to plead a cause. Instead, they depicted the film as an honest portrait of an important, ongoing international event.

That's why Franklin-Trout interviews various Israelis in the film—without telling the viewer that all of the Israelis who appear hail either from the extreme Left of the political spectrum (and are, thus, harshly critical of Israeli policies) or from the far Right (ultranationalists who are likely to put off the average American viewer).

No effort is made in *Days of Rage* to present the mainstream Israeli point of view—and this, as they say, is no accident.

Neither was the way Michael Posner's remarks were distorted.

To cite one example of a passage Franklin-Trout killed, she asked Posner why the human rights situation in Israel received so little attention in the media in contrast to the human rights problem in the rest of the Middle East. "I responded," he reminds her in his recent letter, "that my perception was just the opposite. I said that because the media and international human rights groups have greater access to Israel and the territories than to other Middle East states, the human rights problem in the territories receives relatively greater attention."

It's the fact that Franklin-Trout edited out passages like this, while leaving in Posner's specific criticisms of Israeli policy, that renders her film dishonest. And it's because *Days of Rage* is dishonest that PBS was wrong to air it.

Franklin-Trout feels that presenting a discussion after *Days of Rage*—it was moderated by the neutral Hodding Carter and included some participants who are sympathetic to the Arabs—"simply destroys the integrity of the film."

But integrity is precisely what *Days of Rage* lacks.

Concocting History

February 6, 1993

Liberators—the much-celebrated PBS documentary about how segregated black units in the U.S. Army liberated the Nazi concentration camps at Dachau and Buchenwald—has already been deconstructed by journalists and scholars who see the film for what it is: an ideologically inspired effort to tinker with history.

The message of *Liberators* is plain: Black soldiers, despite the oppression they endured as black Americans and, in particular, as black GIs, sacrificed themselves to liberate Jews suffering under Nazi tyranny.

The film's goal? To forge common ground between blacks and Jews—to calm the tensions that currently afflict black-Jewish relations.

A gala evening at the Apollo Theater in December afforded various politicians and a number of well-heeled New Yorkers—Jesse Jackson was the de facto master of ceremonies—an opportunity to view *Liberators* and experience the emotional bonding the documentary was designed to generate.

The problem, of course—as has been detailed most recently in a *New Republic* article by Jeffrey Goldberg and in various other forums over the past two months—is that the army units featured in the film appear to have played no role whatsoever in the liberation of either Dachau or Buchenwald.

So say a number of the veterans themselves (all of them, of course, black); so say their commanders, so say the various relevant archives, so say many Dachau and Buchenwald survivors.

True, it makes for a good—and politically useful—story. At a less-than-happy moment in black-Jewish relations, such a film—if taken at face value—might well go a ways toward improving intergroup relations in a fragmented city.

But intergroup harmony can't be built on a false foundation. And *Liberators* has a rather distant relationship with historical accuracy. One veteran featured in the film, E. G. McConnell of the 761st Tank Battalion, calls it "a lie." McConnell—along with a Buchenwald survivor and another veteran of the 761st—is shown touring the site of the concentration camp in a scene the film's narrator describes as their joint "return" to Buchenwald. McConnell, however, maintains that the first time he visited Buchenwald was in 1991—"with PBS."

Nina Rosenblum, the film's producer, prefers to describe the scene in question as potentially "misleading." Also potentially "misleading" is the film's patently ridiculous subtext. The implication of *Liberators* is that black soldiers dedicated themselves voluntarily to the task of liberating the camps.

Beyond the fact that the units on which *Liberators* focuses don't appear to have played any such role, it's well to remember an uncomplicated point: Black soldiers were soldiers like all soldiers; they obeyed orders. They went where they were ordered to go and didn't design their own missions. Private concerns and convictions have very little to do with what soldiers do in wartime.

The real issue here is the danger inherent in inventing or "adjusting" history to advance contemporary political goals. This practice—as George Orwell argued for more than a decade—has insidious implications. History is about truth. Yes, past events can be subjected to differing interpretations. But making up facts out of thin air isn't history at all.

Ms. Rosenblum, judging from her response to the author of the *New Republic* piece, seems to feel that questioning the accuracy of *Liberators* amounts to racism. Not so. In fact, the film can easily be seen as demeaning to black veterans. The units discussed in *Liberators* fought gallantly in the Second World War. Much too late, one of them even received a citation from President Carter. The citation did not mention either Dachau or Buchenwald—for obvious reasons: The 761st Tank Battalion—according to veterans of the units and according to its commander—was nowhere near either camp at the time each was liberated.

More to the point—with respect to the question of racism— liberating starving inmates in poorly guarded concentration camps did not require major acts of heroism. *Liberators* cannot be viewed as an effort to confer glory on hitherto unrecognized black soldiers. These *were* brave men; they are in no need of myths to enhance their self-esteem. And to misrepresent their military experiences is condescending in the extreme. Their service records ought not be misrepresented to serve the ideological goals of contemporary film-makers.

For Holocaust survivors, meanwhile, the inaccuracies that plague *Liberators* do reckless damage to fundamental facts about the darkest moment in all of Jewish history. Everything associated with the Holocaust—from the first Nazi pogroms to the moment the camps were liberated—is virtually sacrosanct to those who care about the life and fortunes of the Jewish people. To toy with the hard facts of this tragic period borders on the obscene.

As for the general notion that it's legitimate to "adapt" history for political ends—to build self-esteem, to improve intergroup relations, to deny painful or embarrassing historical episodes, whatever—the phenomenon has a quasi-totalitarian character. Any such effort represents an attack on truth itself. Ignoring or misrepresenting the truth for political reasons leads those who engage in the practice down a slippery slope.

Peggy Tishman, who served as a cohost of the evening at the Apollo and has headed various Jewish philanthropies, seems almost as resentful as Ms. Rosenblum when confronted with evidence that the film's connection with history is limited.

In Mrs. Tishman's view, it would seem, the accuracy of *Liberators* is not an important issue. According to her—Mrs. Tishman's stated goal is to encourage black-Jewish dialogue—"There are a lot of truths that are very necessary. This is not a truth that's necessary."

Interesting.

But what if Mrs. Tishman isn't selected as a judge in some future dispute over which "truths are very necessary" and which are not? What if the next unnecessary truth involves, say, an effort to deny that the Holocaust even occurred—in order to enhance German self-esteem?

Or what if someone proposes a film purporting to demonstrate that the American armed forces were never actually segregated—in order to promote interracial harmony and lay unhappy history to rest? Mrs. Tishman might object. But others will argue that the truths such films deny aren't "necessary."

David Irving's Book on Goebbels

April 12, 1996

As everyone who follows these wars now knows, St. Martin's Press, a reputable New York house, made a last-minute decision a week ago not to publish David Irving's biography of Nazi propaganda chief Joseph Goebbels.

Irving, a British "historian," is a Hitler apologist and Holocaust revisionist who's been convicted in Germany of incitement to race hatred and defaming the memory of the dead. Indeed, by claiming that the whole notion of gas chambers, death camps, and a coherent Nazi scheme to annihilate European Jewry constitutes a vast hoax, Irving—who also argues that Anne Frank's diary is a fraud—has made himself the international Holocaust-denial industry's best-known publicist.

Goebbels: Mastermind of the Third Reich is a 650-page effort to blame such German excesses as Irving is willing to acknowledge on the "satanic" propaganda minister, rather than on Hitler. Not surprisingly, no British house was willing to take the book; Irving self-published it in the United States.

Until last week, however, St. Martin's—despite negative prepublication publicity (*Publishers Weekly* described the biography as "repellent")—was set to press forward. Only after a number of new developments did the firm—which is owned, ultimately, by Holtzbrinck, a German house—reconsider lending its imprimatur to Irving.

A scathing *New York Times* Op-Ed column by Frank Rich detailed Irving's sordid history and noted that *Goebbels* itself is rife with pernicious nonsense. Nobel Laureate and Holocaust survivor Elie Wiesel asked the publishers to kill blurbs he'd provided for other St. Martin's books; Wiesel said he wanted nothing to do with a firm that published Irving. An "open forum" of St. Martin's employees—convened by company chairman Thomas McCormack to discuss the controversy—revealed that 95 percent of the four hundred or so who attended wanted the book canceled. Private protests by influential figures within the industry, along with public declarations of opposition by legitimate Holocaust historians, seem further to have concentrated St. Martin's attention.

The day after Rich's piece appeared, McCormack announced that his firm—having "made a mistake based on our ignorance"—was canceling the book. According to McCormack, St. Martin's had been entirely unaware of Irving's dubious background. Only after the controversy heightened did the company launch a crash internet investigation into David Irving. St. Martin's findings—along with McCormack's own discovery, upon finally reading the manuscript, that the biography itself is animated by the subtext that "the Jews brought it on themselves" (McCormack's words)—convinced the chairman to act.

"We sure wish we knew then [when the book was purchased] what we know now," says McCormack. His point, however, is unclear; after all, the text—which McCormack calls "effectively anti-Semitic"—hasn't changed.

Actually, the "we made an honest mistake" explanation doesn't survive even superficial scrutiny. For starters, Thomas Dunne, the St. Martin's editor who bought the book—other houses to which it had been submitted said no—defended his decision in blistering terms just last month.

Raising the specter of "censorship"—as if nonpublication by an established firm amounts to censorship—and suggesting that Goebbels himself must be "laughing in hell . . . [since] he loved nothing better than burning books," Dunne argued that Irving's prior work had received "scores of good notices" from distinguished scholars. This, as it happens, is false. Most historians—including several cited by Dunne—credit Irving for the scope of his research, but denounce his shoddy methodology and note his eagerness to create controversy by advancing outrageous claims. The key point, however, is that if Dunne actually took even a cursory look at Irving's "notices," he'd have to have learned more than he needed to know about the "mild fascist" (Irving's self-description) who'd been made a St. Martin's author.

In light of McCormack's comments, Dunne's claim that he himself found nothing in *Goebbels* to support the view that Irving is a Nazi apologist speaks for itself. Suffice it to say that the book—which I've just read (no thanks to St. Martin's, which rejected requests for galleys)—isn't an exercise in subtlety.

Two questions remain about this unseemly episode:

What really went on here? And why does it matter whether an established firm—as distinct from a marginal house—publishes an insidious book?

On the latter issue, consider the student who—twenty years hence—heads to a library to research a Goebbels term paper. If he finds a 650-page biography published by St. Martin's, he's likely to take the book a good deal more seriously than if it had been issued by the Institute for Historical Review, a "think tank" for Holocaust revisionists.

The likely explanation for St. Martin's initial decision to take the book is uncomplicated: The deal seemed attractive. Irving, reportedly, was paid a relatively modest sum—twenty-five thousand dollars—for a biography with a guaranteed audience: World War II buffs, Nazi obsessives, even David Irving admirers (it's a big country). And, in fact, as soon as St. Martin's sold the biography to the generally sensible, Doubleday-owned Military Book Club—the club's editor called Irving's study a "strong work of history"—the house probably made back its money.

The decision, in short, reflected a cost-benefit analysis. Only when St. Martin's concluded that the negative publicity certain to attend pressing forward would outweigh the likely financial gain did the firm retreat. Concerns about right and wrong were less than central.

A Bungle at Harvard

August 14, 1997

It's hard to imagine a $3.2 million gift to a school—provided by a generous alumnus seeking to set up an endowed chair in a legitimate scholarly realm—encountering an unending series of university-created impediments. Yet such has been the saga of Ken Lipper—in his effort to endow a Holocaust studies professorship at Harvard.

Actually, the arrogance in evidence here is *not* unique to Harvard. Only two years ago, Yale found it "necessary" to return some $20 million to oil tycoon Lee Bass, who had wanted to subsidize a program in Western civilization. The conservative Texan was distressed by his alma mater's increasing tendency to neglect the Western canon in favor of courses on, say, glass-blowers in late nineteenth-century Lyons.

Had the "Hey, hey, ho, ho; Western Culture's Got to Go" ethos come to New Haven? Bass was concerned. But opposition to the grant on the part of Yale faculty members made itself apparent almost immediately. Many saw no need to enhance Yale's Western civilization curriculum, although most teachers and administrators recognized the difficulty inherent in arguing that the university's offerings in Socrates, Shakespeare, and European history were more than adequate. As a result, Yale simply sat on the gift.

After hearing nothing from the school for an extended period,

Bass inquired as to Yale's plans and was told that no decision had yet been taken. Hoping to see the money deployed during his lifetime, the philanthropist put forward a couple of suggestions.

This step was greeted as an intolerable exercise in audacity. Attacking an utter straw man, Yale pronounced that no outsider—not even a generous benefactor—is entitled to a role in determining faculty appointments or in deciding on prospective course offerings.

In this context, the university returned the $20 million. Meanwhile, by its silence, Yale acquiesced in the false charge that the philanthropist had sought to interfere in areas that remain the exclusive province of the faculty.

At most institutions of higher learning, the Bass affair would likely have led to some sort of inquiry—$20 million, after all, isn't small beer by any standard. But Yale—like Harvard—plays by its own rules. Which returns us to the drama now under way in Cambridge.

A Harvard law graduate and ex-New York City deputy mayor, Ken Lipper made millions at Salomon Brothers. Subsequently, this son of a Bronx shoe salesman—who spent his undergraduate years at Columbia on a city-funded scholarship—gave Harvard $3.2 million to endow a Holocaust studies chair.

Lipper wants to make the Holocaust a permanent feature of Harvard's curriculum. Endowing a professorship would create a tenured post for a first-rank scholar with a continuing commitment to Harvard, a circumstance far preferable to the current practice of designating different instructors to teach the subject on an ad hoc basis.

Lipper's generosity to Harvard, Columbia, and other institutions has been facilitated by the success of his own investment boutique and by a burgeoning film career. He coauthored *Wall Street* and, more recently, produced the Sidney Lumet-directed *City Hall*.

Dr. Evelyn Gruss Lipper has enhanced her husband's capacity for largesse. Her late father, Joseph Gruss, made an oil and gas fortune in America after migrating here from Poland; *his* philanthropy (focused on Jewish education) took on near-legendary proportions. Actually, the chair Lipper would create—tentatively the Helen Zelaznik Professorship in Holocaust and Cognate Studies—would honor the memory of Mrs. Lipper's grandmother, who perished at Bergen-Belsen.

It's hard to imagine controversy attending any such undertaking. Yet Lipper has foes in at least two distinct camps.

A number of Jewish scholars and pundits oppose the establishment of Holocaust studies as a defined scholarly discipline. This camp includes recognized scholars, among them Harvard Yiddishist Ruth Wisse. Calling the notion of a Holocaust studies professorship "a strange idea," Wisse sees irony in the fact that "[Harvard doesn't] have a chair in modern Jewish history, but it [would have] one in the destruction of the Jewish people."

Needless to say, Lipper doesn't oppose modern Jewish history professorships. *He,* however, sees his task as ensuring continuity and excellence in the study of the Holocaust. And unless the folks who are hostile to this endeavor question the legitimacy of the field itself—despite the growth in Holocaust-related scholarly journals and research centers and the rise in the number of books, courses, and Ph.D. dissertations devoted to the subject—it's difficult to grasp their underlying concerns.

In a decidedly different camp are those who "charge" Lipper with trying to influence the actual appointment (Lee Bass redux). Various Holocaust scholars—as well as anonymous members of the search committee—claim the donor wants the new post offered to Daniel Goldhagen, an as-yet-untenured Harvard professor. Goldhagen attained celebrity last year when Knopf published *Hitler's Willing Executioners,* an international best-seller based on his doctoral dissertation.

Not surprisingly, Goldhagen is a controversial personality. The academy allows jealousies to fester. (An old saying has it that campus rivalries are especially vicious because the stakes are so small.) Goldhagen's youth and popular success (rare for a scholar of any age) have not combined to win him friends—not among his Harvard colleagues and not among fellow Holocaust scholars.

To be sure, Goldhagen's dual thesis *is* inherently controversial. He argues that the circle of responsibility for European Jewry's annihilation extends far beyond the SS and Hitler's most radical supporters and that the crime itself required a uniquely German variant of violent, socially pervasive anti-Semitism.

This interpretation of Nazi genocide runs well counter to what passes for received wisdom in this realm. In fact, the whole notion of national character—German or other—lost currency some time ago. So it shouldn't astonish that the relatively small community of established Holocaust scholars has managed to produce Goldhagen's most severe critics. Some in this group, of course, are also his chief rivals for the prospective Lipper chair.

Does Ken Lipper favor Goldhagen's candidacy? There's no evidence to support this claim. But it isn't remotely clear that the benefactor isn't entitled to a preference—so long as Lipper didn't make his gift *contingent* on Goldhagen's appointment.

What *is* clear—and justifiable—is Lipper's opposition to the proposed interim appointment of UCLA's Saul Friedländer, an eminent Holocaust historian. The financier, after all, is creating a chair precisely to halt the ad hoc manner in which Harvard has long handled the teaching of this subject.

Lipper hasn't concealed his frustration at Harvard's inability to make a decision. Indeed, in anticipation of just this rut, he provided the first $1 million in advance—after the university agreed on a job description (a process that itself took a year and a half)—as an incentive for the school to fill the post quickly.

Now the affair is taking on aspects of the Bass fiasco. Harvard, it's safe to say, would be wise to avoid a repetition of Yale's unhappy encounter with generosity.

EPILOGUE:
THE EULOGIES

On March 9, 1997, at Park Avenue Synagogue on Manhattan's Upper East Side, twelve hundred mourners gathered to pay their respects to Eric Breindel. Among those who spoke in his memory were New York's governor, George Pataki; its two senators, Alfonse D'Amato and Daniel Patrick Moynihan; its former mayor, Ed Koch; Housing and Urban Development secretary Andrew Cuomo; and two of the proprietors of the New York Post *during his tenure there, Rupert Murdoch and Peter Kalikow. What follows are three of the eulogies and an article published in memoriam the week after Breindel's passing.*

He Reached Outward

Mayor Rudolph Giuliani

We are gathered here today to say good-bye, too soon, to a man of courage, dignity, and integrity—a man we all admired and loved. I'm here to say good-bye to a very good friend.

I offer my sincerest condolences to Eric's parents, Joseph and Sonia. There is nothing more difficult than seeing your child pass away. It is especially difficult when the child is as gifted and as good, deep in his heart, as your son was . . . when the child is as loving, and loved, as Eric was. As you mourn his loss, the city mourns with you. I know that today, it is hard to think beyond the fact that Eric, who was so alive in so many ways, has passed on.

But you must not ever forget that even though we lost him much too soon, the boy you raised had already become such an accomplished man. It's remarkable how much you taught him about kindness . . . dignity . . . justice . . . and courage.

Eric was young, but he had already accomplished a full life's worth of work. With the strength of his mind and the kindness of his character, he reached people across this city and across the world. He did it on the pages of the *Post,* on television, and in magazine after magazine—but, most of all, every day in the way he lived his life.

Each and every time he wrote or spoke, he reached outward to the world to understand the facts with an open mind . . . and reached inward, to the conscience that his family helped form, to understand the moral questions at hand.

And what emerged of this synthesis, time after time, was a voice of honesty and decency . . . a voice of common sense . . . a voice that took full responsibility for the words it spoke and always remained gracious toward those who disagreed with it. Eric spoke and wrote with a great American voice.

And it was not a voice that sought simply to praise or criticize. Through his entire life and career—whether he was working at PBS on *American Interests* or for Senator Moynihan, the *Post,* or Fox News, or whether he was writing a book on Soviet espionage—Eric was always searching genuinely for the truth.

Eric made a difference in this world, a profound difference. Let it be of comfort that his voice is still with us, that his spirit is alive. We see all those who are here today and all those who have responded to his loss from all over the world. That's because your son, your brother, your friend, and your loved one was willing to take a position on what he believed was right and wrong.

When I recall his voice—when I hear it—it will always be with the urgency and clarity of prayer. Rabbi Abraham Joshua Heschel wrote, "Just to be is a blessing. Just to live is holy. And yet being alive is no answer to the problems of living. To be or not to be is not the question. The vital question is: How to be and how not to be. . . . To pray is to recollect passionately the perpetual urgency of this vital question." In Eric, I will remember a man who always recollected the urgency of this question.

I will remember a good man. Always, I will remember with profound regret that we didn't have him longer, much longer. Oh, what we will miss is not being able to read and listen to the search for truth of this exceptional mind and voice . . . at 50, 60, 70, and more. And I will always miss such a good friend.

But I also give thanks that we had him. I will remember Eric's defense of Israel and his unique understanding of Israel's mission and challenge and his patriotism for America, maybe a more "old-fashioned" patriotism than the more cynical approach of many in New York, but a simple and pure understanding that the goodness and decency of our people and our form of government outweigh our weaknesses.

When I remember my friend Eric, I will always see him sitting next to his father at Holocaust memorials or when he received the New York Police Department's Man of the Year Award. I'll remember the pride that Eric and his father had because they realized that this was a mutual recognition of courage.

Eric set out to advance justice and condemn injustice, answering to his own conscience. He was unpredictable. He had his own mind, his own unique point of view. If he disagreed with you, you would know it . . . and you might even see it in thirty-point type . . . but that would not prevent Eric from connecting with you as a human being, and it would not stop him from discussing other issues with you and trying in good faith to come to a solution.

As his parents know, a gifted mind is nothing without a strong, loving, courageous soul governing its actions. And this, ultimately, is Eric's legacy.

Rabbi Heschel once wrote about the prophets in a way that makes me think of Eric: "Above all, the prophets remind us of the moral state of a people: Few are guilty, but all are responsible." Rabbi Heschel wrote that "the prophets proclaimed that justice is omnipotent, that right and wrong are dimensions of world history, not merely modes of conduct. The existence of the world is contingent upon right and wrong."

Eric knew this, and he helped us see other sides to arguments.

Eric's award-winning editorials and columns on the Korean boycott in Brooklyn [see part 2] focused attention on a dramatic and destructive practice, on the failure to give equal application of the laws to people entitled to its protection.

It was almost like a prophecy of things to come because in it the same "inequality of treatment" was to play itself out on a broader and even more dramatic stage.

Eric's courage; his independent, logical mind; and his understanding of emotions about the history of the Jewish people made his commentary on the Crown Heights riots the most compelling . . . because Eric had the courage and clarity of vision to describe, in precise terms, the violent attacks on Jews for the sole reason that they were Jewish, realizing that the failure to do so, the discomfort with doing it, would permanently jeopardize our ability to come together. The failure to do so would permanently jeopardize our principles of honesty, equality, and decency.

Some of Eric's opinions and views challenged the intellectual elite of a city that was becoming almost tyrannical in condemning new or revised approaches to thinking about race, religion, welfare, Israel, and the necessity to challenge, with force if necessary, violent dictators, and tyrants.

But as strong as his opinions were, he never looked to exploit people or ridicule their frailties. With respect for people and ideas, he defined a realm of high public discourse— sometimes all by himself—in which the basic questions asked, again and again, were "What is good?" "What is right?" and "Why?"

I think we can all learn from the kind of curiosity, tenacity, and integrity with which he tried to answer these questions.

His ideas, of course, will stay with us—he articulated his positions too well and with too much intellectual force for us to forget them. But he leaves us with something much greater than an ideology or a set of opinions. When we listen closely to Eric's voice, which will always be with us, I think all of us—no matter what we do, who we are, or what we believe—will find a strong example of how to live courageous, moral, and honorable lives.

Too Compassionate to Be Mean-Spirited

Robert F. Kennedy, Jr.

I knew Eric Breindel at Harvard when he was still a Socialist. He wore a black leather jacket and a one-day beard that was so deliberately cultivated that we joked with him that he must be shaving at night. He chain-smoked Marlboros, apparently even when he was sleeping, which made him a fire hazard. And he succeeded one time in burning down his part of a Harvard dorm suite that he shared with my brother David and with our friend Mir Bhutto. I had a preview of the pugnacious style he would later bring to his *Post* editorials when he chased a romantic rival down Plympton Street, throwing rocks at his head. But it wasn't the he-man stuff that attracted attention at Harvard.

Everyone who knew Eric agreed that he was the smartest person we knew. Later, I spent a year in London with Eric when we both attended the London School of Economics, where he made me proud to be an American and his friend by being the smartest person in that school, too.

His genius was recognized by everyone who met him, and his college friends soon left him to a stellar parade of mentors, who wanted to be part of a life so obviously destined for leadership and brilliance. It was not just that he was intellectually grounded and the most prodigious and successful writer of our generation at Harvard. Eric was profound. He had a tragic sense of history. He understood how dark and complicated the world could be, but he also had tremendous optimism, particularly as it related to America. His ability to hold these two contradictory thoughts, along with his religious faith and the physical suffering with which he lived, gave him an early wisdom. He had wisdom that most people don't attain until their fifties, which seems now a tragic precursor to the early death that befell him this week.

He was a left-wing liberal through college and remained sentimental about liberalism and social justice. He loved Eleanor Roosevelt, Al Lowenstein, and Paul Robeson. Despite the occasional harshness of his writings, I always felt he never abandoned his core values. He had a basic decency that never abandoned him, even when he turned to the Right. He had a deep-rooted morality and a deep conviction about the notion of struggle between good and evil in the world and American history. He had genuine passions about Israel, police, crime. He was too compassionate to be mean-spirited, and his intellectual discipline shied away from the simplistic platitudes of the ideologue.

That's what made our conversations so delightful. And he accepted my occasional chiding with warmth, gentility, and the basic decency and civility that characterized Eric's every gesture. Unlike most people who are ideologues, he could absorb contradiction and paradox. And he could laugh at himself. He never lost his understanding of the need for social justice that instructs liberalism. Even when he became a Reaganite, his editorials were about standing up for people who were powerless, righting wrongs, extracting justice out of the ruins of the Holocaust, and returning social justice and a sense of community to New York City, which he was so romantic about and understood so well from the Brooklyn Dodgers to Wall Street, from Aaron Burr to Robert Wagner, from Ed Koch to Robert Moses, from knishes to the New York City Ballet.

Eric should have been secretary of state. He would have been one of the greatest in our history. The fault was with his infrastructure. His systems failed him so often. In all the time I knew him, he was never operating at full capacity. But even at 50 percent, he was far ahead of everyone else. At Harvard and afterward, he was afflicted with a nightmarish progression of maladies: his sinuses, his wrist, his throat— surgery after surgery after surgery. He was in perpetual pain, but he never complained, and he never lost his humor. He laughed in the face of his many disabling agonies. To be with Eric was to laugh. And he used his suffering to help others. His own suffering gave him an almost infinite capacity for sympathy for people under duress.

He could without any condescension make contact with people in pain. He was always calling and asking, "What can I do?" When my brother Michael died, one of the first voices to activate my answering machine was Eric's. His message was simple: Tell me where I have to be and when. That was typical. His love for his friends was unaffected and intimate. He would do anything to be of help, no matter what the physical cost to himself. He had as deep a sense of loyalty as anybody I've ever met, and I come from a family that puts a high premium on that virtue. Another thing that seemed familiar to me was his love for his family. It's hard to speak of Eric without superlatives, but I had no friend with a higher level of devotion of love for his parents or his sister, and I was always sure that it was those relationships that had given him such a large capacity to love others.

Despite the divergent paths of ideology, Eric remained one of my closest friends. He was an usher in my wedding, and he was somebody whom I often called for advice or help or just to laugh. He came to my birthday party every year, and I was expecting to see him this Friday at my home in Bedford. I will miss him.

Very few people understood the persistence and severity of Eric's physical affliction. Even for people who knew him when he was relatively healthy, the memory of Eric as an accomplished athlete is fleeting and faint. But he was. He had extraordinary physical coordination. He had been a high school wrestler and a gifted tennis player. But, piece by piece, his gifts were taken from him, and these were the first to go. It's comforting to think of him now, with no physical affliction and with his wonderful mind released from corporeal pain.

When Abraham died, God said, "Take my friend Abraham into paradise, where there is no trouble nor grief nor sighing, but peace and rejoicing and life unending." It's a comfort that Eric is now also in God's company with his brilliance finally shining unobstructed and uninterrupted.

A Very Good Jew

Norman Podhoretz

I first met Eric Breindel when he was still a student at Harvard, and the qualities for which I came almost immediately to admire and cherish and love him were visible even at a glance. I mean his charm and the warmth that gave it body; I mean the quickness and the reach and the agility of his mind.

But there was also something else, something more unusual, and that was the unconventionality of his outlook on the issues under such fevered agitation in those days. Here, amazingly, was a Harvard student from New York who did not think America was the source of all evil and who did not think that Israel was the guilty party in its conflict with the Arab world.

How, I wondered, did he get away with such heretical views up there, in the People's Republic of Cambridge? How did he get away not only with loving America but also with caring so deeply about and fearing for the safety of Israel?

The answer, I suspected, lay in his charm and warmth and brilliance. But it took a while before I began to understand how he had arrived at these heretical views and where he had found the strength both to hold them in his head and the courage to uphold them in public against all comers. The answer to that question, I eventually began to see, was that Eric Breindel was a very good Jew.

Of course, if the criterion was the number of mitzvoth or commandments observed, Eric was not a good Jew at all. Of the 613 commandments the rabbis of old found in the Bible, Eric followed only a few, and even most of those only desultorily. But there was one that he truly did observe, and exactly as a good Jew is instructed to do—with all his heart and all his soul and all his might. This was the fifth of the Ten Commandments Moses brought back from Sinai: *Kabed et avikhah v'et imekhah*—"Honor thy father and thy mother."

Certainly Eric honored Joseph and Sonia Breindel by being a loving and loyal son. But there was more to his love and loyalty than normal filial devotion. Joseph and Sonia, as we all know, barely escaped Hitler's ovens, and Eric also honored them by absorbing into the deepest reaches of his consciousness the lessons of their experience and the experience of those who had not managed to escape. Indeed, he made that experience into the shaping principle of all his thoughts.

Out of it came his understanding of what totalitarianism means; out of it came his understanding that the major form of this unspeakable evil remaining in the world was communism, as embodied in the power of the Soviet Union; out of it came his